Sat

BRITAIN'S BLACK DEBT

Is This book a joke

BRITAIN'S BLACK DEBT

Reparations for Caribbean Slavery and Native Genocide

HILARY McD. BECKLES

University of the West Indies Press
Jamaica • Barbados • Trinidad and Tobago

Filk

University of the West Indies Press
7A Gibraltar Hall Road   Mona
Kingston 7   Jamaica
www.uwipress.com

© 2013 by Hilary McD. Beckles

All rights reserved. Published 2013

A catalogue record of this book is available
from the National Library of Jamaica.

ISBN: 978-976-640-349-2 (cloth)
ISBN: 978-976-640-268-6 (paperback)

Cover photograph: Queen Elizabeth II with her cousin, the 7th Earl of Harewood,
at his sugar plantation (the Belle) in Barbados in 1966.
This plantation was bought by the earl's ancestor in 1780 with 232 slaves.

Book design by Robert Harris
Cover design by Paul Gibbs and Hilary McD. Beckles

Set in Adobe Garamond 11/14.5 x 27

Printed in the United States of America.

To my grandson, Tajari Daniel Beckles.

· · ⊰⊱ · ·

For the late Chief M.K.O. Abiola; Burning Spear (reggae band); Lord Anthony Gifford;
the late member of Parliament Bernie Grant; Congressman Tony Hall; Barbara Blake
Hannah; Professor Ali Mazrui; Randall Robinson; the late Professor Walter Rodney;
the late Dr Ras Ikael Tafari; Dr Ciakiah Thomas; the late Ambassador
Dudley Thompson; the late Dr Eric Williams; David Commissiong;
and the late Professor Rex Nettleford: their advocacy and scholarship *(Joke!)*
continue to inspire the global reparations movement.

all dead, praise the Lord.

Not one British Black

Woman - Why? They themselves

are racist!

Contents

PART 2

Tables

Foreword

THE EUROPEAN MASS ENSLAVEMENT OF Africans, and its globalization as an economic and social system, *should* have been a crime, European politicians argued at the UN World Conference against Racism, Racial Discrimination, Xenophobia, and Related Intolerance, in Durban, South Africa, in 2001. But it was not, the politicians insisted. Their diplomats determined that it was all very legal and moral. This is as untrue today as it was in the past. Jurists, theologians and philosophers said then that slave trading and chattel slavery were crimes. Their voices were silenced. Europe determined that these crimes were in the national interest of the countries involved because of the enrichment such acts bestowed upon nations. Opposing voices critical of slavery were brushed aside and the wealth-generating slave machine sped through the New World like a juggernaut. On board were the kings and queens of Europe, heads of governments, merchants and mercenaries, bishops and bankers, soldiers and soul savers, and in the end, the men and women in the street.

This book does not set out the case for reparations for the entire global enslavement of African peoples. It addresses a small part of the global phenomenon: that of the English-speaking Caribbean. It does not therefore engage the issues pertinent to the United States, Canada, Brazil and other parts of South America: excellent studies already perform this task, many of which have been pressed into service in these pages. Nor does it deal directly with the recruitment, transatlantic shipment and enslavement by the Spanish, Dutch, French, Swedes, Danes, Norwegians, Germans, Russians and Portuguese. Its primary focus is the case of blacks in the colonies owned and controlled by England, and later, Great Britain. In a subsequent work the participation of European nations will be addressed.

The rationale for this approach is both professional and personal. As a text it follows upon my plenary address at the seminal World Conference on Racism in 2001. There I spoke and negotiated on behalf of many Caribbean nations. Slave-owning nations and their allies determined that Durban passed a declaration to the effect that slavery and slave trading were not crimes at the time they were practised, though they *should* have been. This was a naked display of political power in the form of legal and philosophical discourse.

At no time did the British and Western nations seek to discuss seriously the absurdity and shamefulness of *should*. It was an embarrassment. The historically informed members of the conference know of the denial. For them it was politics. The conference concealed more than it revealed. The British stated their position and lobbied behind the scenes for support. It was backroom politics in the place of historical and intellectual discussion. Truth was buried in the silence. The Caribbean delegates objected and led the opposition. They declared that the historical evidence showed that slave trading and slavery were understood as crimes then, as they are now, and as such are subject to reparatory justice.

This book embraces and continues the post-Durban reparations discourse. Caribbean governments have been urged by their civil society leaders to press ahead with the pro-reparations positions they adopted at Durban. I too have urged them to follow through on their rejections of the Durban declaration. Since Durban, I have been asked by many audiences in the Caribbean, Europe, North America and Africa to prepare a text that sets out the case for a direct Caribbean path of action.

This background explains the Caribbean focus and political intention of this book. It stands, however, in solidarity with the many brilliant works published on this subject by scholars and community activists all over the world. Its intention is to push along the global movement by promoting leadership action in a specific context. The seventeenth-century Caribbean was positioned in the vanguard of the economic process that led to the mass enslavement of Africans. Perhaps the Caribbean has a vanguard duty to the twenty-first-century global movement for reparations.

Acknowledgements

OVER THE YEARS, I HAD many memorable conversations with numerous persons as this manuscript developed. Their views have shaped the contours of my thinking and enhanced the content of my writing. Some persons shared their research and ideas; others assisted with the production of the manuscript. Everyone gave support and encouragement. I offer to each of them my sincere gratitude.

At the World Conference against Racism, Racial Discrimination, Xenophobia and Related Intolerance, sponsored by the United Nations and held in Durban, South Africa, in 2001, I worked with Dudley Thompson, veteran campaigner in the reparations movement; George Belle of the University of the West Indies, Cave Hill; and David Commissiong of Barbados. We fashioned a constructive dialogue to advance the reparations movement and to secure wide support for the objectives of the conference. Together, we deployed legal tools found in the writings on reparations by Lord Anthony Gifford. I have sought to provide historical evidence that bolsters Gifford's arguments.

The impressive historical research on British capitalism, Caribbean slavery and emancipation by Nicholas Draper of University College, London, assisted considerably in defining the empirical content of this work. Our academic exchanges have inspired me, and I thank him. S.D. Smith, of the University of York, has mined the details of Caribbean history in new and innovative ways and has set new standards in family and institutional studies. I value greatly his scholarship, and it influenced me heavily.

Earl Lovelace, Austin Clarke and George Lamming, literary luminaries from the Caribbean, dealt in their work with reparatory issues. I wish to thank them, as well as Heather Russell, whose expert literary criticism of their work I relied upon for insights and inspiration.

Margaret Mongerie, Camileta Neblett, Ena Bowen, Korah Belgrave and Janet Caroo assisted in preparing the manuscript. The University of the West Indies offered study leave in the summer of 2010 and provided the resources that enabled its completion. My colleagues in the Department of History and Philosophy at the Cave Hill campus – Pedro Welch, Henderson Carter, David Browne, Cleve Scott and Alana Johnson – have been solid supporters. My editors at the University of the West Indies Press performed remarkable feats in clarifying conceptual issues and arguments. I thank them for their assistance that served to fashion its tone and texture.

Finally, I am particularly indebted to Eric Williams, whose scholarship underpins much of this work. Not only did he provide brilliant insights into the nature of European colonialism and its dependence upon African enslavement, he also has given generations of scholars a way of looking at the role of Africa's exploitation in the development of Western modernity. I relied heavily on the work of Boris Bittker, Robin Blackburn, Roy Brooks, Selwyn Carrington, Richard Dunn, David Eltis, B.W. Higman, Joseph Inikori, Paul Lovejoy, Kenneth Morgan, Walter Rodney, Richard Sheridan, Barbara Solow, Hugh Thomas, Verene Shepherd and James Walvin. Without their research this work would not have been possible at this time. My graduate students M. Broomes, C. Knight and H. Cummins provided a community of enthusiasm that inspired and encouraged. I thank them all for the accessibility of their scholarship and the generosity of their support when requested.

Note on Currency

THROUGHOUT THE TEXT I HAVE chosen to give the present day (2010) purchasing value of historical sums in order to assist the reader with the assessment
of monetary statements. References are derived from "The Index Purchasing
Power of British Pounds from 1264 to Present" (http://www.measuringworth
.com/ppoweruk/index.php). This index uses average earnings and differs from
the retail price index. Both indices are commonly used by scholars. The latter
gives a more conservative conversion while the former gives a truer impression
of purchasing power.

I wish to express gratitude to Dr Nicholas Draper of University College,
London, for his special assistance in this matter.

"Barbarity Time" was the term used by enslaved Africans in the British Caribbean to describe the period of their enslavement. Chattel slavery, and the slave trade that fed it, were crimes against humanity. They went largely unchecked as millions of Africans were consumed by Europe's criminal enrichment project called colonialism. The enslaved fought for their freedom. Thousands died in this quest. Formal emancipation came in 1838. The struggle continued for justice and liberty as human and civil rights were denied in the post-slavery apartheid imposed upon the emancipated. Today, heading the agenda is the case of reparations for these crimes. The reparation of which I speak constitutes the ultimate liberation, the universal recognition of truth, both conditions being necessary for racial and cultural atonement in post-modern human advancement with dignity and morality. The call for reparations is the call for collective healing and closure.

   —*Hilary McD. Beckles, extract from plenary address, UN Conference against Racism, Durban, South Africa, 2001*

Introduction

My Journey with Slavery and Reparations

All the components – huge disparities in wealth, unfair trading rules with heavy protectionist policies and exploitation of labour without protection – were present to permit slavery on an industrial scale. . . . Until we tackle all those injustices, we will not see an end to the modern versions of slavery in this world. . . . We must examine how we need to change if we are truly to give freedom to everyone.

—*Ann Glasgow, Member of Parliament, Debate on the Bicentenary of the Abolition of the Slave Trade, House of Commons, 20 March 2007*

DESPITE POLITICAL INTIMIDATION IN THE West, the majority of Caribbean citizens believe there is a reparation case to be answered by the British state in respect of crimes against humanity committed during its slave regime and the century of racial apartheid that followed.

The causal link between the crimes of slavery and the ongoing harm and injury to descendants is everywhere to be found in the Caribbean. The pain of enslavement and the injury of its injustice haunt citizens and weaken their capacity to experience citizenship as equals with the descendants of slave owners.

Reparation as justice connects each descendant of enslaved Africans and decimated natives to deep, painful emotions. It means as much to millions of other people beyond the Caribbean whose societies were violently colonized by Britain and who live with the open wounds caused by the crimes committed against their community. Reparation resonates throughout these global communities and requires answers beyond casual conversation and academic discourse.

I have suffered this harm and injury in deep and profound ways as a citizen. I might have escaped its poverty trap and transcended its brutalization, but the majority of Caribbean citizens have not. Slavery and genocide in the Caribbean are lived experiences despite over a century of emancipation. Everywhere their legacies shape the lives of the majority and harm their capacity for advancement.

I chose to write a text that reflects this reality within the context of my personal and professional experiences as an historian and concerned citizen. I have discussed this relationship over a period of thirty years with Caribbean intellectuals from C.L.R. James and Michael Manley to Walter Rodney and Earl Lovelace. All of them, in different ways, have helped to set out the evidentiary basis of reparations as a legal, political and moral right. Dudley Thompson, legendary Jamaican pan-African activist, insisted I prepare a text that presents the historical dimensions of the political and legal case on behalf of Caribbean people.

This book, then, like any living thing, has a social origin. Its shape and form are determined by academic discourse, public advocacy and a specific domesticity. It may even be said to have a social lineage and identity of its own – a genealogy so to speak. It tells a typical Caribbean tale. It is an account of known features of British colonialism; its terrorism of adults and ruthless exploitation of children; its maddening material poverty; and the racial brutality it bred within the prison known as the plantation.

I was born and reared in such a prison: a plantation village inhabited by men, women and children who performed lifelong hard labour for sugar planters who owned everything of worth around us. My maternal grandfather, who helped rear me as a child, was born at the end of the nineteenth century and experienced the full impact of the reformed slavery of the post-emancipation decades. His father was born in the mid-nineteenth century, in the aftermath of the 1838 abolition legislation. My grandfather's grandparents, therefore, were enslaved. My grandfather spoke rarely of his family's history. Shame filled his silence, and we knew it. The memories of his childhood would yield what for us were horror stories of the "Barbarity Time", a term older folks used to describe the slavery period.

As a discursive and activist response to this world, this book erupts from the cemetery of plantation Barbados – the first fully matured slave society in the seventeenth-century Americas. When this colony became an independent nation in 1966, its people, like all those in the region, were still living in the racially oppressive world of white supremacy built by British minds. Millions of impoverished, illiterate, economically disenfranchised descendants of the enslaved were still gridlocked in the plantation world perfected by British hands.

From the West Indies, the British exported the financially successful model of African enslavement to the rest of its colonized world. They made global the ideas and methods that were critical to colonial modes of capital accumulation. The British received credit as the creators and primary financial beneficiaries of chattel slavery. The Caribbean was the place where fortunes were made within this system without an interest in human compassion. For the enslaved Africans, the British built "hell on earth" in these "sugar islands". The enslaved have "a more dreadful apprehension of Barbados than we have of hell", said the English captain of the slave ship *Hannibal* in 1693.

One hundred and fifty years after the emancipation laws, the descendants of enslaved Africans still faced endless fields of sugar cane. The pain they sustained was palpable in their faces. The British state sent out its governors to rule these "wretched of the earth", which they did brutally, with police constables and military regiments. Those who rose up in opposition were shot down or beaten and thrown into prisons. Democratic Britain ran its totalitarian regimes – dictatorships of white supremacy – from Jamaica in the north to Guiana in the south.

My maternal great-grandmother spoke freely about her enslaved grandparents who worked these fields. Slavery, for her, was still alive in the present. It filled her consciousness and dominated her reflections. It was the "devil doing", she would say, and the "Englishmen" who rode horses while driving them to work were the devil's horsemen. She would say that if her enslaved grandparents were to return, they would fit right in. Little had changed in over 150 years.

From British Barbados, my parents – disenfranchised and impoverished – travelled to Britain's Birmingham, where recruited West Indian workers laboured in the factories. It seemed like an entirely domestic movement. From the cane fields of Barbados to the car factories of Birmingham was a journey along a continuum. Birmingham was much colder than Barbados, but the

racial heat that burned the minds of black folks was familiar. Those Englishmen who had built and owned the cane fields in Barbados were financially
intertwined with those who had transformed Birmingham, with the wealth
of slavery, from scattered family farms to concentrations of factories.

What an irony, I thought, as I entered the University of Hull, homeland
of the great William Wilberforce who, we were told at school in Barbados and
Birmingham, had set our ancestors free. In the city of the "great one", there
was evidence everywhere of his deeds as a warrior of humanity. I had gone
there to read philosophy and political science. I was attracted to the discipline
of philosophy because I was fascinated with ways of thinking about issues of
fairness, rightness, justice, equality and, of course, freedom.

My affinity for philosophy classes was short lived. The absence of historical
dimensions in seminar discussions did little for me. I soon found peace of
mind in my new disciplinary home – the economic history programme. Here
we examined how Western imperial modernity decimated the native community of the Caribbean and brutalized Africans, and later Asians, on sugar plantations in Europe's race for wealth without conscience. It was in Hull, then,
the cradle of Wilberforce's tirade against the crime his country perpetrated
and left unresolved, that I saw clearly why the call for reparations should be
made.

Earlier, Eric Williams had constructed the framework for the reparations
case. His magisterial book *Capitalism and Slavery* (1944) still represents the
most persuasive articulation of the evidence. He stopped short, however, of
making an explicit call for reparations. But he did have the "audacity", as his
critics called it, to suggest that Britain's magnificent, enviable industrial civilization emerged from the foul waters of colonial slavery. Slavery, they countered, was a distraction to domestic entrepreneurs who were pioneers in
transforming the economy with internally generated capital. The modern
Caribbean reparations movement is a legal, political and moral response of
grassroots organizations and political networks to the evidence presented by
many scholars, but notably in Williams's seminal study. Since then, there have
been many criticisms, refinements and reaffirmations of this work, but its continued capacity to stimulate further research speaks to its essential correctness.

The broader context of my thinking has as much to do with UNESCO's
decision to launch, in 1994, the Slave Route Project under the title "Breaking
the Silence". The silence imposed by the West, by Britain especially, has made

the call for reparations seem confrontational rather than conciliatory. Traditionally, the British media were silent on the historical information presented by Williams. Initially, his book was rarely used in academic programmes and was ignored by most scholars. The concept of criminal enrichment from slavery that applies to Britain's elite commercial families and institutions has not taken root in the public's imagination, though members of ruling class society are aware, at varying levels of clarity, of their own ancestral links to these crimes.

As a director of the Scientific Committee of the Slave Route Project, I have had the experience of engaging British schoolteachers, curriculum specialists and policymakers about their knowledge and understanding of this historic past. Everywhere I have gone in Britain, and in every conversation, the reaction has been the same: shame, guilt and awkwardness in confronting the legacy of slavery. These emotions have conspired to produce the deafening denial and solemn silence that define the responses of the British nation. Only constructive dialogue based on truth can break this cycle. It is a precondition for the actualization of the process called conciliatory reparations.

During the 1990s, I was invited by His Royal Highness Prince Claus of the Netherlands to serve as a member of his cultural committee. I joined a group of distinguished scholars who sought to recognize and reward brilliant cultural activists in the creative and performing arts for their contributions to social justice, peace and cultural respect. Reparation discourse always lurked on the margins of our work as a committee. Some members were anticolonial advocates, and others campaigned for atonement for the crimes against humanity committed by European states.

The publication in 2000 of Randall Robinson's book, *The Debt: What America Owes Blacks*, served to focus my attention on the procedural aspects of the case for reparations. This study drew attention to the techniques used by the US Congress to defeat the national reparations movement by way of committee strangulation. In addition, it illustrated the extent to which Caribbean leaders have failed to take political responsibility for the case of reparatory justice to which their citizens are entitled.

Against this background, reparation advocates arrived in Durban, South Africa, for the UN-sponsored World Conference against Racism, Racial Discrimination, Xenophobia and Related Intolerance (WCAR) – a historic gathering that saw, for the first time, heads of state and nongovernmental organizations locking horns on the subject of Europe's historical crimes and injustices. The official position of the Caribbean governments was that a global reparations agenda should be established and that there should be meaningful dialogue about repairing the damage caused by slavery and colonization within the context of international law.

Durban produced a dearth of goodwill between those gathered to find pathways to reconciliation. The United States refused to discuss the subject, setting the stage for a near collapse of the conference. Colin Powell, US secretary of state, led the American pull-out. European Union countries agreed to discuss the subject on condition that outcomes were non-binding. African countries were divided, as were those in Asia and Latin America.

The reparations issue bred enough vexation and anger to fill the city beyond the plenary walls. There was palpable rage in some places, as British, Dutch, Spanish, Portuguese and French delegates especially found themselves unable to present coherent arguments to justify indigenous genocide, slave trading and black slavery. European and other Western governments were prepared to go the distance in denying the historical evidence relevant to slavery as a crime against humanity.

In the aftermath of Durban, I presented a public lecture at the Cave Hill campus of the University of the West Indies, Barbados, to a full house that had paid close attention to world reports on the controversial conference. I concluded that the world was in terrible moral shape and that the deep racial hatred evident in many discussions at Durban did not augur well for the future of global racial relations. The Western world was firm in its posture that its colonial crimes, principally African enslavement, were not items for reparatory discussion. Seeking such a dialogue raised the rage of "West" against "the rest". The shape of Europe's anger was unattractive, crafted as it was by excessive vindictiveness. Then came 9/11. I cannot say I was surprised by the terrible, inhumane acts, though the massive shock of the latest evidence of inhumanity, one human to another, still rips my soul.

Some progress, however, was made at Durban. Resolutions were passed that condemned the trading in enchained and enslaved Africans. Adopted resolutions were non-binding on countries that were criminally enriched by these activities. The assertion of political power by the West – the United States and the European Union especially – diminished and derailed the best intentions of the United Nations. Britain, especially, missed an excellent opportunity. Driven diplomatically by denial in a conference rich in potential for engaging truth, the nation that benefited most financially from slavery proved itself least prepared to speak honestly of the past. Against this background I accepted a series of invitations to lecture on British official policy and the reparations movement before and after Durban.

The first of these engagements was the Eric Williams Memorial Lecture, organized by Florida International University in partnership with Williams's daughter, Erica Williams-Connell. Then it was on to Warwick University in the United Kingdom to present the Walter Rodney Memorial Lecture. In Africa I presented the R.P. Balfour Memorial Lecture at the Kwame Nkrumah University of Science and Technology in Kumasi, Ghana. Then it was back to Europe, to Amsterdam, where I lectured on the wider European case before a gathering of mostly academics with an interest in the moral and ethical contradictions of the European Enlightenment. In March 2011, I made my final crossing. From academia and public engagements, I moved to the United Nations to share ideas on post-Durban reflections and agendas. An address at the New York headquarters to mark the recognition of the African diaspora was followed by a plenary presentation on reparations at the Geneva complex. In both interactions the spirit that rose up in response to my interventions was supportive, though cautious in light of persistent Western hostility. It was in Geneva, after intense dialogue with nongovernmental organizations and government officials, that I settled my thoughts on this text.

It was undoubtedly the momentum produced by the convergence of these contexts that drove the direction of my academic research, public engagement and international dialogue that has found expression in this form. This multi-layered engagement with history and politics and migration has created the tone and texture of the text which follows. I take full responsibility for this work and hope it contributes to the case for reparations and as a corollary global peace and justice.

PART ONE

Chapter 1

The Principles and Politics of Reparations

Slavery was not just an event. It was a process of destabilising African society. It produced negative self-images and African deculturalisation, and demonised all things black and all things African.

—*Dawn Butler, Member of Parliament, Debate on the Bicentenary of the Abolition of the Slave Trade, House of Commons, 20 March 2007*

THE THEORETICIANS OF REPARATIONS DISCOURSE have presented a body of creative and innovative literature which has assisted the framing of much of this book. In this regard the people who have contributed this literature have been very influential in guiding the direction of historical research. Much of the evidence presented here represents an affirmation of this conceptual contribution. Theory and empirical research constitute the evidentiary basis of reparations cases. Reliance upon this conceptual work is explicit.

Crimes against humanity have been a central feature of the rise of European imperial modernity. The colonization of three-quarters of the world's people and places by western European nations created rich opportunities for such crimes to flourish. In the Caribbean context, the genocide against indigenous populations, the sexual plunder of their women by imperial soldiers and the appropriation of their wealth by merchants and military leaders preceded the mass enslavement of Africans. Such crimes have had lasting and damaging effects in the psychological, material and social conditions of those victimized and on generations of their progeny.[1]

Postmodern discourse has insisted upon atonement for these crimes, and has linked reconciliation between victimized peoples and the beneficiaries of enrichment as a necessary precondition for mending the mind of a common humanity. The crimes of slavery and slave trading have fractured the human family so deeply as to suggest no possibility of reconciliation without atonement. Happily, recent decades have witnessed the growing capacity to reflect and engage in remorse of some European nations that benefited socially and financially from these crimes.[2]

Since the rise of independent nations in Africa, Asia and the Caribbean, a process which reached a climax in the 1970s, the postcolonial world has witnessed an increase in the number and frequency of formal apologies and statements of regret in respect to imperial crimes. These responses have come from governments acknowledging the evidence of crimes against humanity committed by their citizens. One popular example has been the apology offered by Queen Elizabeth II of Britain to the indigenous Maori people of New Zealand for the genocidal activities committed by the British.

With the defeat and uprooting of apartheid in South Africa, the world watched in awe as former president F.W. de Klerk apologized to the millions of black citizens for the crimes against humanity committed by his regime of white supremacy. The mass media continue to keep the world community abreast of all developments relevant to the apology offered by European states for the genocide they committed on Jewish communities during the Second World War.

The historical record shows that the consciousness and capacity of races and societies to commit crimes against humanity is universal. The record also has shown that few perpetrators have been prepared to repair the damage by offering compensation to the victims and their descendants. Even fewer nations have been prepared to accept that the wealth extracted from such crimes should be converted into a national reparations strategy. Britain falls in this category. While it took the lion's share of the profits from selling enchained Africans and continued to build its fortunes and power from the sweat and blood of millions of the enslaved on Caribbean plantations, it has persistently refused to apologize for its crimes and has generally ignored any call to engage officially in a formal discussion about reparations. The persistent use of avoidance diplomacy and intellectual "spin" of the evidence has been the norm. State officials have also engaged the services of scholars to deny and deflect culpability. Armed with scholarly ammunition, mostly produced in its universities, the British state has set out on a path of denial, refusal and confrontation.

Experts have shown that international law lays out a clear trail linking the crime and the reparations demanded by the crime. This trail shows that the damage caused by crimes against humanity can be repaired when offending parties – whether these are individual persons, governments or civil institutions – make reparations. The legal provision of a right to reparation for crimes against humanity is therefore acknowledged by international law. Many successful cases have been settled under international law. Judicial systems and political institutions in compliant countries have been innovative in setting out pathways to reparatory justice.[3]

The concept of attaining justice for historic wrongs, and a corresponding reparatory action, has been defined by the Permanent Court of International Justice (the predecessor of the International Court of Justice). Recognizing the persistent resistance that has tended to be associated with reparations, in 1928, in the Chorzow Factory Case between Germany and Poland, the court offered a definition that seeks to facilitate rather than hinder the process. The definition is as follows: "The essential principle contained in the actual notion of an illegal act is that reparation must, as far as possible, wipe out all the consequences of the illegal act and re-establish the situation which would, in all probability, have existed if that act had not been committed."[4]

The critical part of the definition that connects to social justice discourse is the notion of returning the victim to a condition that preceded the illegal act. The assumption that the development path of persons and nations can be derailed by an illegal intervention is recognized. It is assumed that societies have available to them the capacity for creative legal and political action. Those who have committed the crime, and benefited from criminal enrichment, including the descendants of the criminal, are liable to make restitution. Legal experts have also shown that the International Court is willing to recognize the validity of cases associated with the historical crimes that have been committed under European colonialism. Such crimes and related wrongs can be brought before the court in the form of litigation which seeks reparatory justice.[5]

The underlying principle within international law is that redress for human injustices, including crimes against humanity, is possible. The critical legal premise is that justice can be attained in this way as a result of judicial recognition of the theory of redress. The use of this principle in reparations cases, however, requires that specific conditions are met to the satisfaction of the court. Successful cases of reparations have generally required concerted political action at the level of the state (for example, the official provision of evidence of damage to be repaired and criminal enrichment by its citizens and institutions; willingness to act as the defendant; willingness to act in compliance with court rulings) in order to meet the required threshold.

It has been shown that legislatures have greater political flexibility than the courts in cases of reparation. Political diplomacy can accelerate cases of reparation, while sitting judges left alone are apt to slow them down. A government, for example, can create a legal body with quasi-judicial powers to hear the evidence. It can also bring the matter to closure. Legal right, then, requires political action in the form of an official policy.

The central question for the Caribbean reparations movement (as it is for all cases of compensation for historical and colonial crimes) is, What constitutes a meritorious claim? Complainants have made many legal presentations based on a careful reading of international law. The influential typology advanced by Mari Matsuda, for example, is one point of departure. Matsuda has suggested that a human injustice that attracts a claim of reparations must meet the following three criteria:

1. The injustice must be well documented; the historical data setting out the specifics of the injustice should withstand scientific scrutiny and be verifiable to the satisfaction of a court or tribunal: In the case of the Caribbean, there is an abundance of evidence generally acknowledged by political and judicial institutions.
2. The victims must be identifiable as a distinct group: The native Caribbean people who survived British European genocidal policy and the descendants of enslaved black people constitute identifiable communities that have suffered criminally at the hands of the British and other European colonists.
3. The current members of the group must continue to suffer harm: The descendants of the native people of the Caribbean, and the blacks enslaved in the Caribbean, experience a post-slavery system of apartheid that focuses on their race and ethnicity. The systems of wealth distribution, political marginalization and institutional racism shape their lives today. Such harm

is causally connected to the past injustice. The institutional racism established and sustained by the British and their Caribbean agents imposed considerable harm and suffering on natives and blacks.[6]

Caribbean indigenous communities, still caught in the grip of British genocidal policies, and blacks who have remained deeply economically disenfranchised and racially targeted as a subordinate ethnicity by racist ideology, suffered considerable harm within the slavery and post-slavery systems maintained by Britain. Accordingly, the nature of such historical crimes is recognized by international law (by the UN Charter in particular), and provision is made for the presentation of reparations cases.

Article 55c of the UN Charter reads, "The United Nations shall promote . . . universal respect for, and observance of human rights and fundamental freedoms for all without distinction as to race, sex, language, or religion." This provision was a reaction in large measure to the crimes against humanity committed by European colonists in the New World.[7]

The fundamental feature of the chattel enslavement of blacks in the Caribbean was their legal reduction to the status of non-persons – property and real estate, to be precise – with no right to life. Blacks were denied any essential right to human recognition and treated as existential beings in ways consistent with the usage of animals. In addition to the provisions of the UN Charter, there are many multilateral and bilateral conventions, covenants, resolutions and treaties that have been ratified by governments which deal with the rights of humans.

In all these documents, the rights of all persons are clearly specified and conditions set out for redress in cases of violation. The critical issue here is that in respect of crimes against humanity, there is no hiding behind national law. International law provides for the prosecution of such crimes even when national law might be used by the perpetrator to justify or "legalize" actions. This is an important aspect of law that supports litigation in respect to slavery, slave trading and genocide.

One example of legal provision outside the ambit of the UN Charter is the International Covenant on Civil and Political Rights of 16 December 1966. This instrument is explicit and speaks on the matter of transcending national laws. The right to be free from arbitrary deprivation of life (Article 6); torture or cruel, inhumane or degrading treatment or punishment (Article 7); and slavery, servitude, or compulsory labour (Article 8) is upheld as a core condition of human existence. In seeking to ensure compliance, provision is made for a measure of retrospection so as to protect victims long after the crime has been committed.[8]

In the case of descendants of victims, international law recognizes that crimes against humanity should stand the test of time, with proof of their causal impact upon the lives of persons still suffering harm. For a meritorious redress claim, harm must be causally connected to a past human injustice. This, says Matsuda, brings into play the issue of "remoteness" that forms a relevant part of British common law. The concept of "remoteness" seeks to establish time limitations upon crimes as a matter of common sense application.

The US courts have used a similar concept referred to as the "Privity Principle". Both concepts, says Matsuda, seek to suggest that slavery took place a "long time ago" and that neither victims nor perpetrators are alive to answer a case of redress. However, the counter to the claim of remoteness is the argument of "living memory", which illustrates that descendants are still trapped within the living context of the crime and can illustrate this in terms of a direct cause and effect.[9]

In the case of blacks, slavery and slave trading targeted them as a specific ethnicity. No other group was enslaved in the way that blacks were. It is generally assumed, for example, that all Jews were victims of the European Holocaust. Like the blacks in the colonial period, Jews were identified in legal pogroms as a specific group of people. While some Jews escaped this context by virtue of their social connections, wealth and usefulness to perpetrators (some Jews were even collaborators), this does not deny the essential truth of the case.[10] Similarly, some blacks did not suffer the common fate in the slave societies of the Caribbean. Many were freed, and some served the specific offices of slave owners. In this regard, the evidence of black collaborators does not deny or diminish the truth of racial targeting for the crimes committed against them as an ethnicity. In some respect, the presence of collaborators within the victimized groups makes the crime even more, rather than less, heinous.

In the face of the publicly disclosed evidence of slavery and genocide, some European governments have issued "statements of regret". They have generally avoided the issue of an apology. As a legal admission of guilt, the apology calls for payments to victims or their families. Most governments prefer to pay money to victims without issuing an apology.

Successive British governments and their supportive national institutions have steadfastly refused to formally apologize for the crimes committed against black people. They have refused to recognize that these wrongs constitute crimes against humanity. By refusing to issue an apology, preferring to issue instead a "statement of regret" – a social rather than legal response – the British state hopes to be legally protected from responsibility for repairing the damage done by slavery. The option preferred by British officials in dealing with the crimes committed in the building of its global empire has been the "settlement". The concept of settlement does not meet the legal threshold of reparations. It seeks to settle the matter without admitting responsibility.

The victim is given cash or other material award by the victimizers, who do not accept any liability for the effects of their actions. In this way the dispute is settled as a single action with no attachment to a time-specified future. A statement of regret is issued and the settlement made. The matter of reparation cannot be "settled" this way since reparation begins with an apology, not a statement of regret, admission of criminal liability, and a willingness to repair the damage.

In law, however, both reparations and settlements can be classified as monetary and non-monetary exchanges in respect to the search for justice and reconciliation. It is important to bear in mind that the objective of reparations is not to punish or penalize the offender, but to establish conditions for a just, reconciled future. Reparation is not an action of confrontation, but a search for unity; that is, the aim is repairing a damaged relationship.[11]

International law is explicit. Reparations must be paid in cases of proven crimes against humanity. Importantly, the statute of limitations is removed in the context of this category of crime, thus allowing for perpetrators to be brought to justice and for victimized descendants to claim compensation within the context of social justice, legal restitution and the need for moral closure.[12]

In 1946, the United Nations General Assembly unanimously affirmed the principle of international law recognized by the Charter and Judgement of the Nuremburg Tribunal. In 1948 it adopted a definition of slavery and genocide as crimes against humanity. Since its establishment in 2002, the International Criminal Court has further affirmed this definition as case law.

The genocide inflicted upon the native Caribbean people was a crime against humanity. So too was the enslavement of black people in the colonial societies. It has become the norm, with prominent exceptions, for British scholars of slavery to support the political position of the British government that there was no genocide practised against the native Caribbean population and that black enslavement was not a criminal action. A significant amount of scholarship joins with the British state in formulating the argument that the chattel enslavement of blacks was legal at the time, since it was provided for by the imperial government which was acting within the context of acceptable European norms.

The political position of the British government, then, is that all other European governments were involved in slavery, and this made it an international standard which was not considered criminal. The racism of Europe, therefore, that enabled the British (the English and Scots principally) to practise chattel slavery by targeting blacks as the only racial group for lifelong property status has, in turn, become the legal basis of a political position held by the current British state.

None of this, however, stands up to historical, legal or moral scrutiny. It is not a serious legal argument that there was no crime in enslaving blacks since all white people were doing it, and that it was a common enough activity for European colonizers. Neither can it be sustained that the African governments were doing it to their subjects, since this is not historically accurate. African states did not define their subordinate workers, political prisoners and others subject to criminal punishment as legal non-humans, perpetual property and reproductive chattels.

In much the same way that the English state facilitated the growth of a colonial labour market in white indentured servants – convicts, political prisoners, vagrants, petty criminals and so forth – the African political process generated subordinate, alienated labour. The English did not allow for the chattel, lifelong enslavement of white servants, whose humanity was recognized in legal and moral codes. Neither did African states propose, practise or permit the legal classification of blacks in the slave trade as legal non-humans no different in law from other forms of property.[13]

The early modern world witnessed various forms of slavery and servitude as systems of labour, but neither in Europe nor in Africa did this subservience involve the branding of persons as chattel. This developed in the Caribbean as a special and specific European practice that targeted Africans. No other racial or ethnic group that entered the English colonial Caribbean received this legal classification. This invented brand of property was developed by the Spanish and Portuguese in the sixteenth century and perfected by the English in the seventeenth century. It was a moral and legal break from any African or European tradition of labour. It constituted, furthermore, the most dehumanizing, violent, socially regressive form of human exploitation known to humankind.

Many influential persons recognized the criminal nature of the English undertakings at the time. John Locke, for instance, the prominent philosopher of the theory of liberty and an advocate of human freedom, arguably England's finest legal and political mind of the seventeenth century, was forced to confront this matter at a time when black slavery was being promoted in England as necessary for the advancement of the national interest. He himself became a substantial investor in slave trading and Caribbean slavery. Locke's lesson, then, was philosophically clear. Being a philosopher of freedom and liberty, while investing in slavery and slave trading, constituted for him no paradox or logical inconsistency. This was so because slavery for Locke was not a deprivation of liberty and freedom since the blacks would benefit from serving the English national interest. Locke's theory was that enslaved Africans were part of the bigger project of sustaining English freedom as a hallmark of the emerging nation.[14]

The British state crafted trade laws, devised imperial political relations and implemented legal frameworks for the slave-based colonial project. The Caribbean world that received the majority of enslaved Africans in the seventeenth century was designed and designated as a place where no constraints, other than those protective of property, were considered necessary in the exploitation of Africans.

Edmund Burke, along with many other fine legal and cultural English minds, objected to the criminal enslavement of blacks. There was also moral outrage about the national descent into backwardness which slavery represented. But the power of profit, the pull of market margins and the corrupting force of unrestrained property rights in humans brushed aside these objecting opinions. The moral and intellectual voice of a poet, a scholar or a theologian, for example, was no match for that of merchants, monarchs, economists, lawyers, philosophers and aristocrats hungry to restore their lost fortunes and make new ones.

English self-awareness of African enslavement as a criminal activity remained in the margins of the eagerness to promote the national interest. The general thinking of the legal fraternity was that the crime was something to be tolerated in the far-flung colonies, but it should not be allowed to take root or gain respectability in England. That is, the crime of slaving can be committed and the profits reaped, but English soil should produce no fruit other than that nurtured in the free air of the nation. There was a fair measure of tolerance in England, since the seventeenth century, of the presence of enslaved blacks. But the laws of England never gave explicit approval. Colonial laws approved by the British government for the colonies were clear that blacks were not human but were property first and foremost.

The chattel enslavement of blacks in the Caribbean, this commerce in enchained African bodies, while being in the national interest as defined by government, monarchy, private investors and other beneficial groups was, nonetheless, a crime. There was an acknowledgement that Locke's philosophical posture could not stand the test of English jurisprudence and that English law would not be bent to serve the specific interest of those who made a living from trafficking bodies against their will and holding them in bondage in the face of their refusal and resistance.

On what basis, then, did the British government enforce the chattel enslavement of three million black people in the Caribbean? How did the English allow positive law to enforce slavery in the colonies and yet allow "negative" law in the metropolitan context? And how was Britain able to proceed in a world in which there was one law for its domestic citizens and another for its colonial chattels? The answers to these questions can be found in the very predicament posed by the need to exploit the African body criminally for national enrichment.

The British Empire needed to promote wealth accumulation rapidly and to new heights which were not possible with free or contracted labour. These systems of labour were provided for by well-established and respected labour laws and social conventions. The wealth of the empire required the abandonment of all known laws, conventions, moral parameters, political practices and legal frameworks and the creation of a new and unprecedented labour system.

But to achieve this paradigm shift, a race of workers other than those within the wider domestic civilization was required. That is, English and western European culture could not allow the enslavement of white workers in the way the colonial elite demanded. Africans were outsiders, and the leap from moral and legal labour relations to the extreme space of criminal conduct was possible, especially as racist anti-black values were already prevalent and proving useful in the project of colonial militarism.

The English state, then, knew that slave trading and slavery were crimes but was prepared to risk seeking their normalization in the interest of nation building. In order to do so, it made active provisions of two kinds of laws. First, it sanctioned the use of colonial laws that established the legal framework for building the slave societies. Second, it provided a legal and financial regulatory framework for the creation of companies that both kidnapped and bought Africans for shipment against their will to the Caribbean and elsewhere.

The first action enabled the possessors of enslaved Africans to claim a legal right to own these bodies and to do with these bodies whatever they considered necessary. That is, the English government imposed upon the colonies a power of ownership over Africans that English law did not allow in England. The second action, while protecting white servile workers in the Caribbean from chattel enslavement, sought their replacement with Africans who would be subject to no constraints on account of their race.

The official position of the British government that slavery was legal at the time it was enforced does not stand up to the strict scrutiny of British law. It is insufficient to argue that it was legalized by the colonial government. Colonial laws were sanctioned by the British government, which in turn understood, from its judicial arm, that its illegality in England created a double standard and a contradiction within English civil and common law.

Furthermore, the basis of all British and European trade law was that the colonies were part of the domestic economic space of the nation, hence the capacity of government to enforce trade laws and investment rights, and ensure compliance with the policies of the imperial Parliament.

The construction by the Europeans of massive forts that served as slave factories and warehouses along the entire coast of West Africa should be evidence enough of the shattering military power of Europe in West Africa. These institutions were the largest walled structures built anywhere in West Africa, and stood as monuments to white military might within the context of the political and financial plundering of African bodies.

Scholars have presented a plethora of papers setting out how some African leaders received a significant share of slave-trading profits and held the upper hand in some specific locales. When faced with the evidence which shows how such collaborating groups were eventually consumed and destroyed by the rising tide of British and European addiction to the trade in humans, there is generally an awkward silence, which suggests recognition of the chronic failure of politically motivated scholarship.

Neither scholars nor the state has been able to suppress, effectively deny or silence the evidence of Europe's hegemonic power in the crimes against Africans. Furthermore, the limitation of this scholarship is found in the empirical evidence which shows that slave ships departed London, Liverpool, Bristol, Glasgow and elsewhere laden with cheap textiles, glass beads, pistols and other such items, to be exchanged for fifteen million African bodies – the youngest, strongest and healthiest. The unwillingness of these scholars to consider the unequal, exploitative terms of trade implicit in this commercial culture remains endemic to the historiography.

The Caribbean reparation case against Britain is not based on any concept or intention to participate in political confrontation with the British society or its government. A confrontational approach to reparation does not hold reconciliation as a primary objective. Reconciliation, however, is the necessary outcome of the claim for reparations, seeking as it does to establish a spirit of mutual respect and obligation between the British state and the descendants of enslaved Africans who continued to be victimized a century after legislative emancipation in 1838.

The transition from formal, legal slavery to a reformed system of slavery took the shape of apartheid in the Caribbean. It constituted the platform for the ongoing criminal enrichment of the imperial state and its principal colonial institutional supporters, particularly those who monopolized via racism their ownership of economic resources in the Caribbean.

There is undoubtedly an emotional component to the reparation claim, but this is merely a reflection of the deep and profound psychological, social and economic marginalization that persists among the descendants of the enslaved and the continuing economic domination in the Caribbean of the descendants of the slave owners and their mercantile backers and partners. The emotional component that typifies the call for reparations has tended to engender in blacks and whites alike a perception that the case has no fundamental basis in criminal and civil law, and is incapable of yielding a legal strategy with viability within the courts or Parliament of Britain. There are many legal and political problems associated with the building of the reparation claim, but all of these can be addressed in an innovative way by the British Parliament and its legal and judicial system.

It is important for British society to acknowledge that its development as a nation-state, the transformation of its economy to sustainable industrialization, and its global standing as a super power among nations were founded upon a crime against humanity in the form of racial chattel enslavement of African bodies and the global trafficking of millions of these bodies for three hundred years.

Acknowledging and accounting for wrongs is deeply enshrined within both British law and society. And as such, the need to engage British society with a reparations discourse is consistent with national, cultural and intellectual norms. Indeed, the British intellectual and moral traditions should insist upon it. Far from seeing reparations claims as confrontational, then, British society should champion the cause as an expression of respect and of celebration of the finest aspects of its judicial culture.

The entire body of tort law is based on this understanding that humans who suffer wrongs should be compensated and that political expediency and moral doubt ought not to preclude the onward march of justice and its conclusion in a fair settlement.

Reconciliation must be the dominant ideology of the twenty-first century, and the sooner societies act, the greater will be the benefits. The reparation discourse seeks to foster and facilitate this process. It does not seek the aggravation of an already tense and divided consciousness. At the same time there should be a recognition that the darkness of slavery will hover overhead until the illumination of reparative discourse takes effect and allows justice to be achieved.[15]

Chapter 2

Exterminate the Savages
Genocide in the Windwards

We must acknowledge in some form that modern British society owes much of its prosperity and many of its institutions to what happened all those years ago.
    —*Vincent Cable, Member of Parliament, Debate on the Bicentenary of the Abolition of the Slave Trade, House of Commons, 20 March 2007*

THE ENGLISH ENTERED THE EASTERN Caribbean in the early seventeenth century with a colonizing policy based on violent land appropriation and dispossession of the indigenous population. The use of military power to defeat native communities was matched with a mentality that made possible their extermination when met with resistance.[1] At the outset, the natives were considered undesirable and dispensable. War was unleashed upon these communities with a view to seizing their land and labour. If they could be enslaved, then the added bonus was welcomed. The English state sanctioned this policy and financed its operations. State and private sectors joined together in the hope of massive material reward.[2]

The Caribbean archipelago, noted Jalil Sued-Badillo, was one of the most densely populated regions in the New World. According to English historian of the Caribbean Michael Craton, between 1492 and 1730, the native population of the Lesser Antilles fell by as much as 90 per cent. They were described as "Indians", "Caribs" and sometimes "Arawaks", although in the Lesser Antilles they called themselves "Kalinagos".[3]

Military officers, private companies and government officials in these islands requested and received permission from the English government to "destroy" the native population. In 1681, for example, the governor of the Lee-ward Islands, Sir William Stapleton, stated in a letter to imperial officials in London, "I beg your pardon if I am tedious, but I beg you to represent to the king the necessity for destroying these Carib Indians. We are now as much on our guard as if we had a Christian enemy, neither can any such surprise us, but these cannibals who never come *marte aperto*. If their destruction can-not be total, they must be driven to the main."[4]

Sir William was given permission to mobilize soldiers and militia for a full war of extermination. If the natives could not be completely destroyed, per-mission was granted for those that remained to be driven from the Caribbean. The king also sent instructions to the governor of Barbados, Charles Dutton, to assist with the financing of the genocidal war.

Kalinagos were prepared to fight for their very survival. They engaged the English and used their knowledge of the region to minimize the full impact of the military onslaught. A century later, the British military and colonial officials, frustrated by their continued resistance, were seeking further direc-tions from Whitehall for the final genocidal push. In 1772, Governor Leyborne of Dominica informed the British government that "nothing else than a total extirpation of these poor infatuated would be satisfactory!"[5]

The Kalinagos, who had informed British officials that "not an inch of their territory" would be given over, did not relent. This stance aggravated the British state. While some imperial officials were not persuaded that the "king's troops" should be used to "enter upon a service hazardous in the execution and uncertain in the event", military men in the islands, such as General Dalrymple, could see no other way to secure Britain's economic inter-ests. In St Vincent, especially, British settlers were convinced that this was wise political policy.[6]

So advanced was the genocidal determination of the British on St Vincent that an article published in *Scott's Magazine* called upon Lord Dartmouth, the governor, to "put a stop to the murderous commission sent out by your pre-decessor to extirpate them [Kalinagos]". The magazine noted that the genocide in the Caribbean was no different from the Spanish actions in the conquest of Mexico, and that it was done to "gratify avaricious merchants, land holders and venal commissioners".[7]

The British in the Caribbean, according to Welsh historian Gordon Lewis, viewed the Kalinagos as a "barbarous and cruel set of savages beyond reason or persuasion". According to him, this racial assessment naturally led to the official conclusion that they "must therefore be eliminated". The movement from race hatred to genocide in English colonial thinking, he showed, was the result of the need to defame the character of the native in order to assert military control and colonial dominance.[8]

English plantation development, Lewis noted, was a "slave-based" system which could not "tolerate any alternative system, nor indeed coexist with any alternative system". It had therefore to "crush any attempt at creating such an alternative".[9]

Lewis linked this early genocidal policy of the English with later expressions elsewhere in the empire of a similar nature. The massacre of the Kalinagos, he stated, "anticipates the later treatment of the Maori tribes in Australasia" for which Queen Elizabeth II of Great Britain has offered an official apology, and her government paid reparations for what was acknowledged as a crime against humanity. Lewis concluded that once they had shown a will to survive by resisting, the Kalinagos, were "vilified" by the English, "which in turn justified their extinction".[10]

The Kalinagos believed they had every right to defend their lands and liberty from the English and other European imperialists. Reference is made to their frequent retort: "We do not covet your land, so why should you take ours?"[11] Kalinago leaders were prepared to trade with the English colonizers. When, however, the English declared an intention to enslave their community and occupy their lands, commerce in the Windward Islands especially gave way to combat, and diplomacy degenerated into genocide. This was also the case in the Leeward Islands where the English financed colonial settlements in the first half of the seventeenth century.[12]

The Kalinagos defied first the Spanish, and then later the English and French, in seeking to preserve their political freedom and maintaining control of their territory. According to Carl Sauer, "As the labor supply on Española declined, attention turned to the Southern islands. By authority of the Queen given in 1503, those designated as Caribs might be taken as slaves. . . . In a later provision (July 13, 1512) these were designated as subjects to capture, because of their resistance to Christians . . . [in] the islands of Los Barbudos, Dominica, Martinino, Santa Lucia, San Vincente, La Asunción, and Tavaco."[13]

By the end of the century, however, the Spanish, having accepted as fact the absence of gold in the Lesser Antilles and the inevitability of considerable fatalities at the hands of Kalinago warriors, had decided that it was wiser to adopt a "hands-off policy" while concentrating their efforts in the Greater Antilles. As a result, the Greater and Lesser Antilles became politically separated at this time by what Troy Floyd described as a "poison arrow curtain".[14]

The English, initiating their colonizing missions during the early seventeenth century, had a clear choice. They could confront the Spanish north of the "poison arrow curtain" or the Kalinagos south of it. Either way, they expected to encounter considerable armed resistance. They chose the latter, partly because of the perception that the Kalinagos were the weaker, but also because of the belief that they were the "common enemy" of all Europeans.

Having secured some respite from the pressures of Spanish colonization by the end of the sixteenth century, Kalinagos were, then, immediately confronted by the more economically aggressive and militarily determined English and French colonists. Once again, they began to reorganize their communities in preparation for counterstrategies. This time they would do so while on the retreat. By the 1630s, their rapidly diminishing numbers were concentrated around a smaller group of carefully chosen islands, mostly in the Windwards but also in the Leewards. Barbados, identified in a Spanish document of 1511 as an island densely populated with Kalinagos, no longer had a resident community.

The English took advantage of this reorganization and resettlement of Kalinago communities and established infant colonies in peripheral parts of the Leeward Islands where their presence was less formidable, and in Barbados where it was absent. They sought the destruction of the Kalinagos for two distinct but related reasons, and over time adopted different strategies and methods while maintaining the ideological position that they should be enslaved, driven out or exterminated.

Lands occupied by the Kalinagos were required for large-scale commodity production within the expansive plantation economy. By resisting land confiscation, Kalinagos were therefore confronting the full ideological and economic force of British capitalism.

British economic activities in the Caribbean were based upon the enslavement of natives and imported enslaved Africans. The principal status and relation assigned to these and other non-Europeans within the colonial economy was that of slavery. The British in the Lesser Antilles, however, were not successful in reducing an economic number of Kalinagos to chattel slavery or other forms of servitude.

Primarily because of their irrepressible war of resistance, which intimidated all Europeans in the region, the Kalinagos were targeted first for an ideological campaign in which they were established within the English mind, not as "noble savages", as was the case with the less effective Taino in the Greater Antilles, but as "vicious cannibals" worthy of extermination within the context of genocidal military expeditions. Voluminous details were prepared by Spanish, and later English, colonial chroniclers on the political and philosophical mentality of the Kalinagos, most of whom called for "holy wars" against "les sauvages".[15]

The English started out in 1624 with the establishment of agricultural settlements in St Kitts. From there, they moved on to Barbados in 1627, and between 1632 and 1635 to Antigua, Montserrat and Nevis. Meanwhile, a small English expedition from St Kitts to St Lucia in the Windwards, the heart of Kalinago territory, was easily repelled in 1639. The following year, Kalinagos launched a full-scale attack upon English settlements at Antigua, killing fifty settlers, capturing the governor's wife and children, and destroying crops and houses.[16]

English settlements in the Leewards struggled to make progress against Kalinago resistance. Barbados alone forged ahead uninterrupted. Unlike their Leewards counterparts, early Barbadian settlers rapidly expanded their production base, made a living from the exports of tobacco, indigo and cotton, and feared only their indentured servants and a few enslaved Africans.

St Kitts colonists, determined to keep up with their Barbadian competitors, were the first to adopt a common military front with respect to Kalinago resistance. During the 1630s they entered into agreements with the French, in spite of their rival claims to exclusive ownership of the island, to combine forces against Kalinago communities. On the first occasion, they "pooled their talents" and in a "sneak night attack" killed over eighty Kalinagos and drove many off the island. After celebrating the success of their military alliance, the French and English resumed their rivalry over the island until 1713, when the matter was settled in favour of the English by the Treaty of Utrecht.[17]

The success of the Kalinagos in holding on to a significant portion of the Windwards, and their weakening of English settlements in the Leewards, fuelled the determination of the English state to destroy all of them. By the mid-seventeenth century, English merchants, planters and colonial officials were in agreement that Kalinagos "were a barbarous and cruel set of savages beyond reason or persuasion and must therefore be eliminated". By this time it was also clear that the slave-based plantation system demanded an "absolute monopoly" of the Caribbean lands.[18]

What Richard Dunn referred to as Carib independence and self-reliance constituted a major contradiction to the internal logic of wealth accumulation within the plantation economy. The need for a full-scale genocidal war against the Kalinagos assumed great urgency with the English. By the time they had successfully established plantation structures based on sugar cultivation and African enslavement, they had taken the lead in attempting the removal of "human" obstacles to the smooth and profitable expansion of the system. In the Caribbean, English colonies contained the largest numbers of enslaved Africans. Slave owners believed that the control of the enslaved could be severely weakened by the resistance of the Kalinagos.

It did not take long for the enslaved Africans to become aware of the Kalinago struggle against the English and other Europeans, and to realize that they could possibly secure their freedom by fleeing to Kalinago territory. Père Labat, the French missionary who studied interisland slave "marronage" in the Lesser Antilles during this period, stated that enslaved Africans knew that St Vincent was easily reached from Barbados and many escaped there "from their masters in canoes and rafts".[19]

Between 1645 and 1660, the Kalinagos generally took "the runaway slaves back to their masters, or sold them to the French and Spanish", but as they came under more intensive attack during the mid-century, Labat noted, their policy towards African Maroons changed. They now refused to return the Africans and began regarding them "as an addition to their nation".[20]

Labat estimated that in 1670, over five hundred African escapees from Barbados were living in St Vincent. This community was reinforced in 1675 when a slave ship carrying hundreds of Africans to Jamaica via Barbados ran aground off the coast of the neighbouring island of Bequia. Survivors came ashore at St Vincent and were integrated in the Maroon communities. That year, William Stapleton, governor of the Leewards, noting the significant presence of Africans among the Kalinagos, suggested that of the fifteen hundred native "bowmen" in the Leewards, six hundred "are negroes, some runaway from

Barbados and elsewhere". By this time, noted Labat, Africans outnumbered Kalinagos in St Vincent.[21]

At the end of the seventeenth century, the English tried unsuccessfully to exploit the sometimes strained relations between Kalinagos and Africans by encouraging the former to return runaways to their owners. Miscegenation between the predominantly male African Maroon community and Kalinago females was a principal source of social tension between the two ethnic groups. Both the French and English alleged that Kalinago leaders occasionally sought their assistance in ridding their communities of Africans.

The significance of such allegations, however, should be assessed against the background of two important developments in African–Kalinago relations. First, by the mid-seventeenth century, the group of racially mixed persons, now known as the Karifunas, was increasing rapidly in numbers and by 1700 had outnumbered both parent groups in St Vincent. Similarly, noted Labat, the English expeditions from Barbados sent to capture St Vincent during the 1670s were repelled by Kalinagos, Africans and Karifunas.[22]

In 1664 a Barbados document titled "The State of the Case concerning our Title to St Lucia" described the island as being "infected" with Kalinagos. Likewise, in 1668, Thomas Modyford, governor of Jamaica, former Barbados governor and sugar magnate, described St Vincent as a place which "the Indians much infect".

The first systematically pursued diplomatic effort by the English to establish a footing within Kalinago territory in the Windwards was the Willoughby Initiative of 1667. William Lord Willoughby, governor of Barbados, recognized the great financial gain that would accrue to himself, Barbados and England if the Windwards, the last island frontier, could be converted into slave-based sugar plantations.[23]

For over a decade, the sugar kings of Barbados had been signalling their demand for lands to expand their operations, and the nearby Windwards seemed the perfect place. Small-scale military expeditions had been repelled by the Kalinagos since the 1630s, and so Willoughby, not yet organized for a large-scale military assault, opted to send emissaries to open negotiations with Kalinago leaders.[24]

The Kalinagos, in response, showed some degree of flexibility, as is often the case with peoples involved in protracted struggles. Willoughby wanted a peace treaty that would promote English interests by removing obstacles to slave plantation expansionism. The Kalinagos were suspicious and vigilant. In 1666, they were tricked by the English into signing away by treaty their "rights" to inhabit Tortola and were driven off the island. The Windward Islands were their last refuge, and their siege mentality was now more developed than ever.[25]

On 23 March 1667, Kalinago leaders of St Vincent, Dominica and St Lucia met with Willoughby's delegation in St Vincent to negotiate the peace. At the signing of the treaty were Anmwatta, the Grand Babba (or chief of all Kalinagos), Chiefs Wappya, Nay, Le Suroe, Rebura and Aloons. The conditions of the treaty were everything the English slavers wanted:

1. The Caribs of St Vincent shall ever acknowledge themselves subjects of the King of England, and be friends to all in amity with the English, and enemies to their enemies.
2. The Caribs shall have liberty to come to and depart from, at pleasure, any English islands and receive their protection therein, and the English shall enjoy the same in St Vincent and St Lucia.
3. His Majesty's subjects taken by the French and Indians and remaining among the Indians shall be immediately delivered up, as also any Indian captives among the English when demanded.
4. Negroes formerly run away from Barbados shall be delivered to His Excellency; and such as shall hereafter be fugitives from any English island shall be secured and delivered by as soon as required.[26]

The Willoughby Initiative was designed to pave the way for English colonization of the Windwards, using Barbados as the springboard for settlement. Within two months of the Kalinago-Willoughby Treaty, a party of fifty-four English colonists from Barbados arrived at St Vincent to pioneer a settlement. The Kalinagos, Karifunas and Africans objected to their presence, drove them off the island, and broke the treaty with Barbados. The collapse of the Barbados diplomatic mission angered Governor Willoughby, who swiftly moved to the next stage of his plan – a full-scale genocidal offensive.

Willoughby's opportunity came in March of the following year, when English military commander Sir John Harman left behind in Barbados a regiment of foot soldiers and five frigates. Willoughby informed the Colonial Office that since he knew not how to "keep the soldiers quiet and without pay", the only course open to him was to "try his fortune among the Caribs at St

Vincent". Once again, the Kalinagos proved too much for Willoughby, and the expedition returned to Barbados having suffered heavy losses.[27]

English awareness of Kalinago solidarity and efficient communications throughout the islands of the Lesser Antilles meant that they had reasons to expect reprisals following the Willoughby offensives, anywhere and at any time. Governor Modyford of Jamaica, a man knowledgeable about Eastern Caribbean affairs, had opposed Willoughby's war plan. He told the Duke of Albemarle that while Willoughby was "making war with the Caribs of St Vincent", he feared the consequences for settlers at Antigua, and other places. Such an untimely war, he said, "may again put those plantations in hazard, or at best into near broils". "It had been far better", he continued, "to have made peace with them". Not to do so would be "the total ruin of all the English islands" and a "waste of the revenue of Barbados".[28]

Modyford was perceptive in his assessment of Kalinago responses. A report sent to the Colonial Office in London from officials in Nevis, dated April 1669 and titled "An Intelligence of an Indian Design upon the People of Antigua", stated that "the Caribbee Indians have lately broken the peace made with Lord Willoughby, and have killed two and left dead two more of His Majesty's subjects in Antigua". Reference was made to twenty-eight Kalinago warriors who arrived from Montserrat in two canoes and who participated in the raid upon Antigua in response to Willoughby's war in St Vincent.

In addition, Governor Stapleton of the Leewards, in a separate document, outlined his fear for the lives of Leeward Islanders, including those who had gone to work in a Dominica silver mine under an agreement with the Kalinagos. The Barbadians also offered their criticisms of Willoughby's war effort. In 1676, Governor Atkins described it as a "fruitless design", whose overall result was that there remain "no likelihood of any plantations upon Dominica, St. Vincent, St. Lucia and Tobago". Meanwhile, the Antiguans were forced to keep "fourteen files of men", "doubled three days before and after a full moon", as a protective measure against Kalinago warriors.[29]

Governor Stapleton, reflecting on the collapse of the Willoughby Initiative, and considering the prospects for English settlements in the Leewards and Windwards, quickly moved to the front stage what had been Willoughby's agenda. Only the total destruction of "all the Carib Indians", he concluded, could be the "best piece of service for the settlement of these parts".

In December 1675, a petition from "Several Merchants of London", addressed to the Lords of Trade and Plantations in support of Governor Stapleton's extermination plan, called for the granting of a commission to Philip Warner, Stapleton's deputy, to raise soldiers to go into Dominica to "destroy the barbarous savages".[30]

Stapleton, however, had pre-empted the Colonial Office in their response to the London merchants and had already sent Warner "with six small companies of foot", totalling three hundred men, into Dominica to take "revenge" on the "heathens for their bloody perfidious villainies". One William Hamlyn, who participated in the Warner expedition, described the assault upon the Kalinagos as a massacre. At least thirty Kalinagos, he said, were taken and killed on the first round, not including "three that were drawn by a flag of truce" and then shot.[31]

After these executions, Hamlyn reported, another "sixty or seventy men, women and children" were invited to Warner's camp to settle matters over entertainment. These were given rum to drink, and when Warner "gave the signal", the English "fell upon them and destroyed them". Included in those killed by the English was Indian Warner, Philip Warner's own half-brother, whose mother was a Kalinago and who had risen to become a powerful leader among them. The London merchants described Philip Warner as "a man of great loyalty" whose service to the crown in the destruction of the Kalinagos, "who have often attempted to ruin the plantations", should be commended.[32]

In spite of losses sustained in Dominica, the Kalinagos continued to use the island as a military base for self-defence. In July 1681, three hundred Kalinagos from St Vincent and Dominica, in six canoes, led by one who named himself "Captain Peter" and who was described as a "good speaker of English having lived for some time in Barbados", attacked the English settlements in Barbuda. The English were caught by surprise. Eight of them were killed and their houses destroyed. The action was described as swift and without warning.[33] Frustrated again by his inability to protect English lives and property in the Leewards, Stapleton reiterated his call for a war of extermination against the Kalinagos. He was aware, however, of the inability of Leeward Islanders to finance a major war effort, and had also become respectful of the Kalinagos' ability to obtain "intelligence" with respect to their plans.

Given these two circumstances, the Leewards' governor instructed London to order the Barbados government to prepare the grand design against the Kalinagos. Barbados, he added, was closer to the Kalinago-"infested" islands of St Vincent and Dominica; also, on account of the colony's wealth, it would be the "best piece of service" they could offer England.[34] Colonial officials in London accepted Stapleton's plan in its entirety. They instructed him to make plans to "utterly suppress" the Kalinagos or "drive them to the main". They also directed Governor Dutton of Barbados to make all possible contributions to the war effort. Dutton, however, would have no part of it, but, not wishing to contradict the king's orders, informed the Colonial Office that though he was in agreement, Barbadians would support no such design against the Kalinagos, as they considered the affairs of the Leeward Islands none of their business.

The Leeward Islanders, therefore, had to look to their own resources to finance their military operations. In June 1682, a bill was proposed to the Leewards Assembly requesting funds to outfit an expedition against the Kalinagos in Dominica. The council agreed, but the Assembly of Nevis dissented on the grounds that since they had not been attacked by the Kalinagos in over "twenty years", they did not intend to endanger their peace. Months went by and Stapleton failed to get his settlers to agree on a financial plan for the expedition.[35]

By 1700, the grand design had not yet materialized, but the constant state of war continued to reduce Kalinago numbers. By this time, adult Kalinagos in St Vincent and Dominica, according to Labat, "did not exceed 2000" and warriors were "too weak in numbers to do any serious harm" to English colonies. Nonetheless, settlers in the "outlying districts" still had reason to believe that any night, Kalinago warriors could take them by surprise and "cut their throats and burn their houses".[36]

In 1772, Lord Hillsborough, secretary for state in London, issued instructions for the launching of a military offensive against the large and growing Karifuna population at St Vincent, and a major naval force arrived at the island. The British governor of the island reported that the Karifuna struck against the British settlements as soon as they saw the fleet approaching, killing 72 men and wounding 80; another 110 lost their lives to diseases within a month of the outbreak of war.[37]

Unable to hold out against increasing military pressure, however, Chief Chatoyer of the Karifunas and twenty-seven other leaders found it necessary to settle a peace treaty with the English in May 1773. The Karifuna were promised amnesty and sovereignty over a stretch of land in the north of the island

(35 per cent of the island) in return for their allegiance to King George III.[38]

Peace could not be maintained. The expansion of the sugar plantation sector and the persistent racist postures by the British made the political environment volatile. The French revolution and British reactions to it in the Caribbean offered a further opportunity for Karifuna strategic adjustment. The treaty of 1773, which never sat well with the Karifunas, was rejected and war was declared against the British. But the enormous build-up of British military power in the region easily swept away Karifuna resistance.

In the second half of the eighteenth century, political developments in local and international affairs created a context within which British imperial aggression resolved to push aside all indigenous claims to life, liberty and land. The Seven Years' War had offered the last opportunity for the Karifunas to maximize opportunities for resistance by forging alliances with the French against the British. The British won and the peace treaty of 1773 permitted British settlement and was subsequently used as the basis for British proprietary claims upon Karifuna lands.

The British wasted no time after the war in encouraging Sir William Young, chief commissioner for the sale of lands in the Carib territories of St Vincent, to accelerate the pace of British settlement. The commissioner's position was that either a full-scale war against the Karifunas or a strictly enforced peace treaty was a precondition for settler expansion. He told the Colonial Office,

> We have the greatest reason to think that suffering the Charaibs to remain in their present state, will be very dangerous, and may at some period prove fatal to the inhabitants of the country, as their situation, surrounded with wood, makes any access to them for the purpose of executing justice impracticable; and they will from thence be capable of committing all outrages unpunished; or harbouring the slaves of the inhabitants of this island, as well as of all the neighbouring islands; of sheltering amongst those, vagabonds and deserters from the French, and in case of a rupture with France, it is probable they will join in distressing the inhabitants, and in an attempt to conquer the colony.[39]

The final defeat of the Karifunas in St Vincent and St Lucia during the 1790s drew whatever poison was left from the arrows of the greatly reduced indigenous community.

Joseph Chatoyer, paramount chief in St Vincent, was put to death during a bloody clash with British soldiers in March 1795. Hundreds of survivors fled to sanctuary in Dominica. Those who could not do so amounted to some five thousand. These were rounded up by British troops and herded together on the tiny island of Balliceaux in the Grenadines, pending imperial instructions for a final destination. One third of them starved to death on the island during the four months of incarceration before being transported to Rattan, an island off the coast of Honduras on which, it was said, not even iguanas easily survived.[40]

The transportation of Karifuna communities from St Vincent and St Lucia left the Dominica community as the Caribbean island core of the fragmented, militarily defeated indigenous nation. In 1804, lands in St Lucia and St Vincent conceded to the Karifunas by treaty with the British government were forfeited by the Crown. In Dominica, the surviving community eked out a tenuous living in the rainforest and took whatever advantage they could find in selling their craftwork in towns and their labour on neighbouring plantations.

By refusing to capitulate under the collective military pressure of Europeans, however, the Kalinagos, and then the Karifunas, had kept the Windward Islands in a marginal relation to the slave plantation complex for two hundred years, and in so doing made a principal contribution to the freedom traditions of the Caribbean. This history speaks to the origins and legacy of the British official policy of genocide in the Caribbean. The native community experienced the full impact of this policy. Survivors today struggle to sustain what is left of their "nation". Defeated in battle, scattered and politically marginalized, victims continue their rebuilding efforts. They have a legal right to reparations claims. No legal claim is clearer. Only political will and community organization are required to present the case.

Chapter 3

King James's Version

Royal Caribbean Slave Voyages

We have only to look at the names of buildings and roads in Bristol, Liverpool and London. . . . The profits from the slave trade were astronomical.

—*Jeremy Corbyn, Member of Parliament, Debate on the Bicentenary of the Abolition of the Slave Trade, House of Commons, 20 March 2007*

THE BRITISH OBTAINED AFRICANS FOR enslavement and transatlantic trading by all means possible, including widespread kidnapping, and destroying states that opposed them and assassinating their political leaders. During the middle of the sixteenth century, when they began formally to participate in the selling of enchained African bodies across the Atlantic, it was understood in England as a criminal commerce, and slave merchants knew it to be so.[1]

The four slave-trading voyages of John Hawkins between 1562 and 1568, for example, received considerable financial backing from prominent investors, including city magnates and Queen Elizabeth I. When the queen, however, read reports that in order to recruit a "cargo of nigers" for shipment, Hawkins had engaged in weeks of kidnapping, she recoiled, condemned the criminal practice, and forbade any further criminal conduct by English slave traders. The organization of English slave trading, by the stroke of a royal decree, was outlawed and criminalized.[2] To carry off Africans without their consent, she informed her court, would be a thing "which would be detestable and call down the vengeance of Heaven".[3] But royal objection to kidnapping as a recruitment method was ineffective given her policy support and financial commitment to slave trading. The "English being greenhorns as slavers", as P.E.H. Hair and Robin Law remarked, meant that Hawkins had little choice but to "first attempt to obtain slaves by raiding" African villages.[4] But the expectation of huge profits from slave trading pushed aside the royal objection, and the criminal raiding of African villages by Englishmen became the norm. Records suggest that following Hawkins's first voyage there were many English voyages to West Africa.[5]

By the end of the seventeenth century, the English had become exceedingly brutal at slave raiding and had adopted the practice of assassinating African kings who opposed their interest. Hair and Law tell us that during the seventeenth century

> European powers, including the English, did exercise a degree of political influence over African societies on the coast. . . . The English, for example, supported Komenda in a prolonged war with the Dutch in 1644–99. On one notorious occasion, when the king of Komenda had made peace with the Dutch, he was assassinated by the English on a visit to Cape Coast Castle – though as a means of securing a friendly regime in Komenda this proved counterproductive, provoking a violent anti-English reaction.[6]

The murder of an African political leader in order to secure control of bodies for enslavement indicated the lengths to which English merchants were prepared to go in search of enrichment. The "relative strength of their military presence and the political fragmentation of the local African societies" created political environments, in many parts of West Africa for most of the seventeenth and eighteenth centuries, which enabled the trade to thrive.

From being "greenhorns" at the end of the sixteenth century, the English came to dominate the transatlantic trade in African bodies by the mid-eighteenth century. By this time, noted Moira Ferguson, Britain's share of the Atlantic (slave) trade amounted to about 50 per cent of the total, involving the forcible transference and brutal acculturation of probably two million Africans.[7]

The British took the lion's share of the eighteenth-century trade and its profits. They developed control of the trade by wreaking military and political havoc upon African societies, fighting bloody and costly wars against European rivals, and mobilizing the economic power of their domestic manufacturing base and financial institutions.

The greed that led to the crime of slaving had to be justified and sold to citizens at home. In attempting to "sell" this crime to an unsuspecting public, the slave trading interest went to great lengths to suggest that Africans were not human and were deserving of enchainment and enslavement. This doubled the nature of the crime rather than justified it. Of all the European slavers, the English presented the most detailed and sustained literary and ideological effort to deny the African people their right to be recognized as human beings.

The English actions, then, had the greatest impact upon the black race. First, they globalized the trade so that, by the eighteenth century, they were the largest shippers; second, they produced the most abundant body of writing that established, within the intellectual and social consciousness of the world, the racist philosophy that African people were not entitled to the freedom they cherished.

During the seventeenth century, the English generally believed that black Africans were an inferior people. This view was expressed in the laws and customs used to govern them as enslaved persons. It was also stimulated by writing about the slave trade. Together these texts constituted a source of cultural authority used to justify slavery and the slave trade as entrepreneurial activity. The English justification of slave trading was a large-scale literary and intellectual project. The notion that Africans were non-human, or subhuman at best, and that their right to humanity could be denied and ignored was an intellectual construct that required considerable literary focus and sustained articulation. A mountain of published materials was produced supporting this justification of slavery. As a body of writing, it represents the moral descent of the British mind into the darkest pit of racial hatred.[8]

Seeking to deny the human status of Africans also required the theological support of the church. The English public would support the crime only if it was presented to them as "right" and in the national interest. This is exactly what was done. It was a two-pronged assault on public sensibility: proving that slavery was not a crime and demonstrating that it was in the national interest.

Blackburn has noted that the trade in African bodies had to be packaged as "a commerce to be patronized by royalty, blessed by the clergy, and practised by the aristocracy and gentry". All of this was achieved in England by the mid-seventeenth century. It was a triumph of the soldier and scholar, monarch and merchant, priest and philosopher, investor and industrialist – all banded together and cloaked in nationalism.[9]

The English state believed it needed to commit the slavery crime in order to advance its economic, political, military and social power in an increasingly nationalistic Europe. The national interest had to be served and given top priority. This is where Locke committed his political advice to king and cabinet, and attached a greater importance to economic and political interest over moral and legal right and reasoning. Blackburn concludes, "Locke endorsed colonial slavery because he thought it an institution necessary to the productive exploitation of English colonies."[10] Locke, in so advising, was aware of the objection to slave trading on moral, ethical and legal grounds.

As a royalist, Locke knew of Queen Elizabeth I's earlier forbidding of the crime of kidnapping Africans. As an administrator of slavery, he would have known of early rejections of slave trading by English commodity traders in Africa who were investing in the redwoods and gold trades. Richard Jobson, for example, an English trader in Gambia in 1623, objected strongly when invited to add enchained African bodies to his cargo of wood and gold, and made it clear that he was an honest, reputable merchant. "I made answer," he replied, "we were a people, who did not deale in any such commodities, neither did wee buy or sell one another, or any that had our owne shape."[11]

Jobson's refusal to buy and sell "commodities" that "had our owne shape" reflected the legal ground that had been established by Queen Elizabeth I, but the growing weight of the argument that England's wealth and health as a nation required the slave trade pushed him into a minority "eccentric" position.

Five years earlier, in 1618, King James I of England had granted royal approval for the establishment of a firm called "The Company of Adventurers of London Trading to the Ports of Africa". The company was granted a royal monopoly to trade "forever" in Guinea and Benin, so as to secure the royal investment and that of those in the inner circle. The African trades were proving to be so attractive to the English elite investors that the royal monopoly was taken to Parliament in 1624 and severely criticized as an exclusion of the rights of Englishmen.[12]

In 1631, another firm was established called "The Company of Merchants Trading to Guinea", and in 1640 the private-sector interest that backed the political cause of the English Parliament against the king took control of these corporate enterprises. In this process of corporate development, expressed in the formation of large joint-stock companies, merchants were given a free hand in England to "sail to Guinea to take 'nigers' and carry them to foreign parts".[13]

The restoration of the English monarchy in 1660 represented the beginning of the political effort to place the trade in enslaved Africans on a sustainable and more profitable path. The king and Parliament combined to establish England as the premier slave-trading nation. This policy required the mobilizing of the investing public and the full backing of the government.

The market for enslaved labour in the West Indies was in full bloom following the financially successful introduction of the sugar industry. It was consequent upon the inability of the English working class to supply enough workers for plantation employment as indentured servants and the legal and cultural constraints that prevented the enslavement of white contracted workers.

The instrument the royals chose to revolutionize the English engagement in the trade in African bodies was a fully capitalized joint stock company, more financially secure than any that had been established previously. The prime leader in this project was the Duke of York, the soon-to-be King James II of England. The business established under his governorship was "The Company of Royal Adventurers Trading to Africa", a re-chartered operation with wider scope. It was given a royal monopoly for one thousand years by his older brother, Charles II, to trade in African bodies on the Gambia coast, with powers to take over the military fortifications on the Gold Coast in order to expand its operations. As governor, the Duke of York saw to it that the royal investment was secure and profitable.

The charter obtained on 10 January 1663 was explicit: the company would "trade for the buying and selling, bartering and exchanging of, for or with any negroes, slaves, goods, wares and merchandises whatsoever". The duke "faithfully held weekly board meetings in his apartment at Whitehall". From his home, he made public declarations calling on the "king's subjects in England to subscribe for shares"; the response was always impressive. One hundred thousand pounds sterling (£172 million in 2010 value) was raised in three subscriptions to fund the purchase of twenty-five slave ships. "The company therefore undertook this task, realizing that in the Negro trade it would find by far its most lucrative returns."[14]

With a fleet of slave ships outfitted, "the Duke of York . . . informed Governor Willoughby (of Barbados) that the company had made arrangements to provide Barbados and the Caribbee Islands with 3,000 slaves per annum". The duke also pledged that the company's "negroes imported into the island should be sold in lots, as had been the custom, at the average rate of seventeen pounds per head [£26,100 in 2010]".[15]

Between 11 August 1663 and 17 March 1664, the company delivered 3,075 enchained Africans to its agents in Bridgetown. Of these, 1,051 men, 1,018 females, 136 boys and 56 girls were sold at an average price of £16. The adults were sold at the agreed £17, while the children fetched less. By 1668 the island's population was estimated at sixty thousand, of which forty thousand were enslaved Africans.[16]

The Africans delivered to Barbados were branded "with a burning hot iron on the right breast" with the letters "DY", representing the Duke of York. This made for effective inventory keeping, while dehumanizing the Africans to the status of cattle and chattel. With the duke's brand and the profits flowing, the "English now became the leading trader in Guinea". The Dutch shipped the most gold, Law concluded, "but the English were shipping the most slaves".[17]

The winding up of the Company of Royal Adventurers and the establishment of a new company in 1672, with the name Royal African Company, signalled to the English investor community that the profits in selling African bodies were too great to stay within the confines of royal insiders.

The excluded elements of the private sector cried foul and insisted upon access to the trade. The "black gold" was too lucrative a commodity not to allow all investors an equal opportunity to participate. What ensued in the last quarter of the seventeenth century was a national campaign to allow the English private sector to participate fully in the wealth generated by the trade.

The swarming of the slave trade with private investors demanding free trade and an end of royal monopoly speaks to the reality that the trade in African bodies was the most attractive investment nationally available. Like bees around the hive, all traders and investors wanted a taste of the honey. The farce of minority dissent meant that the private sector would win the national debate, and in 1698 the royal monopoly of the African Company was broken and free trade was imposed upon the English illegal commerce.

The national campaign to "free up" the "slave trade to all investors was conducted within the political context of the Bill of Rights demanded in the English Revolution of 1688". The Scottish insisted on their share, and outfitted dozens of ships for the West African coast. Parliament, then, saw to it that free trade in enchained African bodies became the national policy of England, an initiative that was considered in the national interest.

According to Law, "the company was quickly swamped" by free traders and in 1708 it was estimated that the latter had imported around seventy-five thousand Africans into English colonies since 1698. The English, then, had converted the trade in enchained African bodies into being its principal international trade and its most lucrative business investment. For the remainder of the eighteenth century, when the transatlantic trade reached its maximum in terms of volume, Britain had "seized the largest share".[18]

The slave trade, noted Christopher Brown, "mattered to the emerging wealth and power of the British Empire" and to the English "nation as a whole". A national consensus held that the fortune generated by slave trading was critical to nation building and to imperial power, and that its contribution to the growth of wealthy towns such as London, Bristol and Liverpool was obvious. To oppose the slave trade was to oppose the national interest. For this reason, the beginning of a movement to end the trade was surrounded by "fears of national decline".[19]

The political argument that slave trading was tied to the national interest, and defended in this way, had its loudest voices among government officials and parliamentarians who, as private investors, were major traders. In the 1720s, for example, Humphrey Morice transported hundreds of enslaved Africans. When Henry Lascelles entered Parliament in 1745, noted Brown, he had been trafficking in enslaved Africans for more than three decades. At least three merchants with seats in the House of Commons – George Aufrere, Anthony Bacon and Samuel Touchet – enjoyed lucrative contracts to provide the British trading forts in West Africa during the 1760s and 1770s. Four other members of Parliament, Brown showed, served on the executive committee of the Company of Merchants Trading to Africa between 1750 and 1764: Samuel Dicken, Charles Pole, Peregrine Cust and Edward Lewis.[20]

The British Parliament, then, was well populated with slave traders whose task it was to ensure that the traffic in African bodies fuelled the national development of Britain. These voices, added to those who benefited financially, as well as their political constituents, defined and defended the notion that the slave trade was necessary to advance the national interest of Great Britain. They also constituted a critical part of the governance arm of the state. For this reason, the abolitionist Granville Sharp argued that "because the slave trade was a national project", it was also by extension a national "crime", though he preferred to use the word "sin".[21]

State power, argued Daunton and Halpern, "was central to the creation of slavery and the dominance of a planter class in the Caribbean", and for this reason, they concluded, it is "possible to develop a radical critique of the state, at home and in the colonies, as exploitative and corrupt". This is but the statement of a half-truth. The British state, in its slavery dealings, was not "sinful", as Sharp argued, nor "corrupt" as stated above; it was engaged directly in criminal enrichment.[22]

British slave traders sought to deflect the criminal nature of their undertaking by proclaiming in Parliament and in communities that their "commerce (was) a national undertaking" and that they were entitled to "secure financial assistance from the state". Indeed, slave traders in the mid-eighteenth century argued that they operated their businesses as licensed agents of King George III. Both Whitehall and Westminster created and sustained the legal, fiscal and financial infrastructure for the slave trade to operate as a profitable British enterprise. It is therefore misleading to argue, as does Christopher Brown, that "British merchants, not the British state, directed the traffic".[23]

Brown concedes, however, that the state made critical financial investments in the traffic, and offered good returns to King James II, formerly the Duke of York, chairman and governor of the board of directors of the Royal African Company. The British state used taxpayers' money to maintain the slave forts in West Africa, without which there could have been no viable national slave trade. Brown states,

> The important exception lay with the management of the British trading forts that dotted the West African coast from James Island in the Gambia River to Fort William at Whydah on the "slave coast", in present day Benin. The Royal African Company owned and operated these forts until 1750. After its dissolution in 1752, parliament established a Company of Merchants Trading to Africa, to oversee the forts. . . . At the direction of parliament, the treasury awarded an annual subsidy first to the Royal African Company, and then to the Company of Merchants Trading to Africa to maintain and provide the British establishment on the coast.[24]

The annual subvention from the public treasury confirmed that the British slave trade was officially deemed a part of the national interest and that the government was prepared to act accordingly.

When parliamentarians and other civil society leaders objected to "the use of taxpayers' money to fund the slave trade . . . parliament simply authorized the annual request". This is a typical example of how the state and the private sector came together in defining and promoting "the national interest". When Parliament legislated in 1698 to open the traffic in African bodies to free trade, enabling a private sector feast in search of quick fortunes, it had also provided that the investors would pay a 10 per cent tax to the company in order to maintain the slave factories on the African Coast. The reason for this tax, Parliament decided, was that the "forts and castles are undoubtedly necessary for the preservation and well-carrying-on the said trade". Brown concludes, "The House of Commons declared the forts essential to English interests in the region on seven occasions."[25]

The slave traders were aware that their profits advanced the emergence of the British nation. They were prepared to demonstrate this, and occasionally boasted that all citizens of Great Britain shared in the benefits. In 1730, an official spokesman for the Royal African Company made the point forcefully: "There is not a man in this kingdom who does not more or less partake of the Benefits and Advantages of the Royal African Company's Forts and Castles in Africa."[26] In Parliament, members rose in support of an increased subvention, providing the company with £10,000 annually (£18.7 million in 2010) to protect the slave trade so that slavers "along the coast could fill their ships with enslaved men, women, and children, in weeks rather than months".[27]

In the seventeenth century, the state had set the trade in motion, and during the following century it reaped the rewards of the investment. By the 1750s, "330,000 or so British seamen" were engaged in the slave trade. This was a massive dedication of maritime human resources and speaks to the enormity of the trade within the context of British international interests. These 330,000 workers assured British dominance as the largest slave trader in Europe, and Britain as the country best placed to extract the greatest profits.[28]

Most Africans who found themselves on slave ships were kidnapped in raids upon their communities. The trade stimulated political instability and social chaos, and facilitated spiralling warfare and conflict. As a result of social disruption, larger numbers of Africans were exposed to the practices of kidnappers. It was a vicious cycle, and over time these developments served to increase the volume of humans available to the trade.

In 1702, for example, the Africans near Cape Mesurado complained to William Bosman of the Dutch West India Company that "the English had been there with two large vessels and had ravaged the country, destroyed all their canoes, plundered their houses, and carried off some of their people as slaves". The English, in turn, wrote that it was common for the Dutch in the Gambia to entice the Africans by shows of fireworks and then kidnap them by force of arms. Kings and other nobles who opposed the trade were undermined by European traders. Slave traders armed and financed neighbouring groups to launch wars against them.

To oppose the trade was to invite hostility. Africans, noted James Walvin, "quickly became accustomed to staring at the guns mounted on the ships and trained on their canoes and settlements, or carried by sailors on the coast". Naturally, in order to protect themselves and even out the military power of Europeans, "Africans were especially keen to acquire firearms". As a result, says Walvin, "the export of arms to Africa was a massive business", and by the peak of the trade in the mid-eighteenth century, Europeans sold "between 283,000 and 394,000 guns each year into West Africa". The militarization of West Africa facilitated the trade, as communities were drawn into a violent orgy of self-defence, conducting raids upon neighbours – oftentimes to protect themselves – and fighting Europeans.[29]

Increased state militarization and politically supported violence against communities were sponsored directly and indirectly by English slavers. Such client states sprang up within the vicinity of slave forts. The Bambara State of Segu, formed about 1712, has been described as "an enormous machine to produce slaves". The British provided horses and guns to its client leaders, who supplied the captives. In the early seventeenth century, one good horse could be exchanged for fifteen healthy enslaved Africans. This value transaction was considered by the British as a way of obtaining enslaved labour on the cheap.

African villagers, then, whether or not they lived within client states, were exposed to the raiding forces of British slave traders and African professional warriors. From Senegal to Angola, these client states sprang up or were recreated from old states. One of their primary functions was to subvert and displace states and their leaders that opposed the slaving business.

Some African communities, however, learned how to defend themselves within this new context, and developed a cultural politics of resistance against the British and their client collaborators. They rejected the trading interest of their leaders and established a mass opposition movement.

Popular rebellion forced its way through the compliance of political leaders and set in motion a tradition of resistance that spread through West Africa. By so doing, Africans themselves established an anti-slaving movement that was as significant politically as the client arrangements between kings, nobles and British slavers.

Captain William Potter of the ship *Perfect*, a Liverpool slaver, experienced the force of community resistance in 1758. He had almost completed the purchase of over three hundred Africans and was preparing to sail. His ship was attacked on the River Gambia by the members of the community who had witnessed the sale. The entire crew was killed in the assault. Hugh Thomas has also shown that slave ships were frequently assaulted on rivers by warriors on rafts. Heavily armed with guns and knives, they would often board ships and free captives.[30]

There were hundreds of similar occurrences. Some events had a greater impact on the conduct of the trade than did others. One seminal case took place at Calabar in 1767. Seven British ships – five from Liverpool, one from Bristol and one from London – were awaiting "human" cargoes on the Old Calabar River, where captains and agents had established trading relations with the king of New Calabar. An armed contingent of over thirty Africans from Old Calabar attacked the English, who were defended by the king's soldiers. The leader of the Old Calabar warriors was captured and beheaded; others were sold into slavery in the West Indies.[31]

Descriptions of resistance to slaving on the coast and at sea are quite vivid. Thousands jumped to their death. The captain of the English slave ship *Hannibal* wrote in 1694, "The negroes are so wilful and loth to leave their own country, that they have often leap'd out of the canoes, boat and ship, into the sea, and kept under water till they were drowned, to avoid being taken up and saved by our boats, which pursued them; they having a more dreadful apprehension of Barbadoes than we can have of hell." Furthermore, he said,

> We had about 12 negroes did wilfully drown themselves, and others starv'd themselves to death; for 'tis their belief that when they die they return home to their own country and friends again. I have been inform'd that some commanders have cut off the legs and arms of the most wilful, to terrify the rest, for they believe if they

lose a member, they cannot return home again: I was advis'd by some of my officers to do the same.[32]

Some captains of slave ships went to great lengths to deter captured Africans from this practice. In 1774, Oliver Goldsmith recounted two instances he had recorded from slave ship captains. In respect of the first case, he wrote,

> The master of a Guinea-ship, finding a rage for suicide among his slaves, from a notion the unhappy creatures had, that after death they should be restored again to their families, friends, and country; to convince them at least that some disgrace should attend them here, he immediately ordered one of their dead bodies to be tied by the heels to a rope, and so let down into the sea; and, though it was drawn up again with great swiftness, yet in that short space, the sharks had bit off all but the feet.[33]

A second case, wrote Marcus Rediker, was even more gruesome. A captain seized upon a woman and sacrificed her "as a proper example to the rest". He ordered the woman tied with a rope under her armpits and lowered into the water: "When the poor creature was thus plunged in, and about half way down, she was heard to give a terrible shriek, which at first was ascribed to her fears of drowning; but soon after, the water appearing red all around her, she was drawn up, and it was found that a shark, which had followed the ship, had bit her off from the middle." Other captains, Rediker wrote, practised a kind of sporting terror, using human remains to troll for sharks. He cited a slave trader who wrote, "Our way to entice them was by towing overboard a dead Negro, which they would follow till they had eaten him up."[34]

The British in Africa, like their counterparts in the Caribbean, believed that beheading the bodies of Africans before throwing them into the sea was the most effective way to stamp out the practice of suicide. By this action, slavers sought to impress upon Africans that their journey to the ancestors was precluded since the head and body were disposed of separately. But suicide as an act of resistance remained commonplace.

The Atlantic voyage witnessed the continuation of resistance. Slavers knew that Africans would revolt if any opportunity was offered. Maximum security was therefore the order of the journey. They used the terror of guns and cannon mounted on deck, pointing at the storage holes to secure order. Africans were always vigilant and expectant.

In 1770, the captives aboard the Dutch slave ship *Guinniese Vriendschap*, led by Essjerrie Ettin, seized control of the vessel but were soon overpowered by the warship *Castor*. In 1795, Africans seized control of a ship called the *Neptunius* and were seeking to return to Africa. An English warship, alerted to the situation and noting that it was not one of their own, opened fire and blew it out of the water. On another occasion, in 1780, Africans aboard the *Vigilantie* overpowered the crew and took control of the ship; the crew fled in life boats, leaving the ship, which was eventually captured by a British warship.[35]

British slavers were not keen to report accounts of successful African rebellion. But a few such cases exist. The 1752 story of the *Marlborough* of Bristol is one such example. The four hundred Africans on board, from Bonny and Elmina on the Gold Coast, rose up and killed thirty-three of the thirty-five crew; two were kept alive to assist with navigation and were ordered to return the ship to Bonny. On the way to Bonny, the Gold Coast Africans objected to the journey, and a clash between the two groups ensued in which ninety-eight persons were killed. At the end of the conflict, the Gold Coast group took control of the vessel and headed for Elmina with one of the white navigators. They, too, vanished from British recorded history.[36]

The social and economic development of West Africa in the seventeenth and eighteenth centuries was subverted by the reign of terror known as the transatlantic slave trade. Many kings and nobles, unable to end the slave trade, tried to impose systems of control in order to minimize the violence and destruction of life. Some sought to outlaw kidnapping in their states and allowed only the sale of persons who were convicted for crimes and political prisoners.

In the 1780s, Dr C. Wadstrom informed the British Privy Council of a case in which a king on the Gambia River forbade kidnapping, but it was practised nonetheless by British slavers. The British vessel in question had departed from Gorée but was followed and captured by Africans who released the victims. The vessel was destroyed along with three other British vessels that were anchored in the harbour; most of the crew aboard these vessels lost their lives.

Anti-slaving activities, then, were an important political feature of West African politics and should, therefore, be understood at both the level of the formal state policy and of the mass resistance of communities. The people who paid the highest price for standing against the trade were the Africans themselves. Today they continue to pay a price because their struggle has been written out of history within Eurocentric texts and their invisibility in abolitionism maintained.

Serious estimates of the numbers of Africans sold into the transatlantic slave trade now range from about 9.6 million on the lower end to about 15 million at the top. In the past three decades, the debate has been centred on the work of Philip Curtin, who in 1969 published the first attempt at a comprehensive census. Curtin estimated that between 1500 and 1900, about 11.2 million Africans departed their homelands and that 9.6 million reached the New World. He suggested that perhaps about 2 million perished in the passage.

Curtin's figures have generated considerable debate, particularly among scholars who see them as conservative, though criticisms have tended to make only moderate upward adjustments. Paul Lovejoy's 1989 calculations yield the figure of 11,863,000 entering the trade, with about 10.2 million arriving in the New World. In 1998, Joseph Inikori, a critic of Curtin's calculations, offered the larger global figure of 12,689,000. He was keen to point out, however, that "this figure has been contested by some scholars, and while the process of revision continues, it seems probable that the ultimate figure is unlikely to be less than 12 million or more than 20 million captives exported from Africa in the transatlantic slave trade". In 1995, Per O. Hernaes offered figures 100,000 in excess of Inikori's, and in 2000, David Eltis presented calculations that showed a grand total of 11,062,000 departures.[37]

Research shows that in the earliest years of the trade, mortality among the enslaved in the Middle Passage was oftentimes as high as 20 per cent and that the rate was reduced to about 5 per cent by the nineteenth century. Declining mortality was an effect of growing efficiency in slavers' operations. An important aspect of this development was the tendency towards standardization in the shipping arrangements across imperial lines.

Ships weighing about two hundred tons, specially designed and constructed, became the norm by the mid-eighteenth century. Herbert Klein maintained that even the drastically reduced mortality rate of 5 per cent still represented a very high figure compared to populations in their home environment.[38]

There is broad agreement that the Middle Passage did not begin with the actual transatlantic voyage but rather with the capture of Africans in the interior, and it ended with their adjustment experience in the Americas. Six distinct stages of the Middle Passage have been identified:

1. Capture and enslavement in Africa
2. The journey to the coast and other departure points
3. Storage and packaging for shipment
4. The transatlantic crossing
5. Sale and dispersion in the Americas
6. Adjustment in the Americas

The conceptual separation of these stages allows for detailed analysis, particularly with respect to the successive experiences of individuals. Not all Africans survived each stage, and some experienced different stages more than once and for different lengths of time. Between regions, also, individuals experienced these stages differently.

Many persons were captured and sold more than once before reaching the coast, and some had already been taken captive by others before their sale to the British. A few were taken quickly to the coast and put on board ships that set sail, while others were stored in forts for long periods of time, or changed hands between different European slavers, before setting out on the crossing. All of these circumstances impacted the overall Middle Passage conditions and determined African mortality.

Enormous loss of life characterized the period before the Atlantic crossing. African coasts were referred to as the "white man's grave", but they were also a veritable cemetery for Africans. Many succumbed to brutality and terror, as well as the diseases for which they had no effective immune response. The psychological impact of social exposure to white slavers, who many Africans thought were cannibals, a hitherto unseen ocean, strange diseases, physical brutality, trauma, degradation by branding with hot irons for labelling, and general malnourishment, constituted a recipe for high mortality for many – and madness for some.

On the Slave Coast – Togo, Dahomey and western Nigeria – Africans were stored in prisons called *barracoons* which were located on the beach front. At Elmina and Cape Coast in Ghana, for example, in the forts, or "castles" as the large barracoons were also called, storage space for hundreds of Africans was available in "dungeons". Many died in these overcrowded, poorly ventilated facilities. Some 8 per cent of Africans died while held in storage on the coast as commodities.

The Royal African Company tried to reduce mortality levels by putting captives to work in the fort while awaiting shipment and by encouraging ship captains to arrive more frequently. The manager at a company fort in 1705, for example, expressed concern in a letter to his employer, which stated, "I recommend that you space the arrival of ships better for we cannot purchase large numbers of slaves if no ships are on the coast or due to arrive, because if slaves have to wait a long time they run a great risk of dying and also cost a great deal to feed."[39] In that year, the company records show that 95, or 14.6 per cent, of a group of 650 Africans in storage died. While this may not be a representative sample, it does suggest the importance of examining the mortality that preceded actual shipment.

Miller's work has shown also that British slavers debated at length the relative merits of the two methods of transporting Africans across the Middle Passage.[40] These were "loose packing" and "tight packing". The latter system was based on the assumption that a loss of about 10 per cent was inevitable regardless of the numbers on board, and that it was more economical to pack the ship full to capacity and seek maximum speed across the Atlantic.

Loose packing was preferred by those slavers who believed that the more physically comfortable the captives were, the lower would be the mortality. They opted to stock ships up to perhaps 75 per cent of capacity with the objective of reducing mortality to less than 10 per cent. Slavers, then, were divided into two schools of thought with respect to the delivery of cargoes. In general, the evidence indicates that tight packing above the usual levels had no discernible impact on mortality rates.

Slavers did not fully understand the ways in which contagious diseases spread within confined environments and the reasons why exposure was fatal for some persons and not others. They dealt with the evidence as it appeared in individual cases. Epidemics of contagious diseases could destroy the better part of a shipment and were usually associated with extraordinarily high levels of mortality. Africans from different disease environments were thrown together on slave ships and thus exposed to new pathogens. The first-time exposure to European diseases had greater effects. Outbreaks of dysentery, measles and smallpox were known killers. Surgeons on board slave ships were expected to examine captives for signs of sickness and disease.

In order to protect seemingly healthy persons, those diagnosed with disease were sometimes thrown overboard. It has been suggested that many such persons were reasonably healthy and, if given an opportunity, would have recovered. Many symptoms recognized by doctors were in fact related more to stress and dehydration. Vomiting, bloody diarrhoea, delirium and skin rashes were recognized as evidence of disease and infection, and some persons with these ailments were thrown overboard. Medical ignorance, then, may have contributed to Middle Passage mortality.

It is important to note that women survived the passage at rates marginally better than men. This difference is noticeable in the slave traders' records. The overall death rate for men has been estimated at about 20 per cent and for women at about 15 per cent. Many reasons have been advanced for this differential. A tendency was for slavers to expose young women for the purpose of sexual exploitation to marginally better physical conditions on board and that may have impacted favourably. It has been said, also, that women are more effective stress managers; that they are better able to physically withstand the effects of shock, pain and malnutrition; and that their immune systems are more resistant to unfamiliar pathogens.

Historians, furthermore, have done more than calculate mortality loss per ship during the passage. Miller's analysis sets out the way to measure the rate of loss – that is, the percentages associated with each week of the voyage. Several observations have emerged from the study of the rate of loss:

1. The highest mortality was experienced during the first twenty days of the voyage. (Many of these persons would probably have died on land if there were a longer storage period.)
2. The rate declined during the middle part of the voyage.
3. The rate rose rapidly again after about sixty to seventy days, caused largely by food and water shortages.

No direct relationship has been established between the mortality rate and ship size. This is not surprising, since the conditions below deck for Africans were unlikely to vary meaningfully according to ship size. It is striking how similar were European ship-building methods, and particularly the storage systems. Slave ships in the eighteenth century, when the trade had reached its most expansive stage, carried on average about three hundred Africans.

The records of the Royal African Company for 1675 to 1725 show that the mean number of Africans per ship was 235 to Barbados and 270 to Jamaica. The mean size of ships used was 179 tons. Half of the ships used by the Company in the 1720s were between 100 and 200 tons, and a third between 200 and 300 tons. The typical French ship, particularly those owned by established traders, carried about 395 Africans, and ships owned by the Portuguese about 350. British ships, then, tended to be smaller.

The horrors of the Middle Passage led many public commentators to adopt critical views on the slave trade while remaining supportive of slavery. Not surprisingly, then, the British rallied against the slave trade long before they made the decision to abolish slavery. Overcrowding was the norm on all slave ships, in spite of the debate about "tight packing" and "loose packing", for all ships carried Africans under conditions that made extreme discomfort the norm. In order to prevent flight, suicide or revolt, Africans were chained together below deck, packed like "stones in a wall" and kept as prisoners on commuted death sentences. The stench on slave ships was sickening even to the slavers, whose mortality from disease and illnesses was sometimes as high as that of the captives.

For the enslaved, however, the Middle Passage over time offered no increasing sense of comfort. Dr Thomas Trotter, a Scottish physician reporting on the British trade, stated that Africans were so tightly packed they had no room to move themselves. He described them as being packed "spoonways" and locked to one another. Below deck, he said, was filthy with bad odour, and filled with the sounds of suffering and sickness. It was normal for the sexes to be stored separately, and the crew considered sexual access to captives a right during the journey. Thousands of women arrived in the New World impregnated as a result of rape and sexual violation. These conditions on board slave ships were discussed on public platforms during the European and American anti–slave trade campaigns.

At least an estimated one million Africans lost their lives within the narrow context of the Middle Passage, and a larger number, says Patrick Manning, died as a direct result of capture and enslavement within Africa. Even more, it is important to add to these estimates that millions of those who survived the Middle Passage died young, in a short time, in the New World.[41]

An effect of increased death rates upon arriving at the plantations in the Americas was that Africans were rarely able to reproduce themselves naturally for most of the slavery period. In fact, the most distinguishing feature of African populations in the Caribbean up to the nineteenth century was that they experienced a natural demographic decline. So, whereas it was normal for white colonial populations to grow naturally, blacks suffered a systematic, long-term inability because of high death rates, particularly among infants, and low birth rates.

In the United States of America, the black population succeeded in growing naturally, an experience that stands in contrast to the Caribbean decline. In effect, the Caribbean holocaust which began with the native "Indian" population continued with the Africans for most of the slavery period because the Indians were sustained only by the arrival of Africans.

The trade in "black ivory", as James Walvin called the enslaved Africans, was profitable enough to attract an unending line of investors on four continents for more than four centuries. Slave trading was big business; it utilized advanced management, complex financial arrangements and state-of-the-art investment instruments. Furthermore, it was not a poor man's business. The investment required to participate in the trade was considerable.[42]

The shipment of over 10 million enslaved people across the Atlantic for near four hundred years was a major management project. Investments were made on all sides of the Atlantic: in Europe, Africa, and North and South America. The trade called for an enormous sense of global enterprise and considerable entrepreneurial confidence. It required a specific, facilitating business ethic.

The records of William Davenport of Liverpool, an accomplished, committed slave trader, have survived for the business period 1757–1785. It is the best collection of records available for a British slave trader. Davenport took most of his captives from Old Calabar and Cameroon. The records of sixty-seven of his voyages have been analysed by David Richardson. These voyages entailed a gross capital outlay of £320,000 (£429.1 million in 2010), generating returns of £380,000 (£509 million in 2010) and a net profit of £60,000 (£80.4 million in 2010).[43]

By the middle of the eighteenth century, the British had established themselves as the most efficient extractors of profits from the slave trade. The relatively advanced development of Britain's industrial and commercial economy was reflected in the tendency for British slavers to experience lower unit costs. The British could certainly outfit slave ships more economically than their rivals because most of the goods put on board for Africa were either locally made or procured in their colonies in Asia and the Americas.

Chapter 4

Not Human

Britain's Black Property

Parliament, prior to that legislation [the Abolition of the Slave Trade Act], had already passed over 100 laws accommodating the slave trade. Those laws allowed slaves to be treated by the courts as property, not as people. Many died and, yes, some were murdered in the most criminal circumstances, with no redress.

—*Deputy Prime Minister John Prescott, Debate on the Bicentenary of the Abolition of the Slave Trade, 20 March 2007*

THE BRITISH LEGALLY DEFINED AFRICANS as "nonhuman". They were not members of the human race. At best they were a subspecies. For this reason, a special body of laws was put in place for their social governance and economic management. Socially, they were considered as "beasts of burden" to be driven to work for British profit and prestige. In law, they were classified as "property", "real estate" and "chattel".[1]

Such legal and social categorizations were not confined to the arguments of philosophers, theologians and lawyers. They were argued by economists and political leaders. These views were embedded within commercial laws, approved by the state. Caribbean economy and society were built with slave labour premised on the legal provision that Africans were not members of the human family.

The dehumanization of Africans in British law and philosophy was a critical part of the nationalism that drove the colonial project. It enabled slave trading and chattel slavery to become part of the core of British identity. When British slave traders purchased the African body, they also sought to purchase the legal rights attendant to property. As such, they could do with their "property" whatever the law allowed. Enslaved Africans could be bought or sold, raped and branded with irons, thrown into the sea to their death and then claims for loss of property be made upon insurers. They could be murdered for disobedience and their offspring sold without their consent. They could be driven to work until their death and forced to reproduce like animals.[2]

After enchained Africans were purchased from the slave ship, the first task of the owner was to brand them, as they did horses and cattle. The name or initials of the owner were scorched into their bodies with hot irons. In 1694, the captain of the slave ship *Hannibal* stated that after the purchase was completed on the African coast, "then we mark'd the slave we had bought in the breast, or shoulder, with a hot iron, having the letter of the ship's name on it, the place being before anointed with a little palm oil, which caus'd but little pain; the mark usually well in four or five days, appearing very plain and white after".[3]

Africans who were purchased for the English Royal African Company in the 1670s were branded "DY", Duke of York, after the governor of the company. The Spanish firm Compañia Gaditana branded Africans with the letter "d", and the Middleburgische Kamerse Campagnie of Holland used the letters "CCN". The German company Churfarstlich-Afrikanisch-Brandenburgische Compagnie branded them on the right shoulder with the letters "CABC".[4]

Once the Africans were popularly defined as "animals" and accepted in society as property, then slave traders and slave owners could proceed to establish an economic system on the basis of an Englishman's investment rights in Africans. In 1709, for example, Sir Dalby Thomas, an officer of the Royal African Company, described the African people thus:

> The natives here have neither religion nor law binding them to humanity, good behaviour or honesty. They frequently for their grandeur sacrifice an innocent man, that is a person they have no crime to charge, and to train their children up to cruelty they give them knives to cut and slash the person that is to be killed, neither have they any knowledge of liberty and property. Besides the blacks are naturally such rogues and bred up with such roguish principles that what they can get by force or deceit and can defend themselves from those they robb [*sic*], they reckon it as honestly their own, as if they paid for it.[5]

Mercantile and medical minds merged. Dr James Houston, a surgeon, writing from West Africa in 1725, informed his readers that Africans were not humans but animals: "[The African's] natural temper is barbarously cruel, selfish, and deceitful, and their government equally barbarous and uncivil. And consequently the men of greatest eminency amongst them are those that are most capable of being the greatest of rogues; vice being left without any check on it, becomes a virtue. As for their customs, they exactly resemble their fellow creatures and natives, the monkeys."[6] The British slave system, then, comprised merchants and money lenders as well as scientists and sociologists. They were all gathered to serve the national interest.

Blackburn states that the denial of African humanity by the British was forceful, and driven deeply into popular culture. English authors, he noted, wrote in unison that Africans "are not human, or are kindred to apes".[7] The literary arena, like medical science, was penetrated and corrupted by the slavery complex. The literary and scientific propaganda reached its apex around the time that slave-trading companies were formed. The crime against humanity received powerful intellectual endorsement. "The fact is," Blackburn concludes, "the British Caribbean was the setting for a prodigious new reality."[8]

The "new reality" was a racial world built on the criminal enslavement of Africans as property. It proceeded from the imagination and machinations of the emerging English nation-state. Prior to the widespread investment in enslaved Africans, English employers used white indentured servants in setting up the colonial economy. They recruited these contracted persons from social sources similar to those that became the norm in West Africa.

Servants were an amalgamation of political prisoners, convicts and the poor and destitute, who were recruited by merchants and formally deported by the state. But they were mostly volunteers, persons who wanted to try their social luck in the colonies. These servants, while being exploited and abused, were not enslaved as chattel. They were not the property for life of those who purchased their indenture.

The British model, then, was clear. In the initial stages of colonial development, white indentured servants were ruthlessly exploited and the profits used to purchase enslaved Africans. Servitude was the stepping stone to slavery. But profits required mass production, which in turn meant enslaved Africans. It took a significant amount of white indentured labour to establish the plantations, but it was massive African enslavement and the wealth the enslaved generated that made the West Indies critical to the British Empire.

The Spanish implemented this model in the Greater Antilles during the sixteenth century. In the seventeenth century, it provided an attractive template for the colonizing efforts of the English in the eastern Caribbean. The English newcomers modified and standardized the Spanish arrangement in order to meet their peculiar needs. To promote clarity and certainty in labour relations on the first plantations, for example, English officials at Barbados in 1636 established guidelines for the colonists. These were explicit. Voluntary indentured workers from "back home" would serve between five and seven years, and those deported by the state would serve ten years. The "negroes and Indians" would "serve for life unless a contract was made before to the contrary".[9] A description of Barbados reflected the application of this labour model:

> The inhabitants of this island are one of four sorts. First, the freeholders who formerly held their land from the Earl of Carlisle. . . . The next sort are those they call freemen, who are such as having serv(d) out their time they contracted for, are freed from their masters, and now serve in the country for wages. The third sorts are of those they call Christian servants for distinction, whose time of service is not yet expired. The last sorts are the negroes, brought thither from the Coast of Guinny who live as absolute slaves to their masters.[10]

The English, then, created laws in which they had "absolute" ownership, control and authority over enslaved Africans.

The "total authority" provision meant that they could dispose of them as property, and generally relate to them as chattels. As legal non-humans, Africans experienced what no other social group did. White servants had legal rights under their contracts; they also had the power of their cultural identity and racial status to protect themselves from dehumanization, even when ill-treated as workers and poor persons.

In 1645, George Downing in Barbados wrote to John Winthrop, governor of Massachusetts, to explain the revised English labour model. If a planter could obtain a good supply of indentured servants, he said, to clear the land, lay out the field and plant the soil, he could "in a short time . . . with good husbandry" be able to "procure negroes out of the increase". Here it was: the generic labour formula that would shape the future and underpin what became the slave plantation complex.[11]

The island colonies were transformed by investors who grew rich with the sugar industry that deepened its dependence on the labour of enslaved Africans. Barbados gave birth to the new dispensation and earned the distinction of becoming the first fully formed slave society in the Americas. By 1700, it was the first to rely entirely on the labour of thousands of enslaved Africans. Barbados, furthermore, became the first English Caribbean headquarters of the Atlantic slave-based sugar plantation complex. In so doing, it attained a reputation among whites as the "richest little spot in the New World", and "hell on earth" for blacks. The Lesser Antilles replaced the Spanish Greater Antilles as the primary site of colonial enrichment. Slave owners were keenly supported by the state and its legal system that invented and endorsed enslavement.

Slave Laws and Racist Ideology

The English kept enslaved Africans violently subordinated by an increasingly powerful system which comprised the local militia, imperial troops, army and navy, reinforced by complex legal machinery. The social order, built upon fear and suspicion, was characterized by extreme tyranny and the need for constant vigilance. Slave owners sought complete control over Africans and tolerated no insubordination – individual or collective. The first comprehensive legal code for the governance of enslaved Africans was passed in Barbados in 1661 under the title "An Act for the better ordering and governing of Negroes".[12] According to Richard Dunn, it "legitimized a state of war between blacks and whites, sanctioned rigid segregation, and institutionalized an early warning system against slave revolt".[13] The preamble to the act states,

> *Whereas* heretofore many good Laws and ordinances have been made for the governing, regulating and ordering the Negroes, Slaves in this Isle, and sundry punishments appointed to prevent many of their misdemeanours, crimes, and offences which have yet not met the effect that hath been desired and might have been reasonably expected had the Master of Families and other the Inhabitants of this Isle been so careful of their obedience and compliance with the said Laws as they ought to have been. And these former Laws being in many clauses imperfect and not fully comprehending the true constitution of this Government in relation of their Slaves their Negroes an heathenish brutish and an uncertain dangerous pride of people to whom if surely in any thing we may extend the legislative power given us of punishionary Laws for the benefit and good of this plantation, not being contradictory to

the Laws of England, there being in all the body of that Law no track to guide us where to walk nor any rule set us how to govern such Slaves, yet we well know by the right rule of reason and order, we are not to leave them to the Arbitrary, cruel, and outrageous wills of every evil disposed person, but so far to protect them as we do many other goods and Chattels.[14]

In an attempt to ensure its continued relevance, the act was amended in 1676, 1682 and 1688. Revisions provided for the treatment of Africans described as "heathenish", "brutish" and a "dangerous kind of people", whose naturally wicked instincts should at all times be suppressed. It provided that Africans found guilty of crimes, other than those of a public nature, should be branded with hot irons, have their noses slit and be dismembered.[15] Dunn noted that castration was a "favourite slave punishment" even though it was not embedded in the code. For crimes of a public nature, such as rebellion, capital punishment was provided and the island's treasurer was empowered to compensate the slave owner for loss of capital.[16]

The 1688 revision declared Africans to be real estate as opposed to mere chattels. This meant that enslaved Africans were legally tied to plantations and could not be easily alienated. The act stated,

Whereas a very considerable part of the wealth of this island consists of negro slaves . . . it is hereby ordained and enacted . . . that . . . all negro slaves in all courts of judicature, and other places within this island shall be held, taken, and adjudged to be Estate Real, and not chattel, and shall descend unto the heir and widow of any person dying intestate according to the manner and custom of lands of inheritance held in fee-simple.[17]

This development enabled the property holders of enslaved labour to attain greater security in courts in cases of inheritance and probate challenges. Enslaved Africans could now legally be tied to the land in much the same way as houses and other physical structures. The plantation, then, was constituted as "lands, houses, buildings, and slaves". The enslaved were chattels and therefore could not own property, the basis of social mobility. In addition, the slave laws emphasized that they were, foremost, assets with market values. The 1688 code provided that an owner who "wilfully" murdered an enslaved person would be fined £15 (£28,600 in 2010). If, however, the enslaved died while being punished, the owner was compensated at market value. Africans were not allowed to give evidence in court against persons defined as "white". This remained the case until the early nineteenth century.

It was not until 1805 in Barbados that the murder of an enslaved person by a white person became a capital felony. On the other hand, an enslaved African could be punished by death for striking or threatening a white person or stealing property. Large numbers of enslaved persons were executed for the theft of livestock. The preamble to the 1688 act noted,

> Whereas the plantations and estates of this island, cannot be fully managed and brought into use without the labour and service of great numbers of Negroes and other slaves; and forasmuch as the said Negroes and other slaves are of barbarous, wild and savage nature, and such as render them wholly unqualified to be governed by the Laws, customs and practices of our Nation: It therefore becoming absolutely necessary, that such other constitutions, laws, and orders, should be in this island framed and enacted for the good regulating or ordering of them, as may both restrain the disorders, rapines and inhumanities to which they are naturally prone and inclined.[18]

These laws provided that slave owners should give the enslaved leave to go off the estate with a signed ticket that sets out the terms and conditions of leave. A white person who identified an African on their property without such a ticket was expected under law to apprehend and whip the captive. Failure to do so attracted a fine of 10 shillings sterling, half of which was paid to the informant. In addition, it became lawful, "for all masters, overseers, and other persons whatsoever, to apprehend and take up any Negro, or other slave or slaves, that should be found out of the plantation of his at any time, especially Saturday nights, Sundays, or other Holidays, not being on lawful business, or with a letter from their master, or a ticket, or not having a white man with them".[19] The 1688 Code also stated that Africans were not lawfully allowed to "beat drums, blow horns, or use other loud instruments", and their houses were to be "diligently searched . . . once every week". Any white person who entertained a "strange negro" was upon conviction to forfeit £2.10s (£4,770 in 2010). A series of punishments was provided for Africans who traded in stolen goods, struck a Christian, ran away, burned canes or stole provisions. In addition, white persons were liable to fines for inadequate policing of Africans, assisting them to escape, murdering them or exposing them to seditious doctrines.[20]

Enslaved Africans received limited legal protection, as the act recognized the need to "guard them from the cruelties and insolences of themselves, and other ill-tempered people or owners". Clause 6 provided that "all slaves . . . shall have clothes once every year, that is to say, drawers and caps for men and petticoats and caps for women". These legal codes, therefore, played an important role in the development and maintenance of the racist, apartheid social order which emerged. They excluded Africans from the socio-economic processes of property accumulation, social mobility and freedom, and ensured that they were materially impoverished.

British slave owners did not recognize any human or civil rights of Africans until the final decades of slavery. This was a key part of the system of control. Enslaved Africans had no rights to entitlements such as a family life, leisure time or the practice of religion. Legal codes from Barbados served as the blueprint for colonists in Jamaica and the Leeward Islands in the seventeenth century and for the Windward Islands (St Lucia, St Vincent, Tobago and Dominica) in the eighteenth century. In all instances, Africans were described in the act as having "a barbarous, wild and savage nature", which rendered them "wholly unqualified to be governed by the laws, customs and practices" of the "English Nation". The British state, therefore, thought it necessary that "such other constitutions, laws and orders" should be put in place in the Caribbean for "the good regulating, or ordering" of Africans, the purpose of which was to "restrain the disorders, rapines, and inhumanities to which they are naturally prone and inclined". Under these laws, Africans were gibbeted, castrated, branded with hot irons, dismembered and locked in dungeons for unlimited periods as punishment for insubordination. These socio-legal perceptions of Africans, and the punishments they received, reflected the British definition of them as property, chattels and real estate, and the belief that they were non-humans deserving of their enslavement.

By the end of the eighteenth century, the British slave system had reached full maturity. The Barbados model, developed by Englishmen in the 1650s and perfected by 1700, was exported to all other parts of the empire. Blackburn argued that "property rights in persons was the fundamental legal principal advocated" in the development of the English slave system and that the enforcement of these laws was the basis for ensuring its sustainability. This principle, he concluded, was "upheld by the English judiciary without difficulty for nearly 200 years".[21]

That white people could treat enslaved Africans as property and retain the concomitant property rights, then, became the order of the day, embedded in all laws and accepted by British metropolitan and colonial society. In 1788, the British Privy Council summarized the legal state of affairs in the Caribbean as follows:

> The leading Idea in the Negro System of jurisprudence is that which was the first in the Minds of those most interested in its Formation; namely that Negroes were Property and a species of Property that needed a rigorous vigilant Regulation. The numerous Laws passed in the different Islands immediately upon their Settlement, and for a considerable Time after, with all their multifarious and repeated Provisions, had uniformly this for their Object. To secure the Rights of Owners and maintain the Subordination of Negroes, seem to have most occupied the Attention and excited the Solicitude of the different Legislatures; what regards the Interests of the Negroes themselves appears not to have sufficiently attracted their notice.[22]

The general correctness of this assessment is not undermined by references to the few, and very limited, provisions in most laws that held slave owners accountable for the adequate clothing, feeding and housing of enslaved Africans. Rather, such references would reinforce slave owners' perception of the enslaved as property, since it was expected that even inanimate properties ought to be properly maintained with due regard for their social and economic significance.

In general, similarities in the perception of Africans – as an inferior species whose role Europeans conceived in their colonial mission as that of enslaved labour – could be found in the structure and wording of all Caribbean slave codes, irrespective of their different imperial backgrounds. There were, however, important philosophical differences that informed their origin and content, if not their social applications.

In 1801, white Barbadian historian John Poyer provided a precise formulation of the English notion of black inferiority and how it impacted on social structure. He stated,

> In every well-constituted Society, a state of subordination necessarily arises from the nature of civil Government. Without this no political Union could long subsist. To maintain this fundamental principle, it becomes absolutely necessary to preserve the distinctions which naturally exist or are accidentally introduced into the Community. With us, two grand distinctions result from the state of Society: First, between

the White Inhabitants and free people of Colour, and secondly, between Masters and Slaves. Nature has strongly defined the difference not only in complexion, but in the mental, intellectual and corporeal faculties of the different Species and our Colonial code has acknowledged and adopted the distinction.[23]

Poyer described a crystallized social structure based on the racial targeting of Africans and the legal denial of their humanity and freedom.

Ending White "Slavery"

With the chattel enslavement of Africans well established and the legal power of slave owners "absolute", white indentured servants working alongside Africans in the field became an embarrassment to the English state. In the racialization of slavery and its association with Africans in law and ideology, the existence of labour gangs made up of white servants represented a significant contradiction to English policy.

The English state that had legitimized the "traffic" in white workers, and had racially targeted Africans for enslavement, moved to put an end to the image and rhetoric of white workers in a slave-like condition in the Caribbean. The English Parliament of 1659 was presented with the opportunity to put the final touches to the racial enslavement of Africans by declaring the colonial subjection of white bonded workers a disgrace to the nation and subversive of the national interest. Only Africans should be enslaved; only Africans should be linked to the language of slavery.

Two Englishmen, M. Rivers and O. Foyle, petitioned the English Parliament on the grounds that, in 1656, they were rounded up as political prisoners and "sold into slavery in Barbados" as indentured servants. They described the nature of their work and social usage in the Caribbean as not dissimilar to the Africans around them. They described being "bought and sold from one planter to another, attached to horses and beast for the debt of their masters, whipped at the whipping post for their masters' pleasure, and many other ways made miserable beyond expression or Christian imagination". English parliamentarians were horrified by the details set out in their petition. Some were moved to anger, others outraged that white men could be treated like Africans.[24]

The petitioners wanted to know by what authority so great a breach could be made upon the free people of England "by merchants that deal in slaves and souls of men". Not even the "cruel" Turks, according to the petitioners, enslaved their own countrymen in the acquisition of profits, wealth and power. Martin Noell, a West Indian merchant with significant Barbadian property interests, was called upon to give evidence concerning this trade "in the bodies and souls of men" from which, in the previous year, he had sold a small cargo of political prisoners in Barbados for £100 (£192,000 in 2010). He told the Commons, "I abhor the thought of setting £100 upon any man's person. It is false and scandalous . . . the work is hard but . . . not so hard as is represented to you; It [Barbados] is a place as grateful to you for trade as any part of the world." Parliament was angered. Colonel White argued that the Cavaliers got what they deserved, for which he would not be apologetic, but nevertheless he insisted, "if every justice may commit a man because he cannot give a good account of himself", it would certainly be a practice "against the freeborn people of England".[25]

Sir Henry Vane was quite firm in his conviction that the issue of "white slavery" in Barbados transcended party politics, and was basically one of "human rights and individual liberty". He stated in reply to Colonel Birch, "I do not look on this business as a Cavalierish business but as a matter that concerns the liberty of the free born people of England – to be used in this barbarous manner . . . and sold there for £100." As far as he was concerned, the word "Barbados" was a place that represented the reversal of the English historical experience, which was the growing freedom of the lower orders.[26]

Mr Annesley informed the Commons about the legality of "Barbadosing" English subjects. He stated, "I am sorry to hear Magna Carta moved against this house. . . . I know no law of banishment." The petitioners are English and "why should [they] not have the benefits of it?" Sir John Lenthall stated that he hoped "it is not the effect of our war to make merchandise of men". The English, he said, are "the freest people in the world". He wanted all English servants removed from the field gangs of Caribbean sugar estates, leaving such work only for blacks and Irishmen.[27]

In this racial division of labour, Lenthall got the support of Mr Boscawen, who stated that he was "as much against the Cavalier party as any man in these walls . . . but you have Paul's case before you. A Roman ought not to be beaten or our lives will be as cheap as those of negroes". This was the critical statement

in the debate and the marker in the construction of African enslavement by
the English state.[28]

Boscaven injected the racial comparison into the debate because he had
vested interests in Jamaican slavery and was fully aware of the importance of
African enslavement in the West Indies. Mr Gewen wanted a full debate of
the race issue and an investigation into indentured servitude. He informed
the House that he "would not have men sold like bullocks and horses. The
selling of a [white] man is an offence of a high nature". Sir Arthur Haslerigge
was moved to tears by the plight of Englishmen "sold into slavery amongst
beasts". That white men should be forced to labour in gangs with Africans
represented a heresy, he claimed, that Charles I would himself find unacceptable.[29] The petitioners served out their contracts. Parliament did not interfere
in the contracted rights of employers in servant labour, but opted to suppress
the servant trade.

Between 1659 and 1662, the House of Commons supported plans for
African slave trading, which led to the establishment in 1663 of the Company
of Royal Adventurers Trading to Africa. Serious discussion of any significance
concerning the "human rights" and liberty of the West Indian labour force
would not take place in the British Parliament for another 150 years.

Chapter 5

The *Zong* Massacre

Jamaica-Bound Africans Murdered

The slave trade was part and parcel of British economic and political life for more than 300 years.

—*Diane Abbott, Member of Parliament, Debate on the Bicentenary of the Abolition of the Slave Trade, House of Commons, 20 March 2007*

THE IMPOSITION OF THE STATUS OF "property" and "real estate" upon Africans by the English state and its colonial representatives meant that a pattern of criminal conduct in relation to black people could follow. The social reduction of people to the legal status of property and the commercial enforcement of property rights in humans meant that Africans would be treated and used as property.[1]

Branding enslaved Africans with hot irons to demonstrate property ownership was but the beginning. After African bodies were bought, they were stored, packaged and shipped, like any other commodity. The process of buying, branding, storing and shipping was provided for in insurance law since the risk of owning human cargo and property had to be assessed and managed. British maritime law as it pertained to the shipment of property was a critical part of the economics of slavery. These laws were backed by the full power of the state. The entire property process, then, from purchase to shipment, to deployment in the Caribbean, required the enforcement of law.[2]

Without the effect of property laws as they pertain to blacks, the colonial economy and its role as a vital part of the larger British economy would have collapsed. The wealth of British investors was protected, preserved and accumulated in the application of property rights to owning blacks. The bodies of enslaved black people represented at least 50 per cent of the wealth of the British West Indies economy. The "human" investment was oftentimes greater than that in lands and machinery; it was always greater than that in livestock. In estate inventories, "slaves, horses, cattle, sheep and goats" were bracketed together for accounting purposes. For example, at Lowther plantation in Barbados, between 1825 and 1832, the increase and decrease of slaves, cattle

Table 5.1. Life and Death at Lowther Plantation, 1825–1832

Increase and decrease, 1825		
9 Negroes born	9 Negroes died	
10 calves dropped	2 horses and 3 cattle died	
Increase in value of livestock, 1829		
9 Negroes born and 8 died		balance £75
10 cattle born and 5 died		balance £50
Sum		Total increase £125
Natural increase in value of livestock, 1832		
6 Negroes at £50 each	10 born	
	4 died	
Sum		= £300
Deduct decrease of 3 cattle at £10 each		
5 died and 2 born	–£30	
2 horses died at £30 each	–£60	£90
Total		£210*

*Total equals £151,000 in 2010 value.
Source: Lowther Plantation Papers, Add. MS 43507, British Library.

and horses are listed consecutively within the capital account. Newly born children, inheriting the enslaved status from their mothers, were accounted for alongside other "stock" as a capital gain (see table 5.1).[3]

British National Interests and the Enforcement of Property Rights

Occasionally, the British state was called upon to reaffirm its position on the application of these property laws. One such occasion was the Somersett case. Somersett, an enslaved man, was allowed to stay in England after the court ruled that he could not be removed from the country by his owner, who desired to ship him to Virginia. Judge Mansfield, who made this famous ruling in a 1772 case, went to great lengths to state that he was upholding the slave owner's right to own human property but could find no legal basis in English law to enable the owner of the "property" to transfer him outside the realm. The ruling was therefore not based on opposition to slavery, but was a recognition that property laws in England contained constraints on the use of property.[4]

James Walvin's excellent analysis of Mansfield's ruling in this and other cases deserves widespread discussion and assessment. The judge, he noted, was determined to protect an Englishman's property rights in his enslaved persons. The judge himself was a slave owner; he was also "an expert on commercial law and was loath to make a decision which might disturb the property basis of black slavery".[5]

Walvin noted that "so much commercial wealth flowed to Britain from its slave empire that any judgment which ran counter to that economic interest, even in so minor a fashion as slavery in England, was to be resisted". What Mansfield had not done, he concluded, "was to free all slaves in England". His decision was confined to the specifics of the case and, in Mansfield's own words, went "no further than that the master cannot by force compel (the slave) to go out the kingdom".[6]

The case, however, that became the most famous test of the English application of property rights to enslaved black people was Gregson v. Gilbert, commonly known as the *Zong* case. It pertained to the mass murder of Africans by British slave traders. It remains the most violent recorded event in the British criminal treatment of Africans as property.

As a case, it went beyond mass murder and engaged the courts of England as an event in how human property was treated by owners. Critically, it is a case that reveals clearly the hand of the British state in maintaining the status of enslaved blacks in English law as property.

The *Zong* Massacre: The British State Defends Mass Murder

The *Zong* case, Walvin tells us, "takes us right to the heart of the slave system". In this assessment he is undoubtedly correct. In need of further discussion is his conclusion that the case exposed "the manifest contradictions between the English custom of slave trading, and the basic tenets of English law". English law had supported slave trading for two hundred years prior.

The enterprise of global trading in black bodies required the full practical and silent support of English law and custom. There were no contradictions in English law recognizing enslaved blacks as property and real estate in the colonies. Judge Mansfield's concern was not complicated. You could own enslaved persons as property in England and elsewhere in the British Empire, but you could not sell, trade or transport them outside of England at will. The same applied to other categories of property – horses, sheep and cattle. Special permission was required to move certain livestock outside of Britain.

The name of the Liverpool registered slave ship owned by James Gregson and Associates was the *Zong*. It was commanded by a large crew of seventeen sailors, whose captain was Luke Collingwood. The *Zong* had a well-established record in the shipment of enchained, enslaved African bodies to the Caribbean. The voyage that finally brought the *Zong* and Captain Collingwood to international attention was that of 6 September 1781. The voyage started like any other. After a few weeks on the West African coast, Captain Collingwood secured a "cargo" of 470 enchained Africans. His mission was to traverse the Atlantic with maximum speed, hopefully to arrive in Jamaica in fewer than eight weeks and dispose of his company's property.

Many things went wrong in the captain's calculation. Twelve weeks into the voyage, Jamaica was still not in sight. The crew faced two management challenges. The length of the voyage was taking its toll on both the enchained and the crew. By this time, seven of the seventeen sailors were dead. But more critically, from Captain Collingwood's business perspective, he had thrown overboard more than sixty Africans as being dead or sick. Each day, more Africans were thrown overboard.

The prolonged nature of the voyage highlighted the importance of water availability for the remaining persons on the ship. It was the norm for captains to carry water based on the size of the "cargo", expected length of the voyage and the size of the crew. Walvin tells us, "Luke Collingwood, the *Zong's* captain, called his officers together on 29 November and put forward the suggestion that sick slaves should be jettisoned – thrown overboard – both to secure the rapidly dwindling supplies of water and to allow the shipping company to claim their loss as insurance."[7]

The captain's instructions to his crew were explicit. If the sick Africans died on the ship, the crew would have to bear the responsibility for the death, with financial implications for their level of remuneration. However, if the Africans did not die on board but were thrown live into the ocean in order to protect the safety of the ship, then the cost of the loss would fall to the insurance company, Gilbert and Associates. The relevant insurance law was clear:

> The insurer takes upon him the risk of the loss, capture, and death of slaves, or any other unavoidable accident to them: but natural death is always understood to be excepted; by natural death is meant, not only when it happens by disease or sickness, but also when the captive destroys himself through despair, which often happens: but when slaves are killed, or thrown into the sea in order to quell an insurrection on their part, then insurers must answer.[8]

Captain Collingwood was looking out for the financial best interests of his employers, James Gregson and Associates. For him, it was a simple business decision. It was neither a criminal nor a moral issue as far as he could read the law and the social culture of maritime Britain. During a management meeting, captain and crew assessed the situation. Large numbers of Africans were falling sick and dying daily, but there was adequate water, since heavy rains allowed the crew to catch barrels of water beyond their own needs. The winds were not favouring the ship, and the captain's navigation across the Atlantic was not the best.

There was some disagreement among the crew with the captain's directive that all the Africans be thrown overboard, an action designed to trigger an effective insurance claim for the loss of property. The ship's first mate, James

Kelsall, initially did not agree with the plan but changed his mind. The process of throwing Africans into the ocean commenced. On the first day, fifty-four Africans were released from chains and thrown into the ocean; the following day, 30 November, forty-two were jettisoned; on 1 December, another twenty-six. Ten Africans, choosing to end their own lives, jumped to death once unchained. Reports stated that by "leaping into the sea", they experienced "a momentary triumph in the embrace of death".[9] The choice for these ten, then, was either suicide or murder. It mattered to them that they had the choice. The death ship finally arrived in Jamaica on 22 December.

According to the records, 131 Africans had been thrown into the sea to be consumed by sharks that followed the slave ships across the Atlantic. Aboard were 420 gallons of excess water. The 131 "coolly murdered", noted Walvin, died "for no good reason save the economic calculations of Captain Luke Collingwood and the physical compliance of his crewmen".[10]

When the *Zong* returned to England, the paperwork to claim the insurance for the loss of property began. The owners of the vessel presented documentation to the insurance agents, claiming the full market value of the property lost. The argument presented was that provided for by the law, that the act of jettisoning Africans into the ocean was necessary to save the ship on account of water depletion. This was clearly untrue.

The *Zong* massacre was a common enough event. Two weeks had gone by without much reference to the event until Equiano Olaudah, the prominent free black anti-slavery activist, living in London, brought news of the report to Granville Sharp, who by then had established a reputation as a slave trade abolitionist.

The two weeks of silence over the news of the event signalled to one journalist, who reported the hearing for a newspaper, that the British community had become immune to such acts of murder against black people, and further, that the British state considered it an insignificant event within the scope of things necessary to protect the national interest. The insurance case – Gregson *v.* Gilbert – was reviewed at the London Guildhall. There was little unusual about it – dead Africans and insurance claim on property loss: end of story.

The "endemic violence" against Africans, noted Walvin, was necessary to "keep slavery in place", and for the system to survive in its economic viability, "some Africans had to pay the ultimate sacrifice". This was in the national interest as defined by the state. "It took no great leap of the imagination to appreciate that the logic of pursuing the murderers of the slaves on the *Zong*", concluded Walvin, "would be the first tug which would unravel the entire garment of the slave system".[11]

Neither the owners of the ship nor the British judicial system believed that throwing African bodies overboard was tantamount to murder. To them the case simply constituted an insurance claim for lost property. When Granville Sharp and other anti–slave trade activists sought to bring a murder case against the *Zong* crew, the courts paid no attention. The insurance agent, Gilbert, refused to meet the claim, having heard reports that suggested the Africans were murdered in cold calculation as an act to defraud the insurers. This refusal triggered a court hearing which was brought before Judge Mansfield and two others.

The anti-slavery lobby saw to it that the case took on the highest possible public profile. What was on trial was the principle that British citizens could dispose of human property as they considered in their best economic interest. It is to be noted that neither in Jamaica nor Barbados was the murder of an enslaved African a capital offence. It merely attracted a monetary fine that went towards the replacement cost.

The British authorities that presided over the slave system, and took responsibility for protecting the national interest, showed a direct interest in the case. The owners of the dead Africans were represented in the trial by a senior state official, the solicitor general, John Lee. Lee took the case because he was conscious of the broad implications. Granville Sharp represented the insurance company; he too was equally conscious of the legal implications of the case.[12]

Lee wasted no time in seeking to throw out any possibility of a murder prosecution. As solicitor general of the nation, he used his enormous official status to stamp his thinking upon the proceedings. He told the court that it "would be madness" to consider criminal prosecution against Captain Collingwood and his crew. This kind of event was common on the high seas. But critically, he impressed upon the court that the Africans thrown to the sharks were "property" – no more, and no less.

There could have been no clearer statement of the British state policy on Africans enchained and enslaved. They were chattels, property, real estate, without human identity and persona. Property cannot be killed; hence no murder charge could be brought against the captain and crew. We find the official position of the British government in Lee's words:

What is all this vast declaration of human beings thrown overboard? The question after all is, was it voluntary, or an act of necessity? This IS A CASE OF CHATTELS OR GOODS. It is really so: it is the case of throwing over GOODS; for to this purpose, and the purpose of insurance; THEY ARE GOODS AND PROPERTY; whether right or wrong, we have nothing to do with it. THIS PROPERTY – the human creatures if you will – have been thrown overboard, whether or not for the preservation of the rest, this is the real question.[13]

Lee was a lawyer who knew precisely the essence of the case. He was right and every judge on the bench knew this as well. He was not imagining an evil legal reality. It was British law. Enslaved blacks were property. They had been defined as such for nearly two hundred years. It was written into the slave codes that the enslaved and the British were not to be governed by the same body of laws. The British were human; the Africans were subhuman and therefore not subject to a discourse about human violation.

The judges and the solicitor general were in perfect agreement. They all represented the legal arm of the British state. Judge Mansfield expressed the point even more clearly when he said that they "had no doubt that the case of the slaves was the same as if *horses* had been thrown overboard".[14] The entire proceeding was not about murder. Sharp failed to persuade the British government that murder of humans was the issue. Walvin explained his failure: "He confronted that official silence and inactivity born of the realization that any such action would corrode the system. Once an English court began to discuss murder and cruelty in the conduct of the slaving system, there was no knowing where the question – and the consequent material damage – would end."[15]

The role of the court was to protect the national interest. British national interest was deeply embedded in the investment returns of slave trading and slavery. Walvin concludes, "The benefits of the slave system were clear enough to British contemporaries. How many could countenance destroying so abundant and fruitful an economic system merely from a sense of ethical outrage? . . . To kill a slave, or a group of slaves, was an economic misfortune, but it did not constitute a human outrage which offended or worried those involved."[16]

Chapter 6

Prostituting Enslaved Caribbean Women

If we read the accounts not just of the work that slaves did, but of the extraordinary brutality of the punishments and the torture that they had to endure. . . . the only people a slave was legitimately allowed to love were the children of the slave master, we have to say that 200 years later, that sort of experience must have affected the societies that we see around the Caribbean today.

—*Diane Abbott, Member of Parliament, Debate on the Bicentenary of the Abolition of the Slave Trade, House of Commons, 20 March 2007*

THE SLAVERY SYSTEM BUILT BY the British in the Caribbean led to the legal and customary institutionalization of the slave owners' right to unrestricted sexual access to enslaved women as an intrinsic and discrete product. The circuitous route of wealth accumulation within slavery recognized no clear distinction between the production of material goods and the delivery of sexual services. Production, sexual pleasure and reproduction were indistinguishable within the market economy of slavery. With respect to enslaved women, then, household work, which ordinarily meant manual labour, also included the supply of socio-sexual services and the (re)production of children as an asset that enhanced the wealth capitalization process.[1]

The rape of the enslaved female was, first and foremost, an attack upon her as a human being. But British law denied her a human identity. She could not be raped, for "property" could not be sexually offended. For this reason,

Orlando Patterson, attempting to compare violent rape with the coercive mechanisms of sexual manipulation, laid bare the social reality of plantation life when he stated that rape was often "unnecessary". This argument arises directly from the many assertions found in the tortured texts of slave owners' narratives in which rape is rarely admitted but where clear prominence is given to enslaved women as "sex slaves".[2]

According to Richard Dunn, seventeenth-century English plantation records indicate that "the master enjoyed commandeering his prettiest slave girl and exacting his presumed rights from her".[3] This tradition is further illuminated by John Oldmixon in 1708. Reporting on the domestic lives of slave owners, he noted that the "handsomest, cleanliest (black) maidens are bred to menial services" in order to satisfy their masters in "divers" ways.[4]

As the anti-slavery movement gained momentum towards the end of the eighteenth century, the focus on the sexual exploitation of black women and the destruction of black family life intensified. Increasingly, the sexual authority of slave owners came under intense scrutiny. Indicative of popular British opinion was the reaction of Colonel Hilton. A professional soldier, Hilton reported being horrified in the West Indies in 1816 at the sight of a white woman in the slave market examining the genitals of male slaves "with all possible indelicacy".[5]

Likewise, F.W. Bayley, an English travel writer of the 1820s, found organized slave prostitution in the West Indies rather distasteful but reported that white males considered the use of sex slaves in houses of "ill repute" socially indispensable.[6] Mrs E. Fenwick, an English schoolteacher living in Bridgetown during the 1810s, tried desperately but failed ultimately to accept the social culture in which young white males commonly underwent their sexual apprenticeship with enslaved domestics and prostitutes, "brought into the household solely and explicitly for the purpose of sex". Fearing for the moral character of her young nephew, she prepared to remove him to Philadelphia.[7]

Slave owners seemed undisturbed by such searching critical comments on their social lives. They considered it no evidence of degenerate taste to retain enslaved black or coloured women as sexual objects. The evidence suggests, furthermore, that such a practice was popular in the towns, although estate owners and managers had social access to a larger number of enslaved women. In West Indian towns, organized prostitution and the formal integration of enslaved mistresses into white households were common enough, while on the sugar estates, sexual access to enslaved women took more covert forms and was less visible to outsiders.[8]

Urban society was influenced considerably by the maritime activity on which its economy depended. Here, black prostitution was as much in demand as any social institution. The large, transient, maritime personnel expected to be able to purchase sex, and the liberal values and ideological openness of urban society allowed for the proliferation of facilities that promoted slave prostitution.

Claude Levy informed us that from the seventeenth century, slave prostitution was the norm. With reference to Jamaica, B.W. Higman stated that slave "prostitution was common in the town".[9] The inns and taverns of the towns were very often brothels as well, and the enslaved women attached to them were used as prostitutes as well as domestics. Prostitution was illegal in the colonies, but there is no evidence to show that the laws were enforced – suggesting that this criminal activity was condoned and encouraged by British imperial and colonial officials.

Elizabeth Fenwick could find no significant reason to differentiate morally between urban slave owners who deployed slave women as prostitutes, and plantation owners who used them as "breeding wenches" in search of a greater labour supply. For her, these roles overlapped, because many sex slaves were often the kept mistresses of white males, who also encouraged them, from time to time, to have children so as to benefit financially from the sale of the child.

In Fenwick's value system, slavery in this specific context was "a horrid and disgraceful" institution. She expressed a marked sympathy for "victimized" enslaved women and was particularly disturbed by the manner in which slave prostitutes and resident mistresses (invariably housekeepers) constituted a subgroup within many white households – a kind of informal socio-sexual domestic-service sector. According to her, "The female slaves are really encouraged to prostitution because their children are the property of the owners of the mothers. These children are reared by the ladies as pets, are frequently brought from negro houses to their chambers to feed and to sleep, and reared with every care and indulgence till grown up, when they are at once dismissed to labour and slave-like treatment."[10] Domestic arrangements that sought to conceal the practice of slave prostitution, she added, were "common" to both urban and rural white households and not considered "an enormity".

The data from the 1790s for Newton Plantation in Barbados show that all four field women listed in 1796 as having "mulatto" children – Membah Jubah, Fanny Ann, Jemenema and Little Dolly – were impregnated between the ages of thirteen and sixteen.

White males, including planters who sometimes resided in town, made a gainful business by prostituting enslaved females. William Dickson, an imperial administrator who lived in Barbados during the 1770s and 1780s, found that men would often "lease out" their enslaved mistresses for the purpose of prostitution as a convenient way of obtaining cash. These women, he added, were "rented out" especially to visiting merchants, naval officers and other such clients for specified periods.

The money paid to the owners of enslaved women for sexual services frequently exceeded their market value. During the period immediately after the sugar harvest, the number of enslaved women placed on the urban market as prostitutes by rural slave owners increased, as did the number of male artisans put out to sell their skills on a contractual basis. In both instances, slave owners expected all or a proportion of the money earned.[11]

The question of slave prostitution was raised before the 1790–91 House of Commons inquiry into the slave trade. Evidence submitted showed that in spite of its illegality, it was "a very common thing" for "female slaves to be let out by their owners for purposes of prostitution". The commissioners heard that rural women were sent to town, and town women were sent to the barracks to raise money from prostitution. The evidence suggests that prostitution posed no problems for British colonial administrators.[12]

Early nineteenth-century references to slave prostitution emphasized the distinction between urban and rural contexts. In 1824, Thomas Cooper stated that white women were frequently the suppliers of young black girls to urban clients. J.B. Moreton, however, noted in 1790 that coloured slaves "from their youth are taught to be whores" and to expect their living to be derived from "immoral earnings".[13]

In support of his abolitionist position, Cooper attributed part of the failure of slave populations in the sugar colonies to reproduce themselves naturally to the prevalence of prostitution among young females – on the estates as well as in towns. Slave owners, however, did not accept that prostitution had adverse effects upon the domestic arrangements of enslaved women or their fertility. Edward Long, proslavery ideologue of late-eighteenth-century

Jamaica, echoed the common British sentiments that enslaved black women were predisposed towards prostitution and performed this function with efficiency and without moral reflection.[14]

Captain Cook, a British military officer giving testimony before the 1790–91 parliamentary committee, illustrated the many ways that slave owners prostituted enslaved females. His knowledge of colonial society was derived from several visits to the region in 1780 and 1782. He knew first-hand the domestic culture of the British and was attentive to the sexual practices of empowered males. He described how enslaved domestics, black and coloured, were used as prostitutes in the towns, and concluded that the purchase of sex by maritime crews "was a very common practice".[15]

Enslaved prostitutes, Cook stated, were sent on board ships under special arrangements with port officials for the purpose of selling sex for money. He confessed to accepting this activity on board the ship under his command, since it was part of colonial life, but seemed rather indignant when he discovered that a "negro girl" he knew well was "severely punished on her return home to her owner without the full wages of her prostitution".[16]

The covert organization of slave prostitution was a popular business activity of "well-to-do" white women – especially widows or those without influential or financially sound husbands. White elite society insisted on the projection of images of social respectability, and as such, distanced itself from formal association with prostitution as an enterprise. For financially insecure white women, however, it was the best they could do, and they were described as displaying their involvement without shame or remorse. In 1806, for example, a British naval officer reported that he knew a respectable creole lady who, for a living, "lets out her negro girls to anyone who will pay her for their persons, under the denomination of washer woman, and becomes very angry if they don't come home in the family way".[17]

John Waller, an Englishman who visited Barbados in 1808, made a similar report on the relations between high-society white women, slave prostitution and the "hiring-out" labour system. He stated in his travel book,

> In the family where I lodge, a respectable lady was regretting to company at dinner, that a young female slave whom she had let out for several months was about to return as she would lose twelve dollars a month, the price of her hire, and besides, be at the expense of maintaining her. After dinner, I made inquiry respecting the subject of hiring slaves, and learned that the one in question had been let out to an

officer in the garrison, with whom she had been living as a mistress. I felt extremely shocked at the very idea of so strange a traffic, but I found, a few days later, this very slave advertised in the "Bridgetown Gazette", in the following curious terms: "To let, a Sempstress, a well-looking mulatto girl seventeen years of age, an excellent hand at the needle, etc. To prevent needless application – terms twelve dollars per month. Apply, etc." I had previously noticed advertisements of this description, and I believe that few weeks pass without them; they are however frequently intended only for the purpose literally expressed.[18]

The institutional framework of prostitution, however, was built around taverns, bars and inns. Dr George Pinckard, who frequented the West Indies during the 1790s as a medical officer aboard a war vessel, provides us with insights into the practice of prostitution in Bridgetown's taverns. In any of these taverns, Pinckard informs us, a "bed may be had for half a dollar per night, or three dollars per week; and, for an additional sum well understood, the choice of an attendant to draw the curtains". Prostitutes "were treated in the most cruel manner by their mistresses, whose objectives were to earn as much money from their duties as possible. My considered response to such treatment", Pinckard says, "was much tempered by the realization that these women" showed "neither shame nor disgrace" in their prostitution. Rather, he added, the one "who is most sought becomes an object of envy and is proud of the distinction shewn her".[19]

In 1837, when prominent English abolitionists Joseph Sturge and Thomas Harvey conducted their "emancipation" tour of the British West Indies, most hotels and taverns in Bridgetown were still considered "houses of debauchery where a number of slave women were kept for the purpose of prostitution". Like Sturge and Harvey, other visitors to the colony noted that coloured women, both slave and free, were more in demand than black women, and fetched higher prices for their services.

Coloured women, however, were less available for this role than their black counterparts because they were more likely to be mistresses of white men. The records attest to the favoured status of "yellow-skinned" women, most of whom operated from the more exclusive taverns and hotels. In 1804, for example, an English naval officer made reference to a white woman he knew who made "a round sum" by trafficking her prostitute "coloured" girls to Europeans as "housekeepers" in disguise, or as she preferred to call it, "marrying them off for a certain time".[20]

Chapter 7

Criminal Enrichment

Building Britain with Slavery

Huge fortunes were made from the slave trade by banks and manufacturers. . . . In London, my city, people sometimes minimise or discount its involvement in the slave trade, but it was involved longer and deeper than any other part of the British Isles.

—*Diane Abbott, Member of Parliament, Debate on the Bicentenary of the Abolition of the Slave Trade, House of Commons, 20 March 2007*

ALL WESTERN EUROPEAN NATIONS PARTICIPATED in the traffic in enchained African bodies and reaped the benefits that the enslavement of these bodies conferred on investors. But the British reaped the lion's share and, more than any other European nation, perfected the economic and financial art of exploiting the African. By the end of the eighteenth century, Britain was the slave-trading nation par excellence and the primary Caribbean enslaver. On both fronts, then – slave trafficking and slave driving – the British ruled supreme.[1]

As a consequence of these achievements, Britain extracted more wealth from enchained and enslaved Africans than any other European nation. The wealth of the nation was driven by the wealth of the slave system. It became the first slave-trading superpower and the first industrial giant. Britain benefited the most from the slave-based Caribbean economy within the wider

Atlantic system, an intricate trading web in primary commodities, manufac-
tured goods and enchained people. The spectacular economic results were
symbolic of the relations that constituted Britain's reputation at the end of
the eighteenth century. It had become the leading industrial nation in the
world and the dominant global slave investor.[2]

More enslaved Africans suffered at British hands in the Caribbean than at
the hands of any other colonial power. British hegemony in the slave trade
and its ownership of Jamaica, the largest slave colony in the region in 1800,
established the nation as the market leader and trendsetter. Some three million
Africans were shipped out of Africa during the eighteenth century in British
ships, twice the number of other nations. The British thus established their
status as the nation with the greatest capacity to remove African inhabitants
forcibly from their homes and relocate them finally elsewhere.[3]

By 1807, the end of Britain's slave-trading period, there were some 1.5 million enslaved Africans in English colonies. While many of these were shipped
to the colonies by other European nations, the tragic, almost genocidal system
imposed upon enslaved Africans told the story of the demographic loss. In
most British slave colonies, the enslaved African population could not, and
did not, reproduce itself. For nearly two hundred years, these colonies experienced systemic population loss due to natural decline. With many times
more deaths than births, most colonies resorted to the importation of thousands of Africans to shore up the declining population.

The cruelty and brutality of the labour system subverted any potential for
the enslaved African population to reproduce. Jamaica was a demographic disaster for enslaved Africans. For the British enslavers, the colony was the land
of opportunity. It had replaced Barbados as the most profitable colony but
did not succeed in growing the enslaved population naturally as Barbados had
done. Plantation records speak to the human catastrophe of slavery. In Barbados, the first slave society and England's largest slave-investment project,
English crimes against humanity were staged on the broadest scale.[4]

A considerable body of historical literature speaks to the contribution of
the Caribbean in the eighteenth century to the financial and economic transformation of the British economy. In *Capitalism and Slavery*, Eric Williams
described the West Indian islands as the "hub of Empire". By the end of the
seventeenth century, economic commentators such as Charles Davenant,
Josiah Child and Dalby Thomas determined that the West Indian islands were

Britain's most profitable overseas investment. Eighteenth-century analysts of Britain's colonial trade and domestic economic growth also developed this argument in relation to profitability in the slave plantation complex. For Adam Smith, for instance, the place of sugar among colonial produce was clear: "The profits of a sugar plantation in any of our West Indian colonies are generally much greater than those of any other cultivation that is known either in Europe or America." The sugar colonies, noted Arthur Young, "added above three million [pounds] a year to the wealth of Britain".[5]

In its Caribbean colonies, Britain found the engine to drive its economic growth, an engine fuelled by slave trading and slavery. The Caribbean was the ancestral home of British imperial success as an economic superpower. The Caribbean was the core of a formidable global financial network that would eventually see Britain in command of the high seas. Power, prestige and profits summed up what the Caribbean was to the British. It gave modern Britain its first successful global leap. Britain took full advantage of the Caribbean opportunities. It maximized the benefits, and it has not looked back.

In 1600, England's interests in these "small scraps of land" seemed "more an opposition program" characterized by erratic, but violent, assaults upon Spanish settlements and trade than the projection of a clearly defined policy of colonization. Raiding and plundering became the norm and represented what seemed to be the extent of English capabilities.[6]

During the twenty years of war with Spain, 1585–1604, there was "no peace beyond the line", and the value of prize money brought to England from the Caribbean ranged between £100,000 and £200,000 per year (£263 million and £526 million in 2010). Privateering, linked directly to contraband trades, continued to be important well into the next century. The Elizabethan state, for tactical political reasons, had not wished publicly to support anti-Spanish Caribbean operations. Individual adventurers, however, were confident that they had the means to solve any problem that might be encountered in the Americas. They called on financially experienced representatives of the state for assistance, and received it. Government made covert investments, provided discreet guarantees and offered military assistance.[7]

In these approaches to colonization, the English followed the Dutch, who had formulated ground-plans to trade and settle in the Caribbean. The Guiana coasts, located between Spanish settlements on the Orinoco River and Portuguese possessions on the Amazon River, attracted English as well as Dutch attention. In 1604, nine years after Raleigh's effort, Charles Leigh attempted a settlement on the Wiapoco. There were others: Harcourt's attempt (1609–13), Raleigh's (1617–18) and Roger North's (1619–21). An important outcome of these operations was the opportunity for the English to survey the Windward and Leeward Islands, which the Spanish had left neglected and undefended.[8]

The Spanish had attached little economic value to the Lesser Antilles because the islands could not yield large quantities of precious metals, and the English who first became involved in individual islands also encountered determined opposition from the Kalinagos (the indigenous people) similar to that which had discouraged the Spaniards. The turning point was Thomas Warner's visit to St Christopher (St Kitts) in 1622. Warner was a participant in North's Guiana project, and considered St Christopher ideally suited for the establishment of tobacco plantations. A group of mariners led by John Powell touched at Barbados in 1625 en route from the Guianas and made similar observations. Warner and Powell returned to England to seek financial backing for a novel type of English colonizing activity.

Failed attempts at a Guiana settlement marked the beginning of a new approach by English business interests to Caribbean colonization. The financial collapse of the Virginia Company in 1624 had resulted in a management takeover by the Crown, which signalled a greater determination to convert commercial enterprises into permanent settlements. The furthering of agricultural settlements financed jointly by stock companies, syndicates and individuals symbolized the beginning of a conceptual triumph over the long-standing tradition of piracy.

At the same time, Caribbean opportunities brought to the centre of the colonizing mission powerful groups within the English state. On 2 July 1625, James Hay, first Earl of Carlisle, was issued a grant by Charles I of the "Caribbean Islands". In the next decade the Caribbean islands experienced a veritable "swarming of the English" as more settlers established themselves in the West Indies than in any single mainland colony.[9]

The English established colonies at St Christopher in 1624, Barbados in 1627, Nevis in 1628, and Montserrat and Antigua in 1632. Prior to the campaign of 1655–56, when Oliver Cromwell added Jamaica to the list of English possessions, these small islands were the backbone of England's seaborne empire and the primary location of capital accumulation in the Americas.

The economic importance of these islands far surpassed that of Puritan New England, but that is not to say that Puritans were not interested in the West Indies as well. Individual Puritans, including members of the prominent Winthrop and Downing families, spent some time in the West Indies, but collectively Puritans never attained the political power necessary to promote the West Indies as a location for New Jerusalem evangelism. Even at Providence Island, off the coast of Nicaragua, where they financed a settlement and secured political control, the culture of piracy and smuggling, as well as the cruel exploitation of enslaved labourers, transcended considerations of building a religious utopia and rendered their community indistinguishable from those of other European settlers in neighbouring islands.[10]

By 1640, the English had gained a demographic advantage in the Caribbean over other European nations. Up to 1660, the islands attracted more settlers than did the mainland colonies, which suggests that the colonies were perceived as the destinations that held the best prospects for "material and social advancement". The white population grew rapidly up to about 1660, when it reached 47,000, constituting some 40 per cent of all the whites in Britain's transatlantic colonies. Henry Gemery's estimates suggest that of the 378,000 white emigrants to America between 1630 and 1700, 223,000 (about 60 per cent) went to colonies in the wider Caribbean.[11]

Economic depression and political turmoil of the 1620s and early 1630s, and the effective marketing of the colonies as places of opportunity for all classes, presented an opportunity for English investors and pro-emigration agents. The population of Barbados in particular rose sharply during the 1630s, advancing sevenfold between 1635 and 1639. During this period, no other colony rivalled Barbados as a destination for settlers. The West Indies also forged ahead of the mainland colonies in the expansion of economic activities. Investment and trade increased in direct relation to population growth, and in the early years, West Indian investors were able to secure the greater share of labourers leaving both Ireland and Britain for America.

The organization of staple production – tobacco and cotton – in the formative years depended upon the labour of thousands of British indentured labourers. Unlike the islands acquired by the Spanish in the Greater Antilles, the Lesser Antilles lacked a large indigenous population which could be reduced to servitude. In the absence of a native labour force such as had been exploited by the Spaniards in Mexico and Peru, the obvious alternative supply of workers was found through the importation of indentured servants. This meant – as it also did in the Chesapeake – that the producer who commanded the most servants was the individual most likely to succeed.[12]

Investors in colonies in the first half of the seventeenth century published many works, largely of a promotional nature. Barbados developed the largest labour market in the West Indies during this century by leading the way into large-scale sugar production. The opportunity to switch from tobacco and cotton production was open to planters in Barbados because sugar prices on the European market rose in the 1640s due to production dislocations caused by a civil war in Portuguese Brazil, previously the principal supplier. With considerable Dutch financial and technological support, the more venturesome of the British planters in Barbados moved in and captured a significant market share.

By the early 1650s, Barbados produced an annual crop valued at over £3 million (£5.88 billion in 2010) and was described as the richest spot in the New World. The island's value, in terms of trade and capital generation, was greater than that of all other English colonies put together. Barbados had replaced Hispaniola as the "sugar centre" of the Caribbean, and the French islands lagged behind the English even though their production of sugar also rose steadily over the century.

Richard Ligon captured the nature of this economic explosion in terms of the planters' expectations. He related the case of his friend Colonel Thomas Modyford, son of the mayor of Exeter, who arrived on the island in 1645. Modyford bought a plantation of five hundred acres and provided it with a labour force of twenty-eight English servants and a larger number of enslaved Africans. He took "a resolution to himself not to set face in England, until he had made his voyage and employment there worth him a hundred thousand pounds sterling [£213 million in 2010]; and all by this sugar plant". Modyford's optimism was indeed justified; by 1647 he had made a fortune and was appointed governor in 1660. In the same decade, he expanded his interests into newly acquired Jamaica and became governor of that island in 1664. At his death in 1679, he owned one of the largest plantations in the West Indies, with over six hundred enslaved Africans.[13]

The reorganization of economic activity in Barbados and the Leewards is generally referred to as "the Sugar Revolution". The cultivation of sugar cane on large plantations on Barbados steadily displaced the growing of tobacco, cotton and indigo on smaller farms, and supplemented these activities on the other islands. Sugar planting, with its larger labour and capital equipment needs, stimulated demand for bigger units of land. Landowners foreclosed on tenants, and small freeholders were bought out and pushed off. As a result, land prices escalated and there was a rapid reduction in the size and output of non-sugar producers. In most islands, some small-scale farmers continued to occupy prime lands, maintaining a cash-crop culture on the margins of plantations. But small farmers found it difficult to compete as tobacco and cotton prices fell, and their operations often proved unprofitable. By the 1680s, the "sugar islands" had lost their reputation as hospitable places for poor European migrants, while the progress of sugar cultivation on the island of Barbados effected a more rapid and more extensive manipulation of the natural environment than occurred anywhere else in that part of the Atlantic that was under English control during the seventeenth century.[14]

Impact on Social Structure

Economic transformation had considerable implications for the social structure and political life of West Indian society. The emergence of a slave-owning gentry, considered the richest colonists in America, distinguished the "sugar islands" and set them apart. In most colonies, successive generations of men from elite families dominated political institutions, legislatures and judiciaries, and these were responsible for constructing mansions on the island of Barbados that matched those of comfortable English aristocratic families, as well as port towns and churches that gave a superficial English appearance to all these tropical islands.

On the negative side, the more successful slave owners, especially on Barbados and Jamaica, used systems of exclusion such as property qualifications, membership in professional bodies and the possession of university degrees to aid them in dominating colonial society at the expense of middling and smaller planters, as well as all non-whites. They also played prominent leadership roles in further colonial expansion. The sponsorship of Caribbean settlements in Jamaica, the Windwards, and the Guianas, as well as in Virginia and the Carolinas on the mainland, benefited in large measure from the migration and investments of the Barbadian elite.

In 1645, Barbados and the Leeward Islands were home to fifty-five thousand English persons; at the time, fewer than half of this number lived in the New England colonies. While the French were struggling to settle five thousand in their various Caribbean colonies, the English were establishing their largest overseas presence. The Caribbean was the beginning of the global empire imagined.

Sugar meant enslaved Africans, as it did in Hispaniola and Brazil. Those acquainted with sugar production in Brazil knew that the work regime was sustained with enslaved Africans. The work associated with sugar production was unusually burdensome because it involved a considerable manufacturing input on the plantation as well as harsh agricultural labour. Workers were required not only to clear the ground of lush natural vegetation and to plant, tend and harvest the sugar cane in the tropical sun, but also immediately to crush the juice from the cane in a sugar mill and then to boil the juice in cauldrons before it had time to ferment. Work on a sugar plantation was arduous and labour-intensive throughout the year, but was particularly onerous at harvest time when the sugar works operated incessantly, with the workers organized in shifts to keep the production going. Large profits in sugar during the mid-century meant that the more successful sugar planters could absorb the high labour costs associated with slavery, as they rapidly dispensed with indentured servitude and developed the islands as the greatest British market for enslaved Africans. The capital and credit needed to revolutionize the market for enslaved labour were available. English as well as Dutch merchants and financiers were eager to do business with sugar planters.[15]

The Lion's Share

When England's plunderers entered the Caribbean world at the end of the sixteenth century, variously defined as high seas pirates, freelance buccaneers, anti-Spanish terrorists and such like, they were the underdogs in Europe's exploitation of Caribbean wealth. The Spanish, following the Columbus invasion of 1492, had violently colonized most of the region. They had extracted its mineral wealth, enslaved the inhabitants and tried to exterminate those who resisted. The Spanish military's control of the Caribbean space was designed to enrich and empower the Spanish monarch and mercenaries. Imperial wealth meant domestic political power and, in this regard, Spain soon established its credentials in Europe as a superpower not to be trifled with.

In this age of aggressive nationalism in Europe, the English state feared for its security and sovereignty and felt vulnerable, excluded from Caribbean wealth and denied access to Caribbean glory and imperial prestige. Therefore, the English state unleashed its own nationalism upon the Caribbean world. The Dutch were already ahead, and the French had taken effective measures to establish its Caribbean credentials. The English, therefore, lagged behind not only the Spanish but also the Dutch and the French, whose ascendancy as economic powers it dreaded.

The arrival of the English as colonizers in the early seventeenth century, therefore, took place in a highly charged, political and military European environment. The Caribbean, already a place that Spain had violently redesigned to suit its purposes, became a zone of "total warfare" as the English declared war unofficially in general but officially at strategic moments.

English nationalism was redefined in new and specific ways within the Caribbean, a place that presented real-life activity for the testing of its identity and global interests. Moving tentatively at first, the English state soon felt its confidence, and by the end of the seventeenth century it had broken the back of Dutch and French challenges in the Caribbean and had won the respect and strategic submission of the Spanish. This planned military and political comparative advantage was achieved by way of the mobilization of the wealth that the British had generated in the Caribbean and the wider Atlantic, having effectively engaged in the slave system as trading and agricultural enterprises.

The economic prosperity produced by enslaved African labour in the Caribbean shifted the centre of worldwide wealth accumulation. There was no place like it on the planet for such unrestricted use of humans as enslaved labour. Africans in the Caribbean experienced what the human imagination can only describe as "hell on earth", and the English sugar planters and slave traders were the principal creators of this captivity.

Contemporaries tell us that suddenly these islands became the most valuable pieces of real estate in the world, to be coveted and fought for. Seventeenth-century English political economist Sir Dalby Thomas, an architect of English Caribbean ascendancy, stated that the pleasure, glory and grandeur of England had been advanced more by sugar than by any other commodity. Sugar meant African enslavement. He also quoted another economist, Sir

Josiah Child, well-known articulator of English nationalism in the seventeenth century, who opined that the Caribbean had become the most precious group of colonies ever recorded.[16]

Sir Josiah measured the Caribbean's value to England in terms of the wealth repatriated to generate employment and the market for English manufactures. Barbados in the seventeenth century was worth more to England than all the American colonies combined because it was the heart of English slavery in the New World. By 1775, the British West Indian plantations were valued at £50 million (£71.7 billion in 2010); only three years later they were estimated to be worth £70 million (£97.9 billion in 2010).[17]

As he looked forward to the coming eighteenth century, Sir Josiah Child concluded that England had never been possessed of such burgeoning new wealth. The national interest was embedded in African enchainment and enslavement. The militarized nationalism that gridlocked western Europe in the Caribbean in the seventeenth and eighteenth centuries also served as the prison for Africans caught in the cage of Europe's competitive commercial agendas.

The English directed all their military might against other Europeans and focused all their cultural spite against the Africans. Initially, the Africans were a tool in the war of Europe. Access to enslaved African labour on Caribbean soil was the technology that would give them the economic advantage. It would generate wealth to fund the wider war and serve as a measure of the Englishman's respect for his own liberty and racial identity.

For these reasons, the British state launched wars at will against its rivals in the eighteenth century. These wars were intended to corner the market in enchained African bodies and take control of as much Caribbean soil as possible for the enslavement of these Africans. Unfettered, then, was not just British militarism, but also its entrepreneurial, cultural and industrial power.

The Caribbean was indeed the "hub of Empire", and it served the purposes intended: it nurtured large-scale British mercantile activity, served as a growth market for British manufacturers, stimulated the domestic financial and monetary system, provided occupations for thousands within the mercantile community, enabled the British mind to feel itself mended after the Civil War and superior in the period after the Act of Union, and critically, it spurred British global ambition.

The Caribbean was more than the "hub of Empire"; it was the mother of

British might. In the Caribbean was created the opportunity that sustained imperial efforts in an age of winners-take-all. Enchained and enslaved Africans in the Caribbean made it all possible and profitable. By the end of the eighteenth century, Britain had all the power, profits and prestige it could handle. It also had the largest number of enslaved Africans in the Caribbean and an appetite for an expanded empire with even more.

The three million enchained Africans whom the English shipped across the Caribbean were the basis of this expanded empire. Jamaica, its leading economic enterprise at the end of the eighteenth century, was prison to near three hundred thousand, and when the five hundred thousand in French Saint-Domingue rose up and regained their freedom, the English were left with the status as lead Caribbean enslaver – a nation in possession of nearly four million chattels.

These enslaved Africans, shipped mostly to the Caribbean, were the end product of a chain of value-added that enriched English ports, parliamentarians, public treasuries, financial houses, insurance corporations, shipbuilders and manufacturers. The slave trade, noted James Rawley, "contributed to and benefited English dominion in commerce, shipping and empire". England, he stated, "had a large merchant class that wielded an influence in public affairs", added to which the nation "had industrial products to export, an activity that rapidly grew in the heyday of the slave trade".[18]

Between 1672, with the formation of the Royal African Company, and 1698 when the Company's official monopoly was removed, English merchant tonnage increased from 90,000 to 260,000. By 1700, the English had outstripped the Dutch, their leading competitor, in shipping tonnage capacity. The Royal African Company had computed that it could generate £3 million per annum from its sale of enchained Africans in the Caribbean.[19]

These profits would go to the list of investors, headed by the Duke of York; Prince Rupert, brother to the king; and the Earl of Bath. Trading in enslaved Africans, King Charles II had said, was "of great advantage to our subjects of this kingdom". With the ninety-five voyages between 1680 and 1697, on which Africans were taken from the Senegambia and Sierra Leone regions, "the English earned profits of 38 percent". These were tantalizing profits that lured Englishmen into the trade. While success eluded many, as in all trades, it was this lure of superprofits that enticed the enterprising and sustained the seasoned.[20]

The Caribbean market was the principal site for this rush to riches. Barbados, defined in the seventeenth century as "the brightest jewel in His Majesty's crown", was the largest market; it was surpassed by Jamaica early in the eighteenth century. The "guinney trade", as it was called, worked "to the national advantage" and its influence could be felt everywhere, from Parliament to Palace, from the seat of government to the ghettos around it. It was a feast on the flesh of the enchained Africans.[21]

According to Rawley,

> In the decade of the 1750s England became the Supreme slaving nation in the Atlantic World, a standing she occupied until 1807 [when the trade was abolished]. In the period from 1751 to 1800 England exported 42 per cent of the slaves taken from Africa; 52 per cent in the years from 1791 to 1807, England's annual export of slaves rose from about 7,000 in the late seventeenth century to twice that figure in the 1740s, to nearly 40,000 in the late years of the eighteenth century.[22]

These figures present a glimpse of Britain's pillage of the African population at the height of its reign of terror. But the data available speak to England's nearly three million Africans in the period between 1690 and 1807 (see table 7.1).[23]

As the trade in African bodies began in a dramatic way, with the English monarchy and state as major investors, so too did it end dramatically in 1807. In the last decade of the trade, the British government emerged as the largest single purchaser of Africans. The duplicity of the government, professing

Table 7.1. European Trade in Enslaved Africans, 1701–1800

Nation	Volume
English	2,532,300
Portuguese	1,796,300
French	1,180,300
Dutch	350,900
Danish	73,900
Swedish/German	8,000

Source: Paul Lovejoy, "The Volume of the Atlantic Slave Trade: A Synthesis", *Journal of African History* 22, no. 4 (1982): 483.

abolition on one hand and making mass purchases on the other, was known in the trading centres of London, Bristol and Liverpool. Yet somehow, in order not to embarrass the government, neither side to the abolition debate made an issue of it. Over time, these facts became obscured, and the role of the British government as a major player in a trade it had committed to ending on moral and legal grounds was shrouded in secrecy.

Rawley made much of this evidence in his study of the slave trade, which shows the role of the British state as regulator, purchaser and market manipulator. He wrote, "An extraordinary aspect of the British slave trade during these terminal years has recently been uncovered. Faced with a military manpower crisis in a failure to raise troops for the West India Regiments, Great Britain recruited by buying slaves . . . with emphasis upon 'those of the Gold Coast, Coromantie, or Congo Nations'."[24] The government stealthily dealt with specially commissioned merchants, who sold Africans in small lots, both to keep prices down and to avoid embarrassment. Between 1795 and 1808 the government bought an estimated 13,400 Africans for the West India Regiments at a cost of £925,000 (£712 million in 2010). The expenditure was concealed in an unaudited military account appropriately called Army Extraordinaries. Not only was this duplicity evident in the state's dealings with anti-abolitionists, but officials went to great lengths to cover up that it "was the largest purchaser of Africans in these years when the trade was under attack in press and Parliament".[25] The leadership of Prime Minister Pitt seemed destined to display itself as leader in unprincipled dealings with black people.

C.L.R. James noted that when Prime Minister Pitt saw the opportunity to invade Saint-Domingue (later, Haiti) under the regime of Toussaint L'Ouverture, he eagerly back-pedalled in his support for the abolition of the slave trade. He salivated at the prospect of securing British control over the 550,000 blacks, whom he proposed to re-enslave. The capture and re-enslavement of Toussaint's liberated blacks became Britain's new policy. It led Britain into war with the Haitians in order to overthrow their freedom. Thousands of British soldiers were massacred in the ill-fated operation that revealed the British government's hypocrisy. The wealth in Haiti – large sugar plantations and half a million blacks – was too much for Pitt to ignore. In a sudden turn of politics, he redefined the capture of Haitians and the possibility of their enslavement as being in the national interest.[26]

With the death of Pitt, the British policy of buying Africans for enslavement continued as a strategy to build an army for the defence of the empire. According to Rawley, "Late in 1806, when abolition was imminent, the government frantically negotiated with the great Liverpool slave-trading House of Dawson for '2 to 4,000 slaves of the tribes from the Gold Coast . . . before the act takes effect'."[27]

The stocking-up of enslaved Africans before its own act became law was an action not normally associated with a government. Private sector traders have generally been associated with such conduct within the context of slavery and slave trading. Yet, according to Rawley, "Between passage of the abolition act in March 1807 and 1 March 1808, the last date for landing slaves in the West Indies, the government brought about 1,000 Africans. . . . To its end the slave trade served the national interest."[28]

Slavery Cash for British Cities

The trade in enchained African bodies served as a cash crop for most British port towns and cities, though in the eighteenth century, Bristol, Liverpool, London and Glasgow were pre-eminent. Cities prospered from the wealth generated; thousands of sailors found employment, and banks and other financial institutions sprang up and prospered.

Political and financial careers and fortunes were launched and sustained. The trade in enchained African bodies was the biggest commerce in these towns – the most financially rewarding, exciting and prestigious. The quickest, most recognized way to make a fortune in the eighteenth century was to take the risk and reap the rewards of slave trading, and established merchants were eager to participate in the trade.

In all the port towns and cities of Britain, manufacturers joined in the bounty and loaded slave ships with their goods for sale and exchange in Africa. In Bristol, the local glassworks boomed as demand for bottles and other glass products rose at a rapid rate. Copper and brass factories sprang up and expanded to supply shipbuilders, as also did manufacturers of pots and pans. Bristol's ship building rose to prominence in the eighteenth century on the back of the slave ships; so too did the iron works.

Bristol industries, slave traders and sugar planters from the city, resident in the Caribbean, created a network of wealth organized around the shipment of enchained and enslaved Africans. While politicians in Parliament, like the famous Edmund Burke, showed deference to the city's slave-trading base with considerable cunning and ingenuity, its merchants imported more slave-produced sugar than any other English city in the eighteenth century, and with its slave ships linked to this network of Atlantic trading, Bristol was thriving with business.

This commonwealth of crime was represented and defended at all levels of political governance by its mayors, burgesses and parliamentarians. Bristol in 1740 was ahead by a distance in the competition for the sugar and slave trades. Yet after the 1750s, Liverpool rivalled and outpaced the city, as the manufacturing hinterland of Lancashire developed a more dynamic financial symbiotic relationship with the Caribbean slave system. But the mighty slave-trading companies of Bristol, such as Isaac Hobhouse and Company or James Rogers and Associates, remained in the national slave-trading elite and ensured the city's reputation as an industry initiator.

It required a major investment by Liverpool slave traders to outperform Bristol as the head of the slave-trading industry. Robert Norris, a don of the Liverpool slave-trading fraternity, told the House of Commons in 1790 that the city's investment in slave trading stood in excess of £2,088,526 (£2.56 million in 2010). At least 141 slave ships were registered in the city, he said, and 69 per cent of these were owned by 33 per cent of all the slave traders in the city. Liverpool dominated the slave trade to Jamaica – England's largest slave market.[29]

The link between the slave trade and the rise of the English financial sector first seemed clear at Liverpool. "The growth of the African and West Indian trades", Rawley concluded, "fostered the developments of industry, banking and insurance in Liverpool. . . . Liverpool did not have a bank until 1774, but well before this date, Liverpool merchants began to discount bills of exchange, adding to the fluid capital and purchasing power of the city."[30]

In the city, furthermore, "the bulk of such merchants were West Indian and African traders; Heywood's bank sprang from this source, and the slave trader, Thomas Leyland, became a noted banker". These financial developments that found energy in the profitability of the Caribbean slave system gave Liverpool its reputation as the commercial capital of the northwest by the end of the eighteenth century. Liverpool's banking community, Rawley sums up, "rendered valiant service to the great port during the financial crisis of 1793, when unlike their counterparts in Bristol, Liverpool bankers by accepting Liverpool's own notes issue restored confidence".[31]

Expert political leadership in the city underpinned this and other strategic decisions made to protect the slave-based financial sector. Consider, for example, the benefits that financiers in the city experienced when John Hardman, member of Parliament for the city in the 1750s, was also a leading African slave trader and West Indian sugar trader. When he died, the city lamented his death and considered it a blow to the bloom he had brought to the city market at the end of the eighteenth century.

The big traders in Liverpool were the city's commercial elite, led by merchants such as Thomas Leyland and Company, William Davenport, William Boats and Company, John Gladstone and Company, the Tarleton family, and John Dawson and Company; the industry was well protected in the city and in Parliament. In 1807, when the trade was challenged, member of Parliament for the city, General Gascoyne, summed up the state of affairs in his constituency as follows: "This is a subject of magnitude in a commercial point of view; for it was no small matter of capital which employed two million, with 40,000 tons of shipping and 4,000 seamen."[32]

John Gladstone, the slave trader, had made his future here and laid the basis for his son William to become prime minister of England. He also bought sugar estates in Jamaica, linking his sugar investment with his slaving company. John also expanded his slave operations into Demerara with an investment he made in 1816 of £80,000 (£55.6 million in 2010). There, he doubled his slave labour force, serving as a West Indian coffee and sugar producer. In 1828 he owned at least 1,050 enslaved Africans, with indirect interest in many more.

Rawley noted, furthermore, that "after emancipation of the slaves by Parliament, Gladstone was paid compensation of £93,526 (£69.7 million in 2010) for the 2,039 enslaved Africans he claimed as his personal property". From Caribbean slave-based profits, the careers of distinguished British politicians were launched – landing in and around Number 10 Downing Street.[33]

There were many others. John Tarleton, leading slave trader, would report to city merchants in the 1780s the content of his meetings with the prime minister. He was critical in winning the vocal support for slave trading from His Royal Highness the Duke of Clarence, the future William IV. The duke was fond of Tarleton, and in the two of them, Liverpool slave-trading interests found powerful advocates. In the last quarter of the eighteenth century, 1,754 slave ships left Liverpool for West Africa. In the same period, Bristol arranged the departure of 649 ships. Liverpool took over about 60 per cent of England's slave trade in the 1770s, increasing this to about 80 per cent by 1800. Indeed, "Liverpool had become the premier slave port in the world."[34]

While not rivalling Liverpool as the centre for slave trading, London specialized as the city with the financial know-how and institutions to drive the slave and sugar trades and to enable all the colonial trades to maximize their efficiency. London's focus was on turning the loot into legacy. In this regard, no other city in the world rivalled London by the time the slave system was outlawed in 1838. But by then, slavery had fulfilled its role.

And what a phenomenal role it played in the accumulation of wealth to the British elite. The formation of the Bank of England, as early as 1694, was driven in large measure by the need to regulate and direct the slavery profits from the Caribbean into the provincial institutions that were springing up everywhere. Slave-based profits needed to be directed into the agricultural and industrial sectors, thereby enabling other entrepreneurs to have access to Caribbean capital.

The Credit Act of 1732 was a critical legislative intervention that promoted the freer flow of capital from the Caribbean to England. This development enabled London-based sugar companies, such as the house of Lascelles, to flourish in the safety of knowing that they could litigate successfully against West Indian slave owners in West Indian courts, a privilege traditionally denied.

London merchants controlled the financing of the slave trade, the sugar trade, and ultimately, the insurance sector. The two leading businesses in the Maritime Insurance sector – London Assurance and the Royal Exchange Company – dominated West Indian business. Behind this financial mountain was a massive valley of manufacturing that filled the slave ships and found markets in the sugar plantations. "London industries concerned in the African trade", noted Rawley, "included textiles, guns, metal ware, beer, spirits, and sugar". By 1800, the bulk of Caribbean sugar found its way to London in British ships.[35]

The city was effective in placing its West Indian traders in the House of Commons in order to protect the slave system. In 1788, at least sixty West Indian merchants were London parliamentarians, using their fortunes to buy political seats and to influence voting patterns on colonial matters. They constituted the leadership of the West Indies lobby in Parliament, a formidable pressure group with royal patronage for most of the eighteenth century.

Surrounding the inner core, Bristol, Liverpool and London, were the British network of slave-trading towns. Slave ships went out from almost every port, from Glasgow in the north to Southampton in the south, with Lancaster, Whitehaven, Plymouth, Preston, Hull, Dartmouth, Cowes, Poole, Portsmouth and Chester all participating at a lower threshold. Where there was a port, a slave ship found it because the word was known that the trade was the most lucrative venture in town. Without a slave ship, the port was much the poorer. The risk was great and many voyages were financial failures, but the profits were enormous for those whose enterprises were successful.

The enslavement of Africans was an evil enterprise, but a necessary evil for the economic growth required to protect the English nation from its European rivals. African enslavement was the way the English found to generate wealth at an unprecedented level and to promote English entrepreneurship on a global scale without moral restraint. Africans as chattels meant wealth to the English, as they did to other nations. The English, challenging Spanish and Dutch commercial hegemony, emerged as the nation with the military power to secure the greatest share of the "black gold".

Political economists in the eighteenth century, such as the legendary Adam Smith, also understood that a considerable part of the "wealth of the English nation" was generated by the colonial trades – primarily the trade in African bodies and the prized product of their labour: sugar. The Caribbean economy was the prime generator of the wealth derived from foreign trade.

The merchants of England grew wealthy from the commodities trade and reinvested their earnings back home. They built mansions on large rural estates and maintained town houses; they loaned money to farmers and industrialists; they funded civic institutions, including universities and churches; they invested in government bonds and deposited cash in banks; they financed insurance companies and built up the financial infrastructures of cities. They were celebrated and respected for their contribution to the rise of the English industrial economy.

In the nineteenth century, Karl Marx wrote extensively about the role of African enslavement in the development of British industrialism. Looking at the wider context of slavery and colonialism in British economic development,

Marx considered the interlocking functions of native genocide, black slavery and Asian servitude as critical to its accumulation of wealth. He wrote,

> The discovery of gold and silver in America, the extirpation, enslavement and entombment in mines of the indigenous population of that continent [the Americas], the beginning of the conquest and plunder of India, and the conversion of Africa into a preserve for the commercial hunting of black skins, are all things which characterized the dawn of the era of capitalist accumulation . . . these different moments are systematically combined together at the end of the seventeenth century in England, the combination embraces the colonies, the national debt, the modern tax system, and the system of protection. These methods depend in part on brute force, for instance, the colonial system. But they all employ the power of the State, the concentrated and organized force of society, to hasten, as in a hothouse, the process of transformation of the feudal mode of production into the capitalist mode, and to shorten the transition.[36]

Marx saw this clearly. Slavery did not create the industrial revolution; it facilitated its rise and maturity. It nurtured it, enabling it to grow faster, become stronger.

Economic Growth on the Backs of Blacks

By the early twentieth century, a literature of scholarly denial of this history was in the ascendancy. As Britain celebrated its status as the world's first industrial nation and took pride as a global leader, the marginalization of the role of slavery in its economic development intensified. Within this context, Eric Williams published *Capitalism and Slavery* in 1944. Williams was explicit on points of detail and presented a vigorous statement of the empirical data. By tracking the financial careers of slave traders in the cities that spawned them, and following their journeys into Parliament as prominent men of money, Williams demonstrated that the sugar industry in the Caribbean supplied oxygen to the flagging seventeenth-century English economy.

Empowered by the profits of slaving and slavery, the British economy was energized and transformed in the eighteenth century. The elevation to a high level of sustainable economic growth, Williams argued, was primarily due to the impact of the colonial trades within the Atlantic slave system, of which the Caribbean was the hub. Without African slavery, the Atlantic economy would not have been an attractive investment opportunity for England and Europe. Without the infrastructure represented by the Caribbean sugar economy and its related slave trading and commodity-trading networks, eighteenth-century England's economic growth would not have reached the level that enabled the use of the term "Industrial Revolution".

There was palpable disturbance within academic circles concerning *Capitalism and Slavery*. Conservative English and American economic historians launched a crusade against it. In most cases, their scholarly intention was not always detectable. Instead, there were layers of ideology, distinctly Eurocentric and sometimes with racial undertones. Blackburn has noted that labour historians tended to support the broad contours of Williams's argument since, in fact, various versions of the thesis had been articulated for over two hundred years: "A tradition of British historiography – culminating in Eric Hobsbawm's *Industry and Empire* (1964) and Christopher Hill's *From Reformation to Revolution* (1968) – has argued that British colonial expansion did indeed furnish crucial economic space for British capitalist development."[37] Such scholars "had no difficulty finding seventeenth- and eighteenth-century statesmen and political economists who urged colonial development on the grounds that it would boost the national economy".[38] David Richardson could therefore be challenged when he stated, for example, that "historians resident in Western industrialized nations are generally divided in their explanations of the growth of eighteenth century British exports and in their assessment of exports' impact on the Industrial Revolution. Caribbean based historians by contrast have generally been much more united in attributing to British overseas trade – particularly the slave trade and related trades in plantation staples – a positive and substantial role in fostering British industrialization".[39]

There are, of course, Caribbean-based scholars who have raised questions similar to those of British scholars. Surprising, then, has been the statement from Kenneth Morgan that "the main support for Williams's arguments in *Capitalism and Slavery* has come from black scholars, though not exclusively; the main detractors are white historians".[40]

British scholars who were steeped in the study of labour history, as well as those with a deep intellectual commitment to social justice tended to treat the issues raised by Williams more fairly. Historians of labour recognized the importance of African enslavement to the rise of industrial capitalism in general, knowing as they do the tendency for capital to subject labour to a basic subsistence level. Slavery became the quintessential case of labour exploitation and the commercial classes were exceedingly good at it.

Blackburn's important work on Europe's New World imperial design supports the general argument made by Williams; if he quibbles with specific points that may seem to him overstated, his work serves as a significant endorsement. He states that "during the eighteenth century Britain had constructed an Atlantic system which had nourished its economic strength". By the end of the eighteenth century, the colonial world accounted for two-thirds of all British exports. He concluded that Britain, of all the European nations, was "the leading beneficiary of New World commerce".[41]

Despite this evidence, Blackburn continues, "the so-called 'Williams thesis' became the target of repeated attempts to show that neither the Atlantic slave trade nor the plantation trades had made any large or decisive contribution to British economic growth".[42] Blackburn finds this incredible, stating that two of the most distinguished scholars of the period, Eric Hobsbawm and Christopher Hill, showed that "British colonial expansion did indeed furnish crucial economic space for British capitalist development". Referring to their works as "a wave of revisionism", Blackburn concludes that Williams's critics argue against "the evidence of official statistics", which show clearly the significant contribution to British economic growth of Caribbean slavery and the Atlantic colonial system it nurtured.

Following the early writings of Adam Smith and the mature Karl Marx, Blackburn shows, like Williams, that "it was the commerce of the slave zone that sustained the purchasing power of the entire North American economy; this makes the scope of British exports to all its American colonies" the critical reference point for a study of the English Industrial Revolution. The West Indies was the hub of the "American system". Blackburn shows that in the eighteenth century, "the British West Indies imported more wrought iron than either Africa/Asia combined or the Northern colonies".[43]

For those scholars who used the development of the British metal industries as a barometer of industrialization, this point is more than telling. Here, even the most fervent critics of Williams concede that West Indian demand did more than stimulate English industrialization. Furthermore, "the earliest exports of the cotton industry went almost exclusively to African and West

Indian markets", another telling point for those scholars who have used the cotton manufacturing industry as a barometer.[44]

The research into profitability in the British Caribbean slave economy and its impact on British economic development continues to show the correctness of "the Williams thesis". Richard Sheridan, the American economic historian of the Caribbean, argued that total profits in the West Indian slave economy stood at a phenomenal £2.3 million in 1770 (£3.46 billion in 2010). For the same period, J.R. Ward suggests that £2.5 million was the *annual* profit for all commodity production in the British West Indies. David Hancock suggests that Sheridan and Ward have underestimated these profits, certainly for the London merchants who had considerable plantation investments in the West Indies.[45]

In a masterful critique of the critics of Williams, Robin Blackburn tells us that many of them have not looked at the various trades as a network that constituted the triangular trades. Manufacturing goods were taken out from Britain to Africa, sold or exchanged there for enslaved labour for sale in the Caribbean, after which ships were stocked with Caribbean produce bound for Britain – all in British ships. Blackburn concludes that "triangular trade profits went to the wealthier classes", and that "between 30 per cent and 50 per cent of triangular trade profits were reinvested".[46]

But this is not all. Blackburn goes on to show that "if the reinvestment rate was at the lower end of the range . . . then, according to the basic estimates, triangular trade profits could have supplied 20.9 per cent of Britain's gross fixed capital formation. On the other hand, if 50 per cent of basic profits were reinvested, then the proportion would rise to 28.7 per cent". This suggests, following Williams, that "the profits of the plantations and of the rest of the slave-based trades probably constituted the largest single source of imperial gains".[47]

This is an empirically sound argument. "The oxygen required by the [British and] European furnace of capitalist accumulation, if it was not to succumb to auto-asphyxiation, was supplied by the slave traffic and the plantation-related trades." The Caribbean colonies were producing 80,000 tons of sugar annually. By the end of the century, Europe was taking between eighty thousand and a hundred thousand "young men and women" annually out of Africa, and delivering into Africa an annual average of three hundred thousand guns. The English Merchant Marine employed about twenty-five thousand sailors by 1750, and gave jobs to a similar number of dock workers and ship builders.[48]

By the mid-1700s, "half of all British overseas trade consisted of shipments of sugar or tobacco", as "sugar overtook grain as the most valuable single commodity entering world trade". The Caribbean supplied at least 70 per cent of all the cane sugar entering the markets of the American colonies, and indeed, Europe. This considerable amount of trade wealth was generated from an enslaved African population in British colonies that rose from 64,000 in 1680, to 295,000 in 1750, and 480,000 in 1790.[49]

The enormity of the human price paid by Africans for English economic development becomes clear, even to the blind, when it is noted that England sent about 1.6 million Africans to its Caribbean colonies during the period of 1700 to 1800, and yet fewer than 500,000 of them survived. That is, at least 1 million Africans perished during this period in order to generate the profits that fuelled British industrial development during the eighteenth century. About 75,893 were sold in Barbados between 1712 and 1734, and the island's black population grew from 41,970 to 46,373. Between 1700 and 1774, the English sold about 500,000 Africans in Jamaica, yet the population increased by only 150,000 in the period.[50]

The Caribbean profits were attractive and their expression as investments in British economic development was consistent. The work by David Hancock, going beyond that of Williams, Sheridan and Ward, demonstrated the role of London merchants as generators and appropriators of Caribbean wealth. From a study of twenty-three London merchant houses, he showed that in 1750 they owned 9,000 acres of plantation lands, 21,000 acres in 1763, and 130,000 acres in 1775.[51]

In the Caribbean, these lands were developed as sugar plantations in Jamaica and the Leeward Islands. The London houses also owned estates in South Carolina, Georgia and Florida. Not surprising, "the Caribbean sugar plantations were their most profitable possessions". A leading merchant in the group was Sir Alexander Grant who, in the 1760s and 1770s, owned seven sugar plantations in Jamaica, which generated £3,450 (£5.19 million in 2010) profit per year, a "return on capital outlay of no less than 29 per cent". Across the Caribbean the story was the same.[52]

John Pinney, for instance, inherited a sugar plantation in Nevis in the 1760s. He was a Bristol man, deeply involved in the slave trade and sugar trades. His investments in the British economy were considerable. In 1782 he was one of England's wealthiest men, with a Caribbean-based fortune of £70,000 (£92 million in 2010). When he died in 1818, he was worth a staggering £340,000 (£247 million in 2010), with £146,000 (£102.6 million in 2010) in West Indian lands, slaves and other properties.[53]

Williams's critics have had a difficult time refuting the evidence that profits from the slave trade, the sugar trades, and Caribbean slave-based production and intercolonial trades "fertilised the entire productive system" of Great Britain. David Richardson, for example, an ardent critic, has confined his work to showing that Williams made "broad and sweeping" arguments, but essentially agreed with the fundamental correctness of Williams's research.[54]

In an essay titled "The Slave Trade, Sugar, and British Economic Growth, 1748–1776", after deciding that the relationship between Caribbean slavery and British industry was more complex than Williams suggests, Richardson concluded that

> it appears that Caribbean-based demands may have accounted for 12 per cent of the growth of English industrial output in the quarter century before 1776. Furthermore, the indications are that a similar proportion of the increased output between 1750 and 1775 of Scotland's leading industry, linen, was sold in Caribbean markets. Although West Indian and related trades provided a more modest stimulus to the growth of British industrial production than Williams imagined, they nevertheless played a more prominent part in fostering industrial changes and export growth in Britain during the third quarter of the eighteenth century than most historians have assumed.[55]

Richardson's concession, even if by way of moderating the evidence as presented by three hundred years of economic writers, from Charles Davanent in the mid-seventeenth century to Marx in the mid-nineteenth century and Williams in the mid-twentieth century, represents a significant turn in the literature. Breaking ranks with critics such as Stanley Engerman, Roger Anstey and Nicholas Crafts, Richardson has restored some measure of academic fairness to the treatment of the evidence.

In 2000, Kenneth Morgan presented a general summary of the discussion that sought to assess the extent of slavery's impact on British economic growth. It was a useful commentary on what has been said and why. Its conclusions, however, were somewhat surprising, suggesting the need for more research in the face of deep divides on the "extent" of slavery's fertilization of British industry.[56]

Economic historians often tend not to see the role of human suffering in the enrichment of others, preferring to focus on quantitative relationships. Also, economic historians, particularly those with conservative inclinations, have a tendency to focus on the "average" as a strategy to suppress the lure and frenzy which the upper end generates. By feeding an orgy of the average, the intention is to suggest that slave trading and slavery underperformed and could therefore not have had the impact suggested.

Some slave voyages made super-profits, some made losses, and the average is then presented as the basis of the potential of the slave trade to generate wealth. Likewise, some sugar plantations made their owners some of the wealthiest men in Britain, and some were driven to bankruptcy by their business. The average is then used to suggest the modest performance of the sector in relation to the British economy. Also, no value is placed on the role of slaving and slavery in securing for British businessmen the highest social status, political access to monarchs and prime ministers and to Parliament and elite titles, as well as promoting the reputation of international business as an attractive option for national entrepreneurship. Local businessmen saw slave traders and sugar planters parading as the richest men in town. Such men were envied by "royals". They set new standards for elite society – and all knew that the West Indian planter was the one who could embarrass the king with his display of wealth.

Kenneth Morgan calls for more research. He sits on the fence; he looks back to see the facts on the wall: "Slavery and Atlantic trade made an important, though not decisive, impact on Britain's long-term economic development . . . playing their part in enabling Britain to become the workshop of the world." His final word might appear in contradiction to his earlier call for more decisive data, but it is instructive: "The ever increasing scholarship on these matters now accords a positive role to the connections between slavery, trade, empire and a British economy experiencing the transition to industrialization." No surprises here. The scholarship had been showing this for over two hundred years. For Morgan, the slavery system was not the cause of British development. It was "a stimulus". Williams would not have disagreed.[57]

But for Barbara Solow, Harvard economist, much of the attempt to distance British economic growth from its energy source in slave trading, slavery, and slave-based production and commodity trades has led to a literature of "nit-picking" and anti-intellectual meanness. An attempt to measure the contribution of slave-derived profits and trade as a percentage of Britain's capital formation and gross domestic product is necessary, but to take up academic positions on marginal variations in percentages is rather like arguing that the engine of the vehicle represents 10 per cent of its overall weight and 5 per cent of its physical mass, hence its lack of importance to the movement of the vehicle.[58]

Solow's perspective is that the basic economic truths should not be sacrificed in attempts to diminish "the crucial importance of slavery to the development of the modern world". She is impatient with the "narrow nationalistic approaches that have sprung up", and she calls for a return to truthful academic research. The "richest colonies were those that grew sugar with black slaves", she said, and this centred on the Caribbean. And black slaves, she said, "appeared in greater numbers in colonies that grew sugar".[59]

The slave–sugar complex became the premier institution of European expansion for reasons that are easily understood. The expanding "flows of capital, labor, sugar and manufacture turned these colonies one by one into centers of international trade", uniting Africa and Europe in a "complex web of transactions". These activities of wealth creation centred on the Caribbean. Solow concludes, "This microcosm of capital and trade flows associated with plantation slavery became quantitatively important for British economic development in the eighteenth century".[60]

Efforts to deny or minimize this truth, Solow reminds us, should be met with telling examples of the impact of the Caribbean on British everyday life. The facts, she suggests, exist in abundance and require no special manipulation. She states,

> By 1750 the poorest English farm laborer's wife took sugar in her tea. Rum from West Indian molasses catered to the notorious drinking habits of eighteenth-century Britain and supplied the navy. By 1660 the value of sugar imports exceeded that of all other colonial produce combined; by 1774 sugar accounted for 20 percent of the total import bill, far surpassing any other commodity. The British took a third of Europe's consumption in the first half of the century . . . slave labor produced this sugar.[61]

The West Indian slave plantation, she goes on to say, became the primary

British centre for capital investments, source of revenue inflows, market for manufacturers, and financial services such as banking and insurance.

The "Atlantic network centered on the Caribbean", and it was a vastly greater economic concentration than anything Europe had ever known. "It was important to the economic growth of Great Britain at the beginning of the Industrial Revolution", because "slavery in the colonies raised the rate of return on investment in the empire – made investments more productive – and thereby increased national output". In general, the capital investment in the slave colonies, which amounted to £37 million (£55 billion in 2010) in 1773, "was large enough to make this a significant force".[62]

Solow offers words of comfort to those in denial for "narrow nationalistic" purposes: "The importance of Caribbean slavery to British growth depended on particular circumstances and was confined to a particular historical period." The Caribbean economy, based on slavery, "benefited Britain when investment was lagging, technical change was slow, growth in domestic demand for manufacture was less than that in external demand, and when the North American colonies depended on Britain for manufacture and on the West Indies for the foreign exchange with which to buy them".[63]

To acknowledge, then, the role of the Caribbean in fostering Britain's economic development in the seventeenth and eighteenth centuries is to examine honestly the relations between an imperial country and the colonies it created for purposes of commercial exploitation. The Caribbean slave complex, as Solow tells us, was the principal source of the "foreign exchange" for the North American colonies owned by Britain, and later by the imperial centre itself. "To argue that slavery was important for British economic growth is not to claim that slavery caused the Industrial Revolution." She concludes: "Slavery did not cause the Industrial Revolution but played an active role in its pattern and timing." By the 1820s, when Britain was a self-sustaining industrial nation, "the West Indies mattered less". It had served its purposes. It was time to put it aside and move on.[64]

Chapter 8

Dividends from the Devil

Church of England Chattels in Barbados

> One of the most important battles that William Wilberforce had to fight was with the bishops of the Church of England, not one of whom supported the abolition of the slave trade. . . . The Bishop of Exeter was remunerated to the sum of £13,000 for the 665 slaves he had.
>
> —*Chris Bryant, Member of Parliament, Debate on the Bicentenary of the Abolition of the Slave Trade, House of Commons, 20 March 2007*

THE ENSLAVEMENT OF AFRICANS WAS managed and financed by all the principal institutions that constituted the British state, including the established church. The elected government, judiciary, legislature and the Church of England all sang from the same hymnbook and worshipped the same god: the profits from slave trading and slavery.[1]

The Church of England, represented by its Anglican clergy that spread across the Caribbean throughout the seventeenth to nineteenth centuries, took centre stage as an important player in the slave-based economy. Its relationship to the enslaved was neither pastoral nor spiritual, but financial and entrepreneurial. The clergy engaged in the important ideological work of defending African enslavement. It blessed slave traders and slave ships, and presided over events such as executions of the rebellious. Critically, the clergy were elite private investors in slave plantations which they owned and managed.[2]

Barbados, at the height of the slave economy in the 1780s, boasted the eminence of the Reverend John Brathwaite, rector of the parish church of St John, as the largest slave owner in the colony. The good clergyman was role model and mentor for other men of the cloth who pursued profits in the hell of plantation slavery. As clergymen and commercialists, they preached the gospel to whites and administered the whip to blacks. Africans, they gave witness, had plenty of labour to give and no soul to save. They were brought across the ocean to work the land, and without their hands a place could "scarce be called an estate".

The extent to which the Anglican clergy owned enslaved Africans can fairly accurately be established (see table 8.1).[3] In 1834, for example, 128 Anglican clergymen in Britain and Ireland were owners of enslaved blacks in the West

Table 8.1. Clergy Listed as Recipients of Compensation for Owning Enslaved Africans in the Caribbean

Colony	Number
Anguilla	1
Antigua	16
Barbados	20
Guiana	1
Dominica	1
Grenada	1
Jamaica	62
Montserrat	1
Nevis	4
St Kitts	6
St Lucia	2
St Vincent	6
Tobago	2
Trinidad	1
Virgin Islands	4
Total	128

Source: Nicholas Draper, *The Price of Emancipation: Slave-Ownership, Compensation and British Society at the End of Slavery* (Cambridge: Cambridge University Press, 2010), 303–7.

Indies. There were nearly ten thousand Anglican clergy in Britain at this time, and most of those with West Indian slave investments were among the colonial commercial elite. Many slave-owning clergy were influential leaders of the church and presented its slave-owning theology throughout the empire. African enslavement, they spoke and wrote, was the will of God and consistent with the Bible.[4]

In 1710, the missionary arm of the Church of England, the Society for the Propagation of the Gospel in Foreign Parts (SPG), acquired two large sugar plantations in Barbados, fully stocked with enslaved Africans. The acquisition was occasioned by the death of Englishman Christopher Codrington (1668–1710), scion of a prominent slave-owning family. The Codringtons had led the genocidal war against the indigenous population of the Leeward Islands and established themselves in Antigua and Barbuda, as well as Barbados. Codrington had been a military hero under King William III, and on his death he bequeathed "two plantations in the island of Barbados" to the Society for the Propagation of the Gospel and specified that his "desire is to have the plantations continued entire, and three hundred negroes, at least, always kept thereon".[5]

The Church of England took possession of the two plantations, with the "negro properties", and brought them under its management. The archbishops of York and the bishops of London were the successive principal leaders responsible for the lands and labour for the remainder of the slavery period. They set slave management policy and made sure these were congruent with church theology. The bishops operated these estates with the assistance of hired West Indian agents. According to Harry Bennett, the church "looked to them for necessary profits, and interfered little in their methods of administration". In this respect the church's chattels experienced enslavement in much the same way as other enslaved Africans did. The dividends from "hell" were sent to the bishops in London.[6]

The two adjoining estates consisted of 750 acres in the parish of St John. That three hundred women, men and children were enslaved thereon suggests that these estates were equal to any other on the island. The bishops employed a manager, an overseer and other white persons with supervisory authority. They reported directly to the bishop of London and the archbishop of York. The estates were profitable enterprises, generating in excess of £2,500 (£4.8 million in 2010) net annually from the cultivation of sugar cane. They were inherited at a time of economic boom in the sugar economy. Incomes were high and slave prices moderate; high profits were a cause of celebration in the hallowed pulpits.

Occasionally, the bishops would send out requests to their managers pertaining to the exposure of their chattels to Christian scriptures. The instructions of the Society for the Propagation of the Gospel were always clear. The African should be taught to "look for his reward in heaven, and in this life would abide in the same calling, wherein he was called".[7] They were to be told that, as unfree persons, they should be "useful and laborious servants". As the chattels of the church, they should be obedient, loyal, and hard-working, for the profits of the estates depended upon it. The bishops looked to the Barbados bounty to extend the pastoral work of the church. These funds enriched the coffers of the parish churches throughout England.

Church chattels at Codrington's plantations were branded like other enslaved persons in the Caribbean. In 1724, manager Smalridge paid £1.2s.6d (£2,000 in 2010) for a new silver branding mark, with the letters "SOCIETY" made "in large characters" with which the Africans were "brandished" like "so many beasts". Branding established the identity of the owner. The cattle and horses on the estate were branded with the same instrument.[8]

After Africans were "stamped" and duly registered as the chattels of the church, their new identity was made complete through the allocation of a name by the overseer. The manager would confirm these names and send them to the bishop of London. New names represented a feeble attempt to signal ethnic origins; sometimes they reflected the job to which they were assigned. Africans at Codrington's plantations were renamed "Sloop Johnny", "Cuffy Potter" and "Quashey Boyler". Other names given included "London", "Bristol", "Towerhill", "Caesar", "Hector", "Cain", "Scipio", as well as "Flower", "Rose", "Flora", "Dumb" and "Braveboy". Branded and renamed, these Africans entered the bookkeeper's accounts as Church of England chattels. With the loss of their freedom and of the cultural right to retain the name given by their parents, the enslaved entered the plantation economy as life servers.[9]

The purchasing of enslaved Africans at Codrington's plantations was consistent with the church's role as a major sugar plantation owner. There was a recruitment template which applied to all slave owners. Africans were bought at public auctions in the Bridgetown port and transported to the estates. When they died from overwork, malnutrition, disease and injury, they were replaced.

In 1712, the enslaved population of Barbados was 41,970. In 1734 it was 46,362. Yet between these dates, 75,893 Africans were imported. Some of these were re-exported to other colonies, but the majority died in the colony within a few years of arrival. This staggering demographic disaster typified life on the Codrington estates, and indeed all others. The church responded by hiring and purchasing more enslaved persons to fill the labour gap caused by the high mortality rates. Managers tried to persuade the enslaved women "to breed" in order to reproduce the enslaved stock, but to no avail. This slave breeding policy was deemed "the great failure".[10]

Church chattels were overworked and driven to death at a phenomenal rate. Experts on plantation development in the eighteenth century noted that an estate of 250 acres needed 170 enslaved persons for efficient production. At the Codrington plantations, with 500 acres, there were only 250 enslaved persons. With an understocked operation, managers drove the enslaved to compensate for the shortfall. In 1725, manager John Smalridge pressed the bishop of London to "make up the number 300" as "an absolute necessity". Smalridge and his successors complained consistently to the bishops about the labour shortage on the estates, and impressed upon them the debilitating impact on those who worked from sun up to sun down and deep into the night during the three months of harvest.[11]

But permission to purchase additional enslaved Africans had no long-term effect upon the labour conditions at the estates. More of them continued to die and run away than were purchased. Manager Abel Alleyne was pleased with the batch purchased in 1743, which he described as "the finest he had seen". But within days, "several died chiefly owing . . . to the evil practice of mixing sea water with fresh on board the Guiney (ships) to make it go further". One of them, "Jack, hang'd himself"; "two of them fled to Bridgetown" in an effort to return to Africa. In a state of despair, Alleyne informed the bishops that he begged "God Almighty to preserve their lives".[12]

From 1752 to 1762, the church spent £4,000 (£6.36 million in 2010) on the importation of 107 enslaved Africans. Yet the total number of slaves on the estates fell to 190. God apparently did not hear manager Alleyne's prayer. Altogether, the church, from the time of its acquisition of the plantations in 1712 to 1760, had purchased 453 enslaved Africans at a cost of some £15,000 (£23.3 million in 2010). "Experience has taught us", one manager stated, "how fruitless an attempt it is to aim at stocking [the estates] . . . by buying new negroes".[13]

Between 1712 and 1748, the estate accounts showed that six enslaved Africans died for each one born. In this period there were 69 births and 418 deaths on the estates. Manager Alleyne told the bishops that if he had more Africans, the gangs could be driven less hard and the stock would "hold out many years longer". Critically, he added, "the women would breed".[14]

The church's plantations, then, were places of death without redemption. Africans died in large numbers and were replaced. The replacements died at a faster rate, and the cycle continued as the bishops sought more profits. Added to these deaths were the executions for breaches of the disciplinary code. Jack General, for example, a field hand worth £70 (£96,700 in 2010), was "hang'd for stealing" estate property worth less than half his price. Running away was endemic. In this regard the overseers were kept busy. Fees paid for retrieving fugitives was a major expense. Quashebah, a field woman, ran away three times in 1775, once in 1776 and 1782, and twice in 1784. The rewards paid for her capture ranged from 2s.6d to 18s.9d.

When church chattels were not running away, they were busy sabotaging the estate as acts of resistance. The estates, said manager Alleyne, were filled with "rogues and runaways" and some "that have distempers incurable". Such Africans were described as "a Burden and Charge" upon the estates. The bishops gave strict instructions to maintain law and order, but their chattels were a rebellious and unruly lot.[15]

The pacification of rebellious chattels was always a concern for the church. Some clergy suggested their conversion to Christianity as a strategy. The bishops had serious concerns on this score. Religious instruction, they informed the managers, should "offer no threat to the peace or to profits". Sundays were critical days in the cane cultivation cycle. Managers could not sacrifice the Sabbath as a working day for religious instruction. The bishops preached this policy as a logical consequence of their theology that slavery and Christian conversion had to be handled with no threat to the financial soundness of the business.

The church had no intentions of allowing Christianity to get in the way of running its sugar plantations at a profit. Major financial investments were made in its human chattels and financial returns were expected. This was the perspective from the pulpits presented by the bishops to all their managers.

In 1712, the Reverend Joseph Holt was sent out from London as a missionary to assist the manager in blending "Christianity and slavery" as an effective business proposition. He arrived and soon reported that the Africans were "stupidly ignorant" and not capable of receiving Christian teachings.[16]

This perspective suited the manager, who was keen on keeping the Africans to hard labour on Sundays. The bishops replaced Reverend Holt with Reverend Irvine, who had no interest in the conversion of Africans. Reverend Irvine was soon replaced with Thomas Wilkie, a layman, who was given the title "estate catechist" at a salary of £100 (£138,000 in 2010) per annum. Within Wilkie's first batch of correspondence to the bishops, he admits, "the younger (blacks) I find very docile and capable to learn anything, but that so soon as they are capable of doing they are employed in looking after the cattle and stock so that they have but very little time to learn in".[17]

Child labour was an established part of the plantation system. Children were placed in the "child gang" at about three to four years of age. Wilkie tried to increase his teaching access to the child gang, but found the manager to be non-compliant. He encountered considerable hostility in his effort to constitute a class of enslaved children. He managed, however, to convert a total of fifty-eight children against the will of the manager and the white community in the parish. In the process, Wilkie fell ill and died. He was replaced by another lay catechist, Sampson Smirk, an Englishman, on the reduced salary of £80 per annum. Sampson lacked Wilkie's enthusiasm and soon gave up, with the explanation that he failed "because they [the blacks] are of several countrys and can speak but very little or no English".[18]

The bishops were caught in a contradictory moment. Slavery was approved by the church and investments in the plantations were expected to yield a return. Pastoral care, then, was second to profits. To achieve these ends the church closed "its eyes to the failure of the chaplains" and gave its managers the authority to maintain profitability as their primary objective. Also, the church was keen to reassure other slave owners on the island that it was not prepared to manage its plantations in ways that did not meet with their satisfaction. Neighbouring slave owners, especially, were more than casual observers of activities at Codrington, and managers were instructed to "set a conservative and reassuring example before the uneasy planters".[19]

When profits fell, the bishops became more elaborate in their writings about their chattels. Archbishop Secker, especially, wrote at length during the

1760s about the mystery of spending a fortune on buying new Africans who did not add to the existing stock as reflected in the annual accounts. He wrote, "I have long wondered and lamented that the negroes in our plantations decrease and new supplies become necessary continually." He concluded, "Surely this proceeds from some defect, both of humanity and even of good policy. But we must take things as they are at present."[20]

In February 1768, the bishop of Lincoln, John Green, reflecting on the accounts of the estates, noted the high mortality rate of the enslaved and the moderate profits they generated. He queried whether the managers in the bishops' employ were subjecting the enslaved to "cruelties and abuses". While it was Christian to own enslaved persons and to manage businesses in relation to their enslavement, the bishop stated, it was necessary for slave owners to be humane. He told his fellow bishops and archbishops in a sermon that "though we profit by their labour, it is Christian not to impose on them such hard and rigorous tasks as are injurious to health and incompatible with any degree of self-enjoyment".[21]

In less than a decade, Bishop Shute Barrington was reporting that news from the church's estates was indicating the existence of a "milder treatment (of the enslaved) than formerly experienced". The bishop was also informed of the practical reality of managing the enslaved, a circumstance that required brutality as necessary for discipline, and the use of fear to secure submission. One attorney for the properties was keen to keep the bishops focused on the relationship among production, profitability and proselytizing. He noted,

> The world would certainly expect that the slaves belonging to so hon[oura]ble & reverend a body . . . should be humanely treated . . . [and] nothing shall be wanting on our parts to promote those benevolent and pious intentions which they have so warmly and earnestly recommended. But we must take the leave to observe that to govern upwards of 300 negroes on one plantation is no easy task, it requires a good deal of address, and unless a proper decorum, and subordination is kep'd up they will soon become turbulent and unruly, for after all those who know them best must allow that they are a most inconsiderate and thoughtless race of mortals.[22]

The pious plans for the plantation ran into a sea of trouble, with overseers who had a business to run in an environment cultivated with cruelty. But Beilby Porteus, bishop of Chester, was demanding much more for the church's chattels. He wanted reforms, "real" not "nominal", and he wanted this reflected in the creation of genuine Christian chattels at Codrington. The Africans, he insisted, needed less chastisement and more guidance with instructions based on incentives. Profitability, he said, depended upon their having a personal material interest in their own enslavement. Reform, he insisted, could motivate the enslaved and energize their efforts. In a sermon on the subject, he stated,

> We must, as far as is possible, attach them, and their families inseparably to the soil, must give them a little interest in it; must indulge them with a few rights and privileges to be anxious for; must secure them by fixed laws from injury and insult; must inform their minds, correct their morals, accustom them to the restraints of legal marriage, to the care of a family and the comforts of domestic life; must improve and advance their condition gradually, as they are able to bear it; and even allow a certain number of the most deserving to work out their freedom by degrees.[23]

The bishop did not contemplate the core issue in the attorney's statement. Church chattels had to be held in check by brutal force; that was the only way to manage them profitably. Incentives were for the meek but could not transform the anti-slavery consciousness of the rebellious.

The bishops, however, as absentee landlords and distant slave owners knew that theology would not determine stability and profitability. They gave excellent sermons, filled with instructions for overseers and managers, but at the same time they complied with the policy of the church which was to leave the business of managing the enslaved to their employees on the estates.

Where the archbishops and overseers eventually agreed, however, was on "encouraging the negroes to breed". "To breed, rather than buy" became the holy creed of the church and, by extension, of the Barbados plantation bureaucracy from the last quarter of the eighteenth century. By the 1780s, Bishop Porteus's plan for the "perfect slave plantation" was officially adopted by the church as the way forward. Christianity and slavery, he had argued, were compatible, and the church could prove it so. The policy of breeding rather than buying enslaved persons was put into effect, which meant that enslaved women were targeted for a central role in the new fertility management policy.

Bishop Porteus became the bishop of London in 1787. He was now in an even better position to see to the implementation of his plan. But he found resistance among his colleagues and considerable pushback from estate managers and overseers. Some headway was made, however, with the teaching of the chattel children in basic literacy and numeracy, but abolitionist criticism of the church focused on its hypocrisy in seeking to convert the enslaved while pressuring them to breed for purposes of profit maximization.

From 1800, the Church of England defended its right to own enslaved Africans and profit from their deployment on its slave plantations. It insisted that the enslavement of Africans was "Christian", and that clergymen in the Caribbean were safe within its walls as slave owners and slave traders. It did not join the abolitionist movement but rather became one of its many institutional critics. In the face of growing reforms, the church's slave management emerged as a reactionary force in the West Indies. According to Bennett,

> The whip was still in use in the field, women could still be flogged, no record of punishments was kept, and no program for manumission had been devised. A public announcement in 1823 had stated that the Society's Negroes were usually punished by confinement, but did not mention the use of the whip in the field as a stimulus to labor. In 1825, in fact, the whip had been taken from the negro driver, only to be restored when he and the manager of the estates complained of lax discipline.[24]

During the 1820s, the church was doing all it could to resist emancipation policy. Rather, it countered the emancipationists' argument by presenting its estates in Barbados as "a model of Christian slavery". In confronting the emancipationists and seeking to sustain slavery, the Church of England exposed itself even more directly to the polemical wrath of the anti-slavery movement.[25]

In May 1827, the *Christian Observer*, an anti-slavery magazine published monthly out of London, commented upon the bishops' failures:

> The friends of the Society omitted to mention their own slaves, whose labours on their plantations augment their funds. . . . Let their friends of the unhappy slaves come forward manfully in the Society to plead his cause: and let them never relax their efforts till the Society can fairly expurgate itself from the guilt of being slave holders, and from the incongruity of watering the tree of life planted in India or America, with the tears and blood of unhappy Africa.[26]

Bishop Porteus deepened his defence of slavery from the pulpits across London. As the emancipationists gained support in Parliament, the bishop used the pulpit more intensively to defend slavery as being compatible with Christian theology. To the end, then, the church protected West Indian slavery and practised black enslavement to its profit both materially and theologically. As a major slave owner, the church was enormously influential and provided slave owners with considerable moral and political support in the heat of the abolition discourse.

By practising chattel slavery and systematically providing ideological and theological support for the overall system of African enchainment and enslavement, the church enabled slavery to persist much longer than it otherwise would have done. With the Church of England fully in the slavers' corner, the British state found a powerful ally in linking the perpetuation of slavery with the defence of the national interest. Not only did the church present a strongly influential proslavery front to British society, but it actively demonstrated its racist views towards Africans in its own practice as a slave plantation owner.

The Church of England, then, performed four very significant roles within the world of Caribbean chattel slavery. First, it "bought" into the slave economy as a major investor, manager, owner and financial beneficiary. For over a century, through its missionary arm, it profited from the enslavement of over a thousand African children, women and men whom it bought, branded with hot irons and brutalized further in the gangs on its two sugar estates in Barbados. In so doing, it joined with the British state, and thousands of British families and financial institutions, in committing crimes against humanity. These crimes have left an indelible mark upon the descendants of these enslaved persons, many of whom continue to dwell in villages in the parish of St John, which the church dominated during the slavery period.

Second, the Church of England legitimized the actions of its clergy who were slave owners and slave traders. In most colonies, prominent among the slave-owning elite that constructed and governed the slave regime were parish clergymen who racially excluded their own chattels from churches while preaching the Christian gospel to white congregations. As principal slave owners, clergymen established the Church of England as a prominent global partner in committing crimes against humanity.

Third, the Church of England was the official theological voice of the ideas that Africans were subhuman and not deserving of social recognition within the human family. The racial targeting of African people for the explicit purpose of ensuring their dehumanization on a global scale has done immeasurable harm to the mental health and social esteem of black people today throughout the post-plantation world. The church, in this regard, has done more harm than any other single civic society institution in consolidating and perpetuating slavery in the British colonies in the Caribbean.

The use of scriptural references as the basis of its racial denial of the humanity of Africans penetrated the psychic space of enslaved Africans and their offspring, who have found it necessary to refute these allegations by way of self-defence. For these crimes against humanity, the Church of England is required under international law to pay reparations to the black community of the Caribbean.

Finally, in its official capacity the Church of England provided the moral and cultural blessings upon slave owners and slave traders in their project of personal enrichment by reducing African people in law to the status of property, chattels and real estate. In so doing, the church denied African people in the Caribbean the right to human relations such as family life and the right to possess, nurture and rear their children. For two hundred years, the Church of England as slave owner and as theological articulator of chattel slavery denied black people the benefit of family life and the moral right to motherhood and fatherhood. Children were bought and sold by the church, which in turn legitimized these practices as being legally right.

The spiritual and cultural destructiveness of these actions have damaged the domestic culture of black people to this day. The black community in the Caribbean remains characterized by deeply troubling, negative family values and endemic unsupportive attitudes towards children and youth. This legacy is rarely spoken about, though widely known. The shame has led to silence, which in turn has fostered palpable anger at and latent resentment against the Anglican Church for its refusal to confront this past with the honesty that represents a core value of Christianity.

Chapter 9

Earls of Harewood

Slave Route to Buckingham Palace

The slave trade was . . . at the centre, not the periphery of the British economy. It was something in which all parts of society were implicated . . . and it was the basis of the property of the Church, and one should add, of the royal family.

—*Vincent Cable, Member of Parliament, Debate on the Bicentenary of the Abolition of the Slave Trade, House of Commons, 20 March 2007*

THE MAKING OF FORTUNES SUSTAINED over generations from African enslavement in the Caribbean by British citizens has been well documented. Many families within the present British financial and social elite can trace the origins of their wealth to slavery and the slave trade. The following data detail networks of financial transactions as well as investments in the business of buying and selling enslaved Africans in vast numbers. The property rights in these enslaved Africans held by their owners was an important asset commonly mortgaged in financial transactions. In addition, these families received significant financial compensation at emancipation in 1838, thereby enabling them to rationalize, upgrade and modernize their business portfolios. The British families and institutions converted what began as slave wealth into financial capital to be exploited by subsequent generations in non-slave-related enterprises.[1]

Numerous studies detail British family enrichment from slavery, and

Richard Pares's research on the making of a fortune by the Pinney family of Bristol from slave trading and sugar plantation slavery in the Leeward Islands sets the standard for such studies. S.G. Checkland's excellent work on John Gladstone, father of British prime minister William Gladstone, follows in the same tradition. This study details the profitable exploitation of enslaved Africans in Jamaica and Guiana by John Gladstone, whose compensation cash in 1838 served to expand and diversify the family's business, thus propelling his son William to parliamentary power.[2]

Similarly, the Beckfords of Jamaica lived in Britain like royalty from the proceeds of their slave empire. But arguably the Lascelles family of Yorkshire made the grandest fortune of all; their sons, from the end of the eighteenth century, became the Earls of Harewood. In the ensuing analysis, we rely heavily on a recent scholarly monograph by S.D. Smith about the making of this financial empire. The Lascelles invested their slave profits from Barbados, Tobago and Jamaica in the Britain economy and were rewarded with a hereditary peerage and ultimately with marriage into the royal family. For 327 years, this family exploited enslaved Africans and their free descendants across the Caribbean to amass enormous wealth with which they purchased social prestige and power.[3]

The Lascelles, a lower-middle-class family from the hinterland of Leeds, began modestly with a small slave-owning operation in Barbados in 1648, but within one hundred years, had accumulated one of the largest fortunes in the British Empire. With this financial base, they gained access to the English aristocracy. The Earls of Harewood, as they became known, did not dispose of their sugar plantations in Barbados until 1975, a decade after the country became an independent nation. The history, then, from 1648 (twenty years after English colonization of the island) to 1975 is a startling journey of slave-derived enrichment that gave the Lascelles access to the British economic elite and earned them a place in the line of succession to the British throne.[4]

In 1966, Lord Harewood was honoured to host the young Queen Elizabeth at his Belle estate in Barbados, a sugar plantation his family had owned since 1780. The queen was visiting her family's place, Lord Harewood being her first cousin. It was the latest expression of the old partnership – sugar, slavery and royalty – a "merger" of slavery now consummated by marriage. In 1922, Viscount Lascelles, heir to the fifth Earl of Harewood, had married Princess Mary, the Princess Royal. As owner of the Belle estate in 1966, one of many slave plantations that had enriched the family, the seventh earl, George Las-celles, welcomed his first cousin – Her Royal Highness Queen Elizabeth II. Nothing was unusual about any of this. Barbados was the primary market for the enchained Africans supplied by the Royal African Company (formerly the Company of Royal Adventurers of England Trading with Africa), owned and administered by her ancestor, King James II.[5]

The journey of the Lascelles as slave owners began in 1648 with Edward Lascelles, who bought a small share of a slave plantation in Barbados. The following year he was ready to branch out on his own. He purchased one hundred acres in the parish of St Andrew and launched his career as a slave-plantation entrepreneur. Over the next decade, Edward continued to consolidate his investments in Barbados as a slave owner. He was joined by his three brothers: Philip, Robert and William Lascelles. Together, by 1670, they had established the Lascelles's reputation as elite slave owners, slave traders, financiers, merchants and brokers.[6]

Philip took care of the London end of the business, while William joined Edward in the sugar and slave-trading business in Barbados. Robert preferred slave trading, which he merged into the commodity trade between Britain and Bridgetown in Barbados. The brothers prospered in the slave business, but it was the enterprise and innovations of Edward that laid the foundation for the Lascelles family fortune.[7]

Edward married Mary Hall, daughter of a prominent slave and commodity merchant in Barbados named Hugh Hall and, at the turn of the century, relo-cated to London. He remained involved in the slave trading and sugar business as a financier, merchant and ship owner. Between 1703 and 1709 he invested heavily in the slave trade to "Guinea", or West Africa, outfitting ships with goods in England which he sold in exchange for enslaved Africans, thereby maximizing his returns from the triangular Atlantic business interests. From these profits, Edward invested in British properties, including the acquisition of extensive lands at Stoke Newington in the north of London. When he died in 1727, he left for his heirs a substantial legacy amounting to £8,670 (£15.8 million in 2010) and annuities of £610 (£1.11 million in 2010) per annum.

It was young Henry Lascelles, however, grandson to Edward, who drove the family into the deepest end of slave trading in Africa and sugar and slavery in the Caribbean. Parlaying his financial success into political power, Henry became a member of Parliament for Northallerton in Yorkshire, while his son

Daniel won a seat for Scarborough in 1745. Henry formed a syndicate with seven other merchants and cornered a section of the slave trade. Between 1736 and 1742, he did very well financially. Profits were reinvested in expanding his firm's shipping capacity. He became a leading financier of the slave-owning elite in Barbados. Upon his death in 1753, Henry was one of the richest West Indian merchants in Britain. His will valued his estate at £284,000 (£469 million in 2010), and his assets were calculated at £392,704 (£649 million in 2010).[8]

Henry's obituary described him as "a very great Barbadoes merchant, and sometime member of parliament for Northallerton". In 1748, his eldest son, Edwin Lascelles, for whom he had made a substantial financial provision, was "installed as Lord of the Manor of Gawthorpe and Harewood", two estates that Henry had purchased in 1739 for £63,827. S.D. Smith concludes that "the fortune Henry accumulated probably lies between £408,784 (net) and £565,251 (gross) [£607 million and £751 million in 2009]. While his exact worth may never be known, indisputably Henry Lascelles died one of the richest men in Britain."[9]

Henry, notes Smith, "used his newfound riches to raise his Yorkshire family from respectable gentry to aristocratic eminence". His expanding influence enabled him to draw other Yorkshire families into his colonial projects, particularly those who had established cadet branches in the Americas. Such associations in turn helped him and his sons to acquire landed estates that "bestowed ancestral connections". His death, horribly described as an act of suicide – both wrists slashed – added a gruesome twist to his already violent life as a slave trader and slave owner. He participated in the spilling of African blood for nearly thirty years before shedding his own. But his life ended with a massive financial empire, both built and inherited, while those of his slaves ended as chattel.[10]

By the last quarter of the eighteenth century, the Lascelles were securely positioned in the wealthiest echelons of British society and were ready to make their biggest leap yet – into the nobility and later, royalty. In 1795, the financial empire fell to Edward Lascelles, who had inherited it from his cousin, Edwin Lascelles. Smith sets out the inheritance process thus:

> Following Henry Lascelles' death in 1753, the bulk of his estate was divided between his two eldest sons, Edwin and Daniel. Edwin Lascelles received a university education, toured Europe, and was elected MP for Scarborough. After a brief but distinguished military career, Edwin was installed as Lord of the Manors of Gawthorpe

and Harewood a few years prior to his father's death. Daniel's institution as the co-partner of Serge Maxwell came about in August 1750, when Henry Lascelles nominally retired from business.[11]

The death of Daniel Lascelles in 1784 (heirless), says Smith, coupled with the death in 1786 of his younger brother Henry (also childless), brought about the forced unification of a family fortune that had been split deliberately into separate English and West Indian components. Smith continues: "Upon Edwin's own death in 1795, the Harewood estate passed to this cousin, Edward Lascelles, the Barbadian-born eldest son of old Henry's half-brother Edward. This line of succession resulted in the consolidation of all the West Indian interests accumulated by the family from the early eighteenth century onward into a single settlement trust. Thus was plantation aristocracy established at Harewood."[12] Edward ordered an audit of his slave investments in the Caribbean with a view to enhancing profitability. In addition, he held "repeated conferences with merchants and planters" about the Caribbean slave economy.

Edwin had used his university education to serve the financial interests of his slavery empire by writing one of the most influential works on slave management published in the eighteenth century. He pulled together a team of mostly absentee owners of enslaved persons in the West Indies to produce a literary work dedicated to increasing slave labour productivity and, at the same time, to provide ammunition against critics of the slave trade. The purpose of the book was to increase "slave breeding" and use the evidence of enslaved population growth to demonstrate the argument that if the Africans were "well treated" they could reproduce naturally.

The team that Edwin assembled for his literary project and attack on the abolitionists comprised James Colleton, Edwin Drax, Francis Ford, Reverend John Brathwaite, John Walter, William Thorpe Holder, James Holder, Philip Gibbes and John Barney, the absentee barons of West Indian slave holding. The book they wrote was titled *Instructions for the Management of a Plantation in Barbadoes, and for the Treatment of Negroes*. It was published in London in 1786 and became a popular text among slave owners.[13]

Edwin Lascelles understood, perhaps better than most, the extent to which the demographic crisis of enslaved Africans would be the basis of a major moral assault on slavery. As such, in the introduction to the book's central thesis was printed in bold capital letters "THE INCREASE IS THE ONLY TEST OF THE CARE WITH WHICH THEY ARE TREATED". The work calls for the implementation of a new social policy to encourage slave breeding on a selective scientific basis. Lascelles believed that the fertility and maternity of enslaved women could be targeted and manipulated by such policies, to the financial benefit of the plantations and the overall sustainability of the slave system.[14]

This work emphasized the need for slave owners to implement a series of prenatal policies to assist pregnant enslaved women to deliver healthy babies. Most importantly, it stressed the need to protect fertile enslaved women from excessive physical stress. It paid particular attention to the importance of providing postnatal facilities to assist lactating mothers in an effort to reduce the high rate of infant mortality.

These policies meant the marginal reduction of labour hours for pregnant and lactating field women and improved maternal care. In effect, the authors recommended a significant reshaping of enslaved women's experiences as plantation labourers. For the first time, enslaved women were encouraged to perceive the capital value of their children (reproduction) as important as their labour input (production). The authors outlined their policy as follows:

> Women, who have children at the breast, should not be required to appear in the field till seven o'clock. And in the bad days, during the rainy seasons, they should be employed on some work within doors. As soon as women are known to be pregnant, they should be relieved from all the laborious work of the plantation. In that state they must never carry any load. But they must not be given up to idleness. Let them be employed upon some business that will oblige them to make their appearance, for you must be very attentive that they do not ramble out of the plantation.[15]

Since the poor demographic performance of the enslaved population had long been attributed to high levels of infant mortality the authors emphasized the need for postnatal policies that took into consideration the care of infants and their mothers. Slave owners were encouraged to ensure that lactating mothers did not return to the fields too soon after birth since, in their opinion, available statistics showed a direct correlation between the mothers' health and infant longevity. They instructed managers and planters,

> While children are at the breast, you can do little more than recommend to their mothers a careful treatment of them. Careless and negligent mothers will indeed require a little more of your attention. As soon as the children are weaned, let them

be committed to some careful, good humoured woman, to keep them together, and to attend upon them in the day when the mothers are in the field. . . . The size and strength of the child will be your best direction, when he is fit and able to be put into the children's gang, and to be removed from thence into the second gang.[16]

This was good business, they insisted. Protecting the asset value of the enslaved population was critical to the financial success of a sugar plantation. The money spent on these policies would be minimal, while the financial returns would be substantial.

In 1796, Edward was invited into the nobility and adopted the title Baron Harewood in the county of York. In 1812, the baron was elevated to a peerage as the first Earl of Harewood – a title he held until his death in 1820. Residing at Harewood Castle on the outskirts of Leeds, a monument to the profitability of slavery, the Harewood legacy was now fully established. It had taken over 150 years, and the family had become an iconic brand in the world of slavery. At emancipation, the Harewoods, with three estates in Barbados and two in Jamaica, owned over 1,250 enslaved persons. Their plantations in Jamaica, Barbados and Tobago primarily produced sugar and cotton on 5,529 acres of land, as shown in table 9.1. The 1,250 enslaved provided the human effort that resulted in this production.

The Belle plantation, visited by the earl's cousin Queen Elizabeth II in 1966, was acquired by the Lascelles in 1780, at which time it had an enslaved population of 232. By 1834, this number had increased to 291 in an attempt to expand sugar production. The Harewoods moved the enslaved workers among their Barbados estates and managed the four estates as a unified enterprise (see table 9.2).

In 1816, when the enslaved population of Barbados rose up in revolt against their enslavement, the Harewoods were not spared their wrath. Their own enslaved community would have known that the earl had campaigned against the abolition of the slave trade and that he was a public supporter of enslavement. Three of their plantations – Thicketts, Fortescue and the Mount – were sites for anti-slavery activity during the "war of General Bussa". The rebel army under "General" Bussa's command fought the militia and imperial army at Thicketts plantation, inflicting massive damage upon the properties.

The earl was informed of the rebellion of his enslaved workers by his estate managers. In these correspondences he was notified that the damage to the

Table 9.1. Harewood's Ten Slave Plantations in the Caribbean

Name of Plantation	Parish and Colony	Date of Ownership	Size (Acres)	Principal Activity
Belle	St Michael, Barbados	1780–1975	537 (in 1780)	Sugar
Mount	St George, Barbados	1784–1974	292 (in 1795)	Sugar
Fortesque	St Philip, Barbados	1787–1918	241 (in 1787)	Cotton
Thicketts	St Philip, Barbados	1787–1918	584 (in 1787)	Sugar
Mammee Ridge	St Ann, Jamaica	1777–1797	1,000 (in 1777)	Cattle
Nightengale Grove	St Dorothy, Jamaica	1777–1836	285 (in 1777)	Sugar
Williamsfield-in-the-Vale	St Thomas, Jamaica	1777–1848	1,440 (in 1770)	Sugar
Richmond	St Paul, Tobago	1777–1820	600 (in 1770)	Sugar
Glamorgan	St Mary, Tobago	1777–1820	575 (in 1770)	Sugar
Goldsborough and Goodwood	St Mary, Tobago	1781–1818	1,151 (in 1770)	Sugar

Source: S.D. Smith, *Slavery, Family, and Gentry Capitalism in the British Atlantic: The World of the Lascelles, 1648–1834* (Cambridge: Cambridge University Press, 2006), 262.

Table 9.2. Harewood's Barbados Enslaved Persons, 1817, 1820 and 1834

	1817	1820	1834
Belle	295	290	291
Mount	133	145	188
Fortescue	136	137	183
Thickett	247	254	231

Source: S.D. Smith, *Slavery, Family, and Gentry Capitalism in the British Atlantic: The World of the Lascelles, 1648–1834* (Cambridge: Cambridge University Press, 2006), 263.

Thickett estate was £3,989 (£2.77 million in 2010), while damage at the Mount totalled £5,150.10s (£3.58 million in 2010). The militia had made several arrests of Harewood's chattels; six were taken to trial and seven were released. The managers and supervisors of these estates had been targeted by the rebels. Their homes were attacked and damaged. Harewood, seeking to be supportive of his staff, made a cash payment of £111.2s.3d (£77,220 in 2010) to each by way of compensation.[17]

But the earl did not end there. He celebrated the crushing of the rebellion, and joined in the commendation of Colonel Edward Codd, who was credited with leading the imperial troops against the rebels. At a dinner held in 1819 to thank Colonel Codd for his services to the colony in putting down the rebellion, the earl contributed £200 (£139,000 in 2010) to defray the costs. The Belle estate was not a site of rebellion, so it was minimally affected.

After celebrating the military defeat of the enslaved, the second earl rose to challenge the British anti-slavery movement. He was asked to chair a meeting of "proprietors, merchants, bankers, ship owners, manufacturers, traders, and others interested in the Preservation of the West Indian Colonies" on 5 April 1832 at the City of London Tavern. His opening remarks represented a classical defence of slavery, which was met with applause from his audience. In the earl, the proslavery cause had found an articulate and very wealthy champion.

The earl lamented the "strong feelings of prejudice created" in the country against "possessors of a slave population". He rejected the view that slave owners "were wickedly and improperly deriving profit from the labour" of the

enslaved. He regretted slavery and asserted that he and his slave-owning colleagues "should be most anxious to do without that description of labour if
we could (cheers)". The West Indian proprietors, he continued, "do not wish
to hold a population in that state of existence if we could do otherwise".[18]
Slave owners, then, the earl suggested, were reluctant violators of human rights
– victims, in fact, of history and political circumstance. The earl continued,
"We are in difficulty; it is not of our making; and it is the duty of those who
are so loud in their complaints respecting it, to show us our way out."

The enslaved people of Barbados had tried to show them the way out; the
earl celebrated their defeat and feted the military commander who slaughtered
hundreds of them in his cane fields in that colony. The earl's support for slavery was congenital, and his attempt to appear concerned for the state of
humanity a mere ruse. In his judgement, the slaves, "in their present state of
mind", were not ready for freedom. This was the core issue. How could
enslaved people, whose sweat and blood had been the basis of his wealth and
status, ever be ready for their freedom? "To set them free," he concluded,
"would be to endanger the colony."[19]

The argument of the second earl was buttressed with references to the economic value of the slave plantations to the British state and economy. In his
judgement, emancipation would be a financial disaster for the British people.
"The duties alone", he said, "upon the produce of the colonies amount annually to £7 million, and the amount of British exports to those colonies is annually £5 million; is that revenue to be sacrificed" by those with an agenda to
emancipate the slaves?[20]

The earl was succeeded by his son, the third earl, who sat as member of
Parliament for Northallerton. It was his great-grandson, the sixth earl, Henry
George Charles Lascelles (1882–1947), who married Princess Mary, daughter
of King George V. The Lascelles were now at the centre of British royalty.

The seventh earl, George Henry Hubert Lascelles, born 1923, died on 11
July 2010. He was the first cousin of Queen Elizabeth II and in line of succession to the British throne. It was he who in 1966 hosted the queen, and
showed her around his Belle sugar plantation and great house, a property
known for its rich soil and its profitability as a slave plantation in the inhumane world of the Lascelles. At the time of his death, he was widely known
for his generous contributions to music in general and the English National
Opera in particular.

Chapter 10

Slave Owners in Parliament and the Private Sector

In 1776, it was estimated that 40 Members of Parliament were making their money from West Indian [slave] plantations. William Beckford, MP, owned 22,000 acres in Jamaica; his two brothers and his sons were also Members of Parliament.

—*Diane Abbott, Member of Parliament, Debate on the Bicentenary of the Abolition of the Slave Trade, House of Commons, 20 March 2007*

IN 1824, THE *TIMES* CARRIED an account of British slavery in the Caribbean that placed the crime of slave owning in its proper perspective. It stated the case as follows: "The crime of creating and upholding the slavery of the West Indies is a national crime, and not the crime of slave-holders alone." Two years earlier, the Duke of Devonshire had noted that enslaved persons owned by the British should properly be seen as "stolen goods", since black people had been robbed of their property rights in themselves, and the British state was a party to the crime.[1]

A widespread belief in Britain held that slavery was a crime committed against Africans by British citizens, and that it was a special kind of crime – a "national crime" – in which citizens and state collaborated as "thieves" to rob the Africans of their natural right to self-ownership. The "national crime" argument, Draper noted, was deeply embedded in the anti-slavery campaign, accompanied by name-calling to shame political leaders who represented the British state and benefited from the crime.[2]

The British state was not prepared to accept the criminal nature of its conduct in the face of the charges made by the press and some of its leading citizens. While the legal and ethical issues were clear – that slave owning could not be justified outside of naked self-interest – the influence of the national interest counterargument was formidable. Owning enslaved black people, and legally converting them into the property of British citizens, was defended as necessary for the advancement of the national interest.

It was the role of the state to protect the national interest, especially against citizens who held a different view about how that interest should be defined and best served. Slavery was arguably the most divisive subject in early nineteenth-century British society. The first line of defence was presented by parliamentarians. They represented the political formulation of what was the "national interest". The public looked to them to design national policy and to be advocates of the public good.

The concept of slavery as a national crime gained new life during the first part of the nineteenth century, and politicians became even more aggressive in defending slavery as the national good. Parliamentarians, however, many of them national statesmen with considerable public influence, were deeply embedded within the slave economy as owners and investors. It was hardly surprising that the British political leadership should defend slavery, thus committing the state to a posture of confrontation with the anti-slavery public opinion.[3]

The data on Caribbean slavery show the considerable ownership of enslaved Africans by British politicians. In the 1830s, according to Draper, over one hundred British parliamentarians owned enslaved persons in the Caribbean or were trustees and executors for such owners. This considerable number reveals the level of management and ownership at which the British political elite were involved in the slave trade. Draper identifies fifty members of Parliament in 1831, and forty-two in 1833, with a "direct interest in slavery". This direct involvement, Draper shows, did not include those parliamentarians who, without an ownership stake, defended slavery because it was in their political and economic interests to do so. Neither does it include parliamentarians who were members of large slave-owning families but who did not personally own enslaved persons. Two examples of the latter would be

"Christopher Bethell Codrington's son, who sat for Gloucestershire in 1833 and 1835, and W.S.S. Lascelles and Henry Lascelles, one of whom sat for Northallerton in every parliament from 1820 to 1835".[4]

Caribbean enslavers were ministers of government who "either supported their own colonial interests, or represented constituents deeply involved in colonial property or prejudice". By 1800, the British political culture was deeply embedded in slave owning, which corrupted and enriched both sides of the party divide. Whig political leaders, such as Edward Ellice, were major slave investors during the 1820s. The radical member of Parliament Joseph Hume married into the Bunley clan, a prominent Trinidadian slave-owning family, and thereby secured substantial financial backing for his political career.

A "party" of slave-owning West Indians straddled the Tory and Whig political groups and secured for both parties a strong defence of slavery in Parliament. Slave-owning members of Parliament were prominent public figures who successfully kept the link firm between Caribbean slavery and the national interest. In some regards, they were a typical example of how an interest group dominates the politics of a parliament by infiltrating all sides of the political process and forging a common core of self-interest within the governance system.[5]

Slave owners among the political elite were also key members of the British aristocracy, a social group with considerable influence over the formulation of the national interest, and kept slavery afloat as a critical part of the national economic and social way of life. Well-known aristocrats such as the second Earl of Harewood, one of the leading slave owners in the West Indies, defended the slave system during the 1820s with vigour. He was surrounded by Lord Holland and the Duke of Buckingham and Chandos. In 1834, the slave ownership records show that there were two dukes, one marquis, ten earls, and twelve barons listed as slave owners, while twelve of those also appeared as trustees and executors.[6]

According to Draper, of the 616 members of the English, Scottish and Irish peerages, thirty-seven (or 6 per cent) were involved in "the exploitation of the enslaved". Some of these families, such as the Harewoods, the Seafords and the Scarletts, had investments in slavery over many generations – sometimes over a period of 150 years. Lord Abinger (James Scarlett), for example, was the son of a slave-owning family – the Scarletts – with massive investments in

Table 10.1. British Slave-Owning Dukes, Marquesses and Earls

Persons	Colony
Duke of Cleveland	Barbados
Duke of Buckingham	Jamaica
Duke of Richmond	Jamaica
Marquis of Sligo	Jamaica
Earl of Rosslyn	Antigua
Earl of Lichfield	Barbados
Earl of Harewood	Barbados
Earl of Caithness	Barbados
Earl of Dudley	Jamaica
Earl of Zetland	Grenada
Earl of Balcarres	Jamaica
Earl and Countess of Airlie	Jamaica
Earl of Carhampton	Jamaica
Earl of Thanet	Jamaica
Earl of Romney	St Kitts
Earl of Eglinton	Jamaica
Earl of Stanhope	Jamaica
Earl of Hopetoun	Jamaica
Earl of Northesk	Jamaica
Earl of Brownlow	Guiana
Rt Hon. Countess of Buchan	Grenada
Rt Hon. Earl Talbot	Jamaica

Source: Nicholas Draper, *The Price of Emancipation: Slave-Ownership, Compensation and British Society at the End of Slavery* (Cambridge: Cambridge University Press, 2010), 318–19.

Jamaica since the seventeenth century. He was also the Lord Chief Baron of the Exchequer. The nobles, then, were up to their financial necks in Caribbean slavery, which many used to establish and sustain their own elite status.[7]

Added to this list of peers and nobles were three viscounts and twenty barons, including Lords Seaford, Abinger, Sherborne, Lyons, O'Bryen, Rivers, Combermere, Carrington, Hatherton and Rolle. The women included Hon. Ann Stapleton, Rt Hon. Lady Marjorie Saltoun and Rt Hon. Lady Maria Ann Saunderson. Through marriage, investments in slavery served to bind these elite families into a common sense of their collective responsibility to protect the slave system as a personal and national treasure.

Wealthy slave owners placed their daughters through marriage into the aristocracy and considered this a major achievement, rather like "washing" dirty money with fancy matrimony. The Lowther slave-owning family, with large investments in Barbados during the early nineteenth century, married into the family of the Duke of Cleveland, an independently wealthy British family. Also, Philip Dehany, with large slave investments in Jamaica, celebrated the engagement of his daughter, Mary Salter, to the eleventh Earl of Caithness, linking Caribbean slave-based wealth to mainstream British accumulation and elitism.[8]

Seventy-five baronets were registered in 1834 as slave owners, or with mortgages or slave-based properties. Some 6 per cent of all baronets in Britain, says Draper, "were slave owners or mortgagees and a further 2 per cent were sufficiently connected to assume roles as executors or trustees to men and women whose assets included 'slaves'". Most of them were "substantial slave owners". Edward Hyde East, a judge, "owned 1,211 human beings". These connections show the extent of "the permeation of the landed gentry by slave owners". Many of these families used their slave-based capital to accomplish considerable civil works in British society. Draper, for example, noted that "John Whyte Melville, one of the major forces behind the Royal and Ancient Golf Club of St. Andrews (of which he was elected Captain in 1823 and again in 1883, serving also as Chairman of the merged club in 1877), Grand Master of free masonry in Scotland 1864–6, deputy-lieutenant of the county, whose wife was a daughter of the Duke of Leeds, was a slave owner".[9] He was owner of the Melville Hall plantation in Dominica, on which now resides one of the island's airports.

Many of these slave owners made grants to churches and universities as part of their civic duties. This way the West Indian slave profits flowed into civic institutional development. The list of West Indian slave owners, for example, who made donations to King's College (London University) in the 1820s speaks to the further permeation by educational and research institutions of Caribbean slave profits. In 1828, a sum of over £4,000 (£15.2 million in 2010) was contributed by seventy-eight slave-owning interests from the Caribbean.

George Hibbert, an agent for Jamaican slave owners, was a major institution builder in the cultural life of London. His biographical data show that his family firm prospered well in the City of London during the 1770s and that with his wealth he entered a world of "good works", emerging as co-founder of the prestigious "London Institution", conceived as a City counterpart of the "Royal Institution". He was the president of what became known as "an ornament to the metropolis" that served to disseminate the knowledge of science and literature for the "elevation of the mind". He built up a substantial library and art collection from the profits of his slave businesses.[10]

Large numbers of West Indian slave owners resided in Britain, and they added to the pool of investment capital available for cultural development. These absentee owners increased the number of British owners who either travelled across the Atlantic periodically or who employed Caribbean management teams for their slave plantations. Draper noted, "Such movement was of course part of the process by which slavery 'came home' to Britain and by which the colonies were bound to Britain by ties of kinship, information and commerce."[11] Such sociological insights provide good measure of slavery's tremendous impact upon British culture and economy.

Caribbean slave profits, and the various forms that the investment in slavery took, was so deeply embedded and intertwined in the fabric of elite British society as to make a separate accounting almost impossible. West Indian profits were known to be a vital life-support system for many elite families whose domestic investments were enlarged and sustained by the slave-based financial feed. Draper gives the example of Elizabeth Wood Senhouse, daughter of prominent slave owner Samson Wood, who was born in Barbados in 1755. She married into the Anglo-Barbadian slave-owning, naval Senhouse family, which was deeply connected to elite families in rural Britain. Widowed in 1800, she came to live in England. On her death in 1834, her wealth was passed on to her three sons, Sir Humphrey Fleming Senhouse, Samson Senhouse and Edward Hooper Senhouse. Edward was married to Elizabeth Spooner, daughter of Hon. John Spooner, acting governor of Barbados, who resided in London at Upper Gower Street.[12]

The London and Barbados branches of the family travelled the Caribbean, making investments on both sides of the Atlantic, yet operating as an extended family which was drawing the source of its wealth from the slave system. Thousands of families in Britain had their slave-based West Indian branches, some rich and others modest. The financial feed of slavery sustained them all and demonstrated the importance to Britain of British industrialism and Caribbean slavery.

These domestic bonds oftentimes escape the attention of economic historians seeking to assess the contribution of slavery to British economic and social development. These family links are generally ignored because they appear less obvious than the pattern of direct ownership found in company accounts that link slave traders, plantation owners and national financial accounts. But these aristocratic and influential families were a crucial part of the political governance process of Great Britain. They exercised direct and indirect influence on the parliamentary dialogue that produced policy. The British elite guarded their West Indian domestic and business connections and sources of capital in which the preservation of slavery was as critical as the titles they pursued. At the heart of the British private sector resided Caribbean slavery. It was the major site of spectacular wealth accumulation, a source to acquire social status and prestige, and the basis of a way of life – the empire – that was a vital part of British national identity. Economist Adam Smith noted that by the 1820s the slavery system that once fuelled economic development had become a drag on the national economy. He did not, however, assess the intricate linkages that still existed between the private sector and slavery.

The London bankers, for example, would not have agreed with Smith and would have considered his position premature. They had been banking on Caribbean slavery for two hundred years – more so from the second half of the eighteenth century – and to this end were in receipt of considerable political patronage from parliamentarians and sugar planters themselves. Most London merchants, who had considerable direct management responsibility for these banks, were themselves engaged in the Caribbean slave economy.

By the end of slavery, when national data were collected in order to process compensation claims from slave owners, the ownership patterns of London bankers and merchants were revealed. The evidence showed that "over 150 London merchants have been identified" as slave owners, and "dozens more appeared to have acted only as agents". Of these London merchants, noted Draper, "about one-half were firms that appeared to have had British colonial slavery as their main or exclusive business". Some £2 million (£1.42 billion in 2010) was paid to London merchants as compensation for the enslaved persons they owned in 1838.[13]

Many of these London merchant firms used their investments in Caribbean slavery to launch business projects in other parts of the British Empire. This was standard procedure, as the Caribbean slave economy was used in this way to provide seed capital, management and mortgages for business propositions elsewhere. For example, Andrew Colville, a slave owner in Guiana, after collecting his compensation "slave money" in 1838, invested in the Hudson Bay Company. George Fife Angas collected £7,000 (£4.9 million in 2010) in "slave money" for his English clients who owned slaves in Honduras. Thereafter, he established the South Australia Company, the Bank of South Australia and the Union Bank of Australia.[14]

The Caribbean slave economy and the British banking system established a mutually dependent business relationship. Again, the slave compensation data reveal the number and identities of these banks. Of sixty London banking firms listed in 1835, thirty have been identified by Draper as owners and agents within the Caribbean slave economy. Some of these banks have survived today, illustrating the continuity between slave capital and the current British financial sector. R. Barclay of Barclay, Bevan and Tritton, for example, the forerunner of Barclays PLC, collected £40,358.18s.3d (£28.7 million in 2010) in compensation "slave money". Of Barclays Bank, Eric Williams wrote,

> Two members of this Quaker family, David and Alexander (Barclay), were engaged in the slave trade in 1756. David began his career in American and West Indian commerce and became one of the most influential merchants of his day. His father's house in Cheapside was one of the finest in the City of London, and was often visited by royalty. He was not merely a slave trader but actually owned a great plantation in Jamaica. The Barclays married into the banking families of Gurney and Freame. . . . From the combination sprang Barclay's Bank.[15]

Barclay, Bevan and Tritton acted as bankers for John and Henry Moss of Liverpool, who owned 805 enslaved persons in Guiana. Other banking firms, such as Coutts and Co.; Curries and Co.; Smith, Payne and Smiths; and Williams Deacon, were bankers for West Indian clients and managed their slave plantation accounts. Draper tells us, furthermore, that of these banking firms, Coutts and Co. led the way in the London financial sector in managing the slave plantation accounts for West Indian clients, many of whom were Scottish slave owners. This bank, for example, managed the slave financial accounts for member of Parliament James Blair, who received the largest single slave compensation for a West Indian slave owner – £83,530.8s.11d (£59.4 million in 2010) for the 1,598 enslaved persons he owned on the Blairmont estate in Guiana.[16]

The records also show that ten London banks, having lent money to West Indian slave owners using enslaved persons as security, collected slave compensation money. Leading the way was the banking network owned by Smith, Payne and Smiths. The other substantial bank, Hankey and Co., had investments of £5,777 (£4.11 million in 2010) with enslaved persons in Jamaica as security. The firm of Bosanquet Anderson had mortgages against 243 enslaved persons in Nevis. Furthermore, noted Draper, "Overall, of 21 London predecessor banks of today's Royal Bank of Scotland Group active at the time of Emancipation, six (Dorriens, Magens, Mello and Co., Sir James Esdaile; Robarts Curtis; Smith, Payne and Smith; Vere Sapte, and Hankey and Co.) have been identified" as mortgagees of West Indian slaves. In addition, three other London banks – Coutts and Co., Curries and Co., and Williams, Deacon, Labouchere and Co. – were trustees for West Indian slave owners. Six other banks – Barnard Dimsdale, Joseph Denison and Co., Drummonds, Sir J.W. Lubbock, Prescott Grote, and Glynn Mills – were direct bankers for West Indian slave owners.[17]

The current British banking multinational Lloyds TSB had the bank Bosanquet Anderson as its predecessor and was thus a major beneficiary of slave-based West Indian profits. Lloyds TSB, which can be seen on almost every British high street and in most major global cities, is not the only British bank with roots buried deep within the slave system of the West Indies. Bosanquet, Anderson and Barclay, and Bevan and Tritton were trustees and mortgagees for hundreds of enslaved persons in Jamaica on the plantations owned by James Dawkins.[18]

So too was the case with the Royal Bank of Scotland. The Scots were significant slave traders, slave owners and managers in the West Indies; the money generated by their involvement in slaving was handled by established bankers and financiers. Banks doing business during the period of the slave trade received substantial benefits by means of lending funds to slave owners and by investing in plantations where enslaved Africans were used as forced labour. In time, the Royal Bank of Scotland acquired some of these banks, and thus enjoyed the benefit of profits from the slave trade.

One of the Scottish Royal Bank's predecessor banks, Hankey and Co., lent money to a Grenada slave owner using his enslaved human property as mortgage security. This bank was also an investor, at the end of the eighteenth century, in the Arcadia plantation in Jamaica. It lent money to a Dominican slave owner using his enslaved persons as security. The Royal Bank of Scotland has recognized its roots in the slave economy of the Caribbean and has published a statement that sets out its involvement in funding Caribbean slavery. It has not, however, made any attempts, like its American counterparts, to pay reparations for its criminal enrichment.[19]

British merchant banks were also deeply embedded in the financing of the West Indian slave system and profited from their investments. They guarded jealously their interests in Caribbean slavery and competed fiercely for slave compensation cash when emancipation came in 1838. Two well-known British merchant banking firms, Baring Brothers and the Rothschild banks, were significant beneficiaries of their enterprises in the West Indies and went to great lengths to defend slavery and to receive compensation cash for their slave investments.

The Baring Brothers received compensation for their slave investments and became particularly litigious in guarding these investments. They contended rights to ownership of enslaved persons in Jamaica and Guiana and demanded that their rights be legally recognized by the court. Sir Thomas Baring was aggressive regarding 156 enslaved persons – blacks – that he claimed on the Osborne plantation in Jamaica, while Alexander Baring, senior partner, went after ownership rights to "human property" slaves in St Kitts.

The Rothschild banking empire resided at the heart of the Caribbean slave-based economy. It was a primary financier of slave owners, including the British government and other Caribbean investors. When the British government decided to provide a compensation package for the owners of enslaved

Africans, the question of how its funding should be arranged was answered when Nathan Mayer Rothschild agreed with the government to provide the financing. Rothschild raised a public loan, backed by his enormous financial wealth, to ensure that the government was provided with the £20 million (£14.2 billion in 2010) it needed to pay reparations to West Indian slave owners.

Rothschild was not acting as an independent London financier; he was personally involved as an owner of enslaved persons in the West Indies. In this regard, his roles as banker and slave owner overlapped. According to Draper, "he was also a counter-claimant as mortgagee for compensation for 88 enslaved persons on an estate in Antigua, for which Charles Chatfield, the trustee of Rothschild's executors, was awarded £1,570.18s.0d [£1.12 million in 2010]". After Rothschild's death, Baron James de Rothschild also pressed his claims for compensation for his enslaved persons in the West Indies.[20]

Other members of London's Jewish banking and financial community were compensated for their ownership of enslaved West Indians. Judah and Hymen Cohen had investments in enslaved persons, as did Alfred Latham, the co-founder of Arbuthnot Latham, who owned 148 Africans on the Gunning Hill estate in Jamaica. Ann Latham, wife of Thomas Latham, owned enslaved persons in Antigua and Nevis.

The Rothschild financial empire protected private investors in Caribbean slavery and, in addition to its own investments, reached into the slave system to find wealth and forge political connections. That it should emerge as the government banker in the financing of the compensation claims was therefore an extension of its slavery business. Rothschild had objected to the emancipation of Africans because his connections to the slave owners, including the government, ran deep. In the end, the Rothschilds were thinking long-term, a perspective that assured their financial sustainability.

Merchants and bankers in London, therefore, with private interests in the West Indian slave system represented the elite group within the City. They were "disproportionately represented amongst institutions generally accepted as representing the City elites". These money managers "had larger capital than the average City trader, and greater influence appears to have been the corollary of this greater wealth".[21]

The City was big on slavery, and the slave owners were big in the City. They were located everywhere that mattered; they ran the City. They did what was necessary to enhance the system of slavery. For example, of the fourteen governors of the Bank of England elected between 1807 and 1834, says Draper, nine were slave owners or had inherited rights to the ownership of enslaved persons. Furthermore, he added, of the twenty-four directors of the bank elected in 1821, nine owned property rights in blacks. The City, then, profited from these slave owners and depended upon them for management skills and financial guidance.[22]

The Atlantic slave complex, then, "helped to foster" what was clearly more than a "miniature banking revolution" in British cities. Kenneth Morgan has suggested that "colonial merchants became prominent partners in the first banks established in Bristol, Glasgow and Liverpool". This is an important point, given that in the eighteenth century there was a vibrant relationship between the banking system and British industrial development. "Bristol's sugar, slave and tobacco merchants", Morgan tells us, "were among the founders of the Old Bank (1750), the Miles Bank (1752) and the Harford Bank (1769)". Included among these was "one of the first local banks in Liverpool", Arthur Heywood Sons and Company – a prominent slave trader.[23] "The critical argument here, from the point of view of British economic development, is that: this growth of banking in the provincial ports suited the needs of substantial businessmen by providing available deposit and transfer facilities. In this way, international trade made significant financial and business connections with the internal economy in Britain."[24]

The slave trade and West Indian slavery were vital parts of the growth of the financial services industry that enabled other sectors of the British economy to expand at an unprecedented rate. The provision of credit to local businessmen by these banks was oftentimes a direct result of slave-based profits finding their way into these networks as deposits. It was in this context, then, that Williams also spoke about the fertilization of British industry by profits and revenues generated by the Caribbean slaved-based economy.

Chapter 11

Twenty Million Pounds
Slave Owners' Reparations

> Many of the slave plantation owners in the West Indies had a direct link to Bristol and contributed much to the city's wealth. Ironically, the compensation that they received once full emancipation took effect in 1838 contributed further to the city's prosperity.
>
> —*Stephen Williams, Member of Parliament, Debate on the Bicentenary of the Abolition of the Slave Trade, House of Commons, 20 March 2007*

In 1838, the British people ended their 250-year-old "national crime" of black enslavement with a sum total payment of £20 million to the last slave-owning cohort. From the perspective of the state, the cash payout represented an apology for aborting the property rights of citizens, a legal action that prompted a settlement as monetary reparations.[1]

Slavery, then, came to an end with a festive orgy of public money being showered upon slave owners, who for generations had been financially enriched, socially elevated and celebrated, and politically empowered and protected. Their final pillage came in the form of massive financial reparations from the British treasury. The £20 million were the last grains from the slave-endowed public granary.[2]

When the issue was discussed in Parliament, some politicians argued that the £20 million paid to slave owners was in fact back pay, part of the taxes the state had extracted with fiscal policies from the slave system. Others spoke of pay-up time from the British public that had enjoyed a higher standard of living as a result of cheap slave-produced products. They all recognized that British citizens were socially empowered by the white supremacy culture so effectively institutionalized on a global scale by slave owners. Underlying most statements made in Parliament, however, was an acceptance of the idea that the payment was in part compensation for the role slave owners had played in building the British Empire as a project that successfully enhanced national economic development.

Some ministers of government suggested that the reparation payment to slave owners was a political victory for all sides. Slave owners cashed in their chattel certificates (documents of ownership of black slaves) to the government and collected £20 million; on top of that, they retained access to those same freed Africans by being able to employ them as cheap labour. Blacks were doubly victimized. They got nothing by way of cash reparations to carry them into freedom. No land grants were provided. No promissory notes were posted. Slave owners ran to the banks. Although unchained, the enslaved remained captives of a constitution that rendered them disenfranchised labourers.

Draper has suggested new ways to look at today's value of the £20 million reparations that slave owners received in 1838. "The British state of the 1830s was much smaller than it is today, and at 40 per cent of government receipts or expenditures, £20 million was a huge amount: it would equate to almost £200 billion today. . . . Finally, in relation to the size of the economy, the £20 million compensation would be the equivalent of around £76 billion."[3] The state and its Caribbean slave-owning partners were bonded together, even if on occasion their heads and hearts diverged.

The policy commitment of the British state to the legal principle of property rights vested in enslaved Africans, and the rallying of the political culture around this economic world view, meant that any notion of legislative emancipation would entail monetary compensation. For two hundred years the British had practised the economics of property rights in African bodies. It had become a way of life – a living culture. The colonies may have originated this culture but Britain reaped the benefits equally. The political system of eighteenth-century Britain perpetuated, and traded as its legacy, the idea that Africans were not human, even though, as property, they provided human pleasures to owners. In addition to enforced labour in the fields, enforced warming of the enslavers' beds was a product whose value was not to be understated.

Ending slavery, therefore, was not simply a matter of terminating an economic system. It was also the abolition of a social culture in which white persons had unrestricted social and sexual rights to black bodies and totalitarian powers over their lives.

Many British slave owners were prepared to accept a reduction in profits before losing their right of total access to black bodies. The right to determine the life and death of black people had become engrained in the slave owner's psyche. While it is compelling to suggest that a rational business person would not destroy productive property, the slave owners' desire to exercise total social power often had that effect. The white race had become intoxicated with its power over Africans. This power constituted a psychological asset which did not respond rationally to market forces.

Slavery was an intense social experience. Living in fear in the face of lurking death produced its own social expressions. But in the end, the enslaved were property, and when the British state moved to use its legislative power to impinge upon rights that were considered derivative, citizens had reasons to expect compensation. This argument took centre stage and pushed aside the notion posited by George Canning, in 1826, that slavery was a "common crime" for which slave owners should be censored, not compensated.⁴

While a few politicians did admit that slavery was a "national crime", more were comfortable with the idea of it as a "national sin".⁵ Nonetheless, as politicians, they imposed upon the British Parliament the perspective that emancipation was an attack upon the property rights of British citizens and constituted a breach of social justice. As slave owners, these politicians, ironically, were vociferous users of the term "social justice" in the emancipation discourse as it related to their rights in enslaved property. Africans, they maintained, were non-human chattels and not entitled to be the subject of a debate on freedom and liberty.

The British state had its own specific financial interest in defending the sanctity of property rights in blacks as a paramount legal principle. The state was a major direct investor in enslaved Africans and stood to suffer a significant financial loss. The government, then, played the game on both sides: as a major slave owner and as the abolitionist. The issue, therefore, was wider than the notion of the sanctity of property. It was ultimately about the role of the state in enhancing economy and society. Slavery, all recognized, was central to the civilization that the British had imagined and built into an empire.

An act of Parliament that abolished slavery would therefore test the laws of private property as they related to the rights in owning enslaved Africans, society's ideological belief that black people were first and foremost non-human, and public opinion with regard to who was entitled to compensation. The slave owners understood that the British government had long established a pact with them in securing and protecting their property rights in humans.[6]

Some slave owners understood this bond to be contractual. Augustus Beaumont, owner of a newspaper in Jamaica, made this point forcefully in his contribution to the compensation discussion: "The property in slaves which the British Parliament sold them, is in the rights, the natural – the born rights of the Negro – a right to his labour – to all he can acquire, to the possession of him as a mere chattel – destitute of will – subject to absolute power. Cruel as this may be, it is the contract between Parliament and the Slave Owners."[7] The primacy of such a contract, between state and citizen, based on over two hundred years of conception and practice, brushed away opposing voices with its empirical and political force. Slave owners could not be robbed by the British state in an act of emancipation if it wished to maintain its credibility.

Freeing blacks, some slave owners argued, meant the legal recognition of their status as humans. Furthermore, and equally important, it meant the necessity of devising strategies to ensure British rule and the values of white supremacy in the colonies. For these reasons, the critics of emancipation argued, the new abolitionist policies of the British state were betraying all that was popularly understood as the British way of life.

No one made these points more clearly than John Palmer, a former governor of the Bank of England, who looked at the issue of property rights in the enslaved as indispensable to the financial culture. Emancipation without reparation to slave owners, he said, "would endanger the whole frame of society. The property of the planter had been secured by a hundred acts of Parliament, and no Minister had a right to tamper with that property. (Hear! Hear!) It tended to shake the credit and confidence of the country."[8] The entire British economy, said Palmer, was tied up in the finance and credit surrounding property rights in Africans in the Caribbean. Slavery was at the core of the credit system that kept the British economy on an even keel. To tamper with enslaved blacks as property was to subvert the national economy – and the City of London understood this well.

Palmer was speaking for the City, and the City's voice in Parliament was powerful. Pay the slave owners, the City cried, and let the government, as party to the breach of property rights, fund the reparation. There was no choice in the matter, stated Viscount Howick: "However large the claim of the West Indians for compensation may be, I do not hesitate to say that it should not stand in my way for a moment, as weighed against the importance of putting an end to the sufferings of the slaves . . . the victims of that guilt must not continue for one hour to suffer, while we are haggling about pounds, shillings and pence."9

Parliament expressed less passion for the humanity and future welfare of the enslaved Africans in the Caribbean. The blacks were told to understand that, as chattels, they had no legal cause, and as property they had no right to a political plea. They were to be silent in their enslavement while the British state and its citizens decided "who" or "what" they were and how best to treat them.

The grand revolt of the enslaved in Jamaica in 1831 may have said enough to Parliament about the matter of black silence and stillness, but few persons, Thomas Clarkson being the noble exception, were prepared to press the argument that the enslaved, not the enslaver, should receive reparations. As early as 1807, Clarkson was an advocate of this idea. He wrote, "That compensation is due somewhere there is no doubt. But from whom is it due? Is it due from you to Africa! . . . In all other countries, except in defenceless Africa, or the colonies of nations planted on the discovery of the New World, you would have been condemned to death had you gone there on the same errand."10

The discourse on reparations, Clarkson tells us, was essentially one about power relations. In history it is the influential who receive reparations. The weak merely talk about it. The slave owners were a mighty powerful group in the British Parliament, the cities and civil society. The enslaved had advocates in these forums, but their ability to shape political policy and their economic influence within the economy was marginal and ineffective. There were also those who argued that the enslaved were victors and should instead pay reparations to their enslavers in exchange for their freedom. The injustice of emancipation, they said, is the enslavers' for their loss of investment rights.

The identification of the slave owner as victim was the basis of the emancipation discussion in Parliament. The only serious matter was "who" should compensate the slave owner – the state or the emancipated. Slave owners examined this choice and recognized that the better option was the state. By pressing the point that "someone" should pay, slave owners pushed the state into a corner. Member of Parliament William Hankey argued that the "enslaved could not owe compensation", but the "nation does". The reason he gave is that "slavery is a national act" with "national consequences". He made reference to taxation of £800 he paid to the state on the acquisition of his slave estate and suggested that this constituted evidence of public enrichment for slavery.[11]

On 28 August 1833, the British Parliament passed the Slavery Abolition Act. It contained the expected victory of the slave owners, who would be compensated for the infringement of their property rights in enslaved blacks. The law, titled "An Act for the abolition of slavery throughout the British colonies, for promoting the industry of the manumitted slaves, and for compensating the persons hitherto entitled to the services of such slaves", also bound the emancipated to their owners for another period of four to six years.

The emancipated, then, after 250 years of enslavement, did not receive the courtesy of a compensatory clause in the act. They were assigned to further bondage for a period conceived as the necessary transition for their "owners" to become accustomed to being non-owners.

Critically, the payment to slave owners was a notable example of parliamentarians helping themselves. Most members of the Commons and Lords were financial and social beneficiaries of slavery, in one way or another. The government itself was a major slave owner. In 1824, according to Butler, "thirty-nine members of Parliament identified with the West Indian cause. Eleven West Indian merchants, including John Gladstone and Joseph Marryat, represented London and the outports, while the remaining twenty-eight members were the absentee owners of colonial estates".[12] Gladstone was a Liverpool merchant, while Marryat was a London agent. They "linked their political and trading activities to their positions as members of Parliament". Gladstone had investments in seven estates in Guiana and six in Jamaica. He also "exerted considerable influence over George Canning, the foreign minister, and member of Parliament for Liverpool".[13]

Then there were other parliamentarians, such as Neill Malcolm, member of Parliament for Boston, who "owned nine estates and over 2,080 slaves in

Jamaica". Lord Seaford was recognized as the leader of West India business in the Commons. He owned five Jamaican plantations. Among the peers who owned West Indian slave plantations were "the Earl of Harewood, with three estates in Barbados, two in Jamaica", which were stocked with over 1,250 enslaved persons, as well as the "Marquis of Sligo, later Governor of Jamaica, with two Jamaican estates, and the Duke of Cleveland, who owned one estate and 230 enslaved persons in Barbados".[14]

There was no surprise, then, that the act provided for a massive reparatory sum, plus interest from 1 August 1834, to be paid to themselves as owners of enslaved blacks. In a country, noted Butler, "already burdened with a national debt of £800 million (£569 billion in 2010), this was an enormous amount of money to be found". It was a budget-busting payout to slave owners, but critically, it represented a major injection of cash into the economy by the British state that recognized the importance of slave-based property to the national economy. From a macroeconomic perspective, it was a huge stimulus package, designed to empower the investor class with new possibilities.[15]

Slave owners wanted the last drop of blood from the dying slavery system. Their own calculations were that the enslaved population in the West Indies

Table 11.1. Estimated Values of Some Enslaved West Indians

Colony	Caribbean Values (£)	British Compensation (£)
Jamaica	13,951,139	6,161,927
British Guiana	9,729,047	4,330,665
Barbados	3,897,276	1,721,345
Trinidad	2,352,655	1,117,950
Grenada	1,395,684	611,936
St Vincent	1,341,491	576,446
St Lucia	759,890	333,700
Tobago	529,941	232,400

Source: Kathleen Mary Butler, *The Economics of Emancipation: Jamaica and Barbados, 1823–1843* (Chapel Hill: University of North Carolina Press, 1995), 28.

was valued at £40 million (£28.5 billion in 2010) and that all their other properties were worth £100 million. Apart from the reparations of £20 million,
they demanded "an additional £10M" in the form of a loan, and stated that
failure to comply would "destroy all confidence in British trade and could
affect the property of every British citizen".[16]

A Barbados newspaper lamented that the £20 million "was insufficient and
left the colonists uncompensated for over £27 million worth of property".
Colonial officials did not agree. The governor of the colony, Sir Lionel Smith,
urged the British government to ignore slave owners' greed, as the offer of
£20 million "had given the planters a great deal of satisfaction". The slave
owners, he noted, had inflated the replacement price of their enslaved workers,
and the British government should defend its own best market calculation.[17]

It was upon the British government's own best calculation that the reparation was paid. The divergence with colonial estimates was considerable and
speaks to the attempt by slave owners to extract maximum cash from the
emancipation process.

The British government made its own calculations. It established an average
price for an enslaved person in each colony and multiplied that by the total
number of enslaved in each colony. The figure for each colony was calculated
as a percentage of the total value of all enslaved persons in all West Indian
colonies, which the British government had estimated at £45,281,738. Each
colony, then, said Butler, "received a percentage of the indemnity equal to the
ratio that the value of its slaves bore to the total value of all slaves covered by
the act".[18] In 1834, there were 664,970 enslaved persons accounted for in the
British colonies of the West Indies. Their distribution across the colonies is
illustrated in table 11.2.

Furthermore, the British government paid compensation based on locally
established values for enslaved adults and children. Children played an important part in the labour regimes of plantations and were considered a prime
asset by slave owners. Government agreed and supported the claims made for
child values. The average compensation payment for adults and children in
the colonies varied and was explained in terms of the relative regional prosperity of the sugar plantation economy, as shown in table 11.3.[19]

The actuarial entry of babies and children into slave owners' computations
for reparations was an indicator of the hard-nosed business approach adapted
in relation to their property rights in humans (table 11.4). It also indicated the

Table 11.2. Estimated Enslaved West Indian Population, 1834

Colony	Enslaved Population
Barbados	83,150
St Kitts	17,525
Nevis	8,840
Antigua	28,130
Montserrat	6,400
Virgin Islands	5,135
Jamaica	311,070
Dominica	14,165
St Lucia	13,275
St Vincent	22,250
Grenada	23,645
Tobago	11,545
Trinidad	20,655
Demerara-Essequibo	64,185
Berbice	19,360
Cayman Islands	985
Bahamas	9,995
Anguilla	2,260
Barbuda	505
Total	664,970

Source: B.W. Higman, *Slave Populations of the British Caribbean, 1807–1834* (Baltimore: Johns Hopkins University Press, 1984), 418.

moral degradation inherent in the slave system, which was backed by the British government.

Slavery, Draper noted, had "pervaded particular strata and localities of Britain by virtue of direct slave ownership or indirect financial dependence on the slave economy". The avenues used to travel deep into the social heartland of British societies were annuities, marriage settlements and legacies.[20]

Table 11.3. Average Value of Working Enslaved Adult West Indians, 1834

Colony	£
British Honduras	60.9 [£42,700 in 2010]
British Guiana	58.5
Trinidad	55.5
St Vincent	30.6
Grenada	30.0
St Lucia	29.9
Barbados	24.9
Jamaica	22.9
Dominica	22.7
Tobago	22.3
Nevis	21.4
Montserrat	20.0
St Kitts	19.0
Antigua	17.8
Virgin Islands	16.3
Bahamas	15.4

Source: B.W. Higman, *Slave Populations of the British Caribbean, 1807–1834* (Baltimore: Johns Hopkins University Press, 1984), 79.

Enslaved men, women and children were counted, valued and discounted, and the British government began the process of disbursement. It was a seminal moment in the national history of Britain.

Draper's research has enabled scholars to better understand the mood that dominated British political and economic life as inspired by cash for chattels. Persons who were hitherto ashamed to stand up as slave owners, but who relied on the slave-generated income, found courage in demanding compensation in cash. Those with a marginal claim on enslaved West Indians became aggressively litigious in asserting specific rights. Enslaved West Indians were the prized assets in British claims of poverty alleviation. The scramble to scrape

Table 11.4. Average Value of Enslaved West Indian Children

Colony	£	
Trinidad	22.2	[£15,700 in 2010]
British Honduras	21.6	
British Guiana	19.0	
St Vincent	10.9	
Grenada	10.3	
St Lucia	8.4	
Jamaica	7.7	
St Kitts	5.6	
Tobago	4.8	
Dominica	4.6	
Bahamas	4.4	
Nevis	4.0	
Barbados	3.9	
Virgin Islands	3.3	
Montserrat	2.5	
Antigua	2.4	

Source: B.W. Higman, *Slave Populations of the British Caribbean, 1807–1834* (Baltimore: Johns Hopkins University Press, 1984), 79.

up compensation cash turned friendships, partnerships and family ties into aggressive and at times litigious campaigns.

The state of affairs over reparations money is described by Draper as a "feeding frenzy" which, he says, took over the behaviour of British society. In so doing, it revealed fully how deeply slavery was embedded in the national social and economic spine. It was a "frenzy that drew thousands of Britons into asserting their ownership of the enslaved", Draper notes, "once the state attached specific and immediate monetary value to the claims of ownership". Compensation records set out each claim and the related counterclaims over the property value of the enslaved. Contesting the claims were the rich and the famous, the nobles and commoners. They went to great lengths to get their share and, in the process, the reach of slavery's tentacles was revealed.[21]

That organized public opinion should support compensation for enslavers is therefore instructive. It indicates the depth of slave owning to British popular culture and identity. The extent of infection of the national imagination with racist anti-black sentiments was not always understood and accepted, even by the anti-slavery groups. But the persistent bombardment of the national consciousness with racist ideas and sentiment had its lasting effects. The emerging mass media, intellectual classes, political leaders, corporate elites and the judiciary were vehicles for race-based values that supported the idea of compensation for enslavers and not the enslaved.

The logic of emancipation politics was to ensure that freed blacks remained, as far as possible, located on sugar plantations that would not change ownership. There would be no redistribution of income or economic enfranchisement of blacks. The social structure would remain as closely attached to the slave-based system as possible. The future imagined in Whitehall was one in which black subordination was guaranteed within colonialism. Without black hands, Caribbean lands were useless. Blacks were to be landless as the norm, even if adjustments were necessary in some places in order to secure labour.

In giving effect to slave owners' demand for reparations, the British legal and political system showed considerable flexibility and creativity. It is a feature of all reparations procedures that lawyers, once given the remit by politicians, have shown bureaucratic ingenuity. This was the case in 1834, just as it was with the Nuremburg war tribunals after the Second World War that set in train the prosecution of the German state and citizens for crimes against humanity. The British government was enterprising as it entered a new and innovative legislative league.

The Abolition Act established the Compensation Commission. This body was chaired by a respected legal mind, Charles Pepys, who soon thereafter rose up the political ranks to become Lord Chancellor and the first Earl of Cottenham. Also given an opportunity to chair the commission was the charismatic politician John Carter, member of Parliament for the constituency of Portsmouth. The commission did not rely upon its membership for the critical data relevant to slave owners' reparation. It employed professional staff to work through the complex accounting and financial issues. For example, Charles Willinck was given the job of making actuarial calculations on West Indian "slave values". He was a senior official of University Life Assurance Office.[22]

The commission employed assistants who served as members of boards in each colony, charged with bringing to order the discrepancies in slave owners' property evaluations. This was an impressive governance system for a major legal project. The commission handled "over 45,000 individual claims from owners of 800,000 enslaved", an undertaking that indicated the resolve of the British government on the matter of slave owners' reparations. Individual West Indian slave owners, mostly British-based, received the bulk of the bounty (table 11.5). The remainder was paid to slave owners whose chattel resided in Britain, and slave owners in other parts of the empire.

Table 11.5. Reparations Received by Owners of Enslaved West Indians

Colony	Number of Enslaved	Money Received in £
Anguilla	2,260	35,669
Antigua	29,003	424,391
Barbados	83,225	1,714,561
British Guiana	84,075	4,281,032
Dominica	14,266	277,737
Grenada	23,729	615,671
British Honduras	1,896	100,691
Jamaica	311,455	6,121,446
Montserrat	6,392	103,556
Nevis	8,792	149,611
St Kitts	17,514	293,331
St Lucia	13,232	331,805
St Vincent	22,786	579,300
Tobago	11,592	233,367
Trinidad	20,428	1,021,858
Virgin Islands	5,135	72,635
Total	655,780	16,356,661*

*Total equals £11.6 billion in 2010 value.
Source: Nicholas Draper, *The Price of Emancipation: Slave-Ownership, Compensation and British Society at the End of Slavery* (Cambridge: Cambridge University Press, 2010), 139.

In addition to the dozens of politicians and merchants, most British banks cashed in on the compensation. These banks later evolved into the institutions recognized today on the high streets and in the international arena. Many American banks, for example, have made strategic reparations contributions when the evidence became public of their historic enrichment from slavery. In Britain, Barclays Bank, Lloyds Bank and the Royal Bank of Scotland head the list of major banks with slavery origins.

Barclays Bank

The predecessor banks of Barclays were Barclay, Bevan and Tritton; Cocks, Biddulph and Biddulph; Stone, Martin and Stones; and Goslings and Sharpe.[23] They all received reparations money on behalf of themselves, and for acting on behalf of clients and customers. Barclay, Bevan and Tritton, for example, was banker for the Scott family, who received £6,501 (£4.63 million in 2010) for the enslaved on their Jamaica estate. R. Barclay also collected £40,353 (£28.7 million in 2010) for the enslaved on the Guiana estates of John and Henry Moss of Liverpool. Barclay, Bevan and Tritton also received £35,908 (£25.5 million in 2010) as beneficiary for enslaved persons in Jamaica. It acted as agent for banker Stone, Martin and Stone in collecting £3,605 for H.A. Earle, who owned enslaved persons in St Kitts. There are many other cases in which it acted as agent for slave owners, and also on its own behalf as holder of property rights in enslaved blacks.[24]

Lloyds

The predecessor firms of Lloyds were Barnetts, Hoares and Co.; Bosanquet Anderson; T.H. Farquhar and W.S. Davidson; Praed and Co.; and Stevenson and Salt. They all claimed reparations on behalf of clients. They collected £26,426 on behalf of P.J. Miles, £3,529 for Viscount St Vincent, and £2,652 for Lieutenant General John Mitchell, all Jamaican slave owners.

Royal Bank of Scotland

Draper relates that six of the predecessor firms of the Royal Bank of Scotland received reparations money. He notes,

Overall, of twenty-one London predecessor banks of today's Royal Bank of Scotland Group active at the time of Emancipation, six (Dorriens, Magens, Mello & Co.; Sir James Esdaile; Robarts Curtis; Smith, Payne and Smith; Vere Sapte; and Hankey & Co.) have been identified as receiving compensation as mortgagees of slave property, partners in three more (Coutts & Co., Curries & Co., and Williams Deacon Labouchere) acted as trustees or executors of slave owners, as well as agents in the case of Coutts and Williams Deacon; and six acted solely as banking agents (Barnard Dimsdale; Joseph Denison & Co.; Drummonds; Sir J.W. Lubbock; Prescott Grote; and Glynn Mills).[25]

As executor trustee, for example, the Royal Bank of Scotland collected £15,379 (£10.7 million in 2010) for Job Raikes and £20,027 for J.G. Campbell, Jamaican slave owners. It also collected £10,197 (£14.2 million in 2010) for the Earl of Liverpool for his enslaved persons in Guiana. It acted on behalf of itself when it claimed £2,064 for enslaved persons in Tobago, and £4,121 for enslaved persons in Jamaica. Many other cases are recorded in which the predecessors of the Royal Bank of Scotland, acting as beneficiary, made claims on the value of enslaved West Indians.

· · ⟻ · ·

Butler noted that slave owners, despite demanding more, were content with the reparations received: "Such generous compensation was unprecedented." They hoped, she concluded, "that repaying at least part of their outstanding debts would encourage investment and make new working capital available". Reparations, then, was read as a strategy by which the British government capitalized the national economy and the empire.[26]

The accounts of the Gladstone family tell the story of how slave owners were able to use reparations money to refinance, expand and restructure their business operations. By 1830, John Gladstone was a major slave owner in Guiana, in both the coffee and sugar sectors. He received £110,000 (£78.3 million in 2010) in reparations for his enslaved workers in Guiana and Jamaica. Critically, "he did not re-invest the money in either colony". Rather, he bought ships for deployment in the India trade and invested in Britain's transport sector. He bought £40,000 (£28.5 million in 2010) worth of shares in canals, which gave him control of the Forth and Clyde Canal Company. He

Table 11.6. Reparations Received by British Financiers for Enslaved Jamaicans

Name of Company		Reparations (£)
W., R., & S. Mitchell	(London)	93,965
W., G., & S. Hibbert	(Manchester)	59,545
Judah & Hannah Cohen	(London)	38,247
Biddulph & Cockerell	–	36,260
Timperon & Dobinson	(London)	35,441
Currie, Pearse & Tunno	(London)	35,406
Davidson & Barkly	(London)	35,122
P.J. Miles	(Bristol)	28,188
J.H. Deffell	(Bristol)	26,804
T. & M. Hartley	–	23,385
Andrew Colville	(London)	20,830
John Gladstone	(Liverpool)	19,605
Sir John Rae Reid	(London)	19,400
Stewart & Westmoreland	(London)	17,361
Hawthorne & Sheddon	(London)	15,520
Purrier & Purrier	(London)	15,211
Jeagan & Rutherford	(London)	13,227
Dickenson & Harmon	–	11,978
Sir Alexander Grant	(London)	11,709
S. Boddington	(London)	10,413
Baker & Phillpotts	(London)	7,990
Barrow & Lousada	–	6,370
Charles Horsfall	(Liverpool)	5,196
Pitcairn & Amos	(Yarmouth)	6,806
Total		594,339*

*Total equals £423 million in 2010 value.
Source: Kathleen Mary Butler, *The Economics of Emancipation: Jamaica and Barbados, 1823–1843* (Chapel Hill: University of North Carolina Press, 1995), 53.

continued to downsize his West India investments and divert his interest to the British domestic economy.[27]

Slave owners, then, won three decisive battles in securing reparations for their property rights in enslaved Africans. First, they received cash to refinance their business (see table 11.6); second, they were able to make new investments, mostly in British stocks; and third, they succeeded in holding on to their West Indian enterprises and thereby rendering the "freed" persons largely landless and second-class in the colonies where they had been enslaved.

The impact of reparations money on slave owners' finances was immediate. They used the funds to pay off debts and to reduce mortgages on their plantations held by British merchant companies to manageable levels. Reparations funds saved most slave owners from the bankruptcy they faced in 1830 as a result of excess credit consumption. Reparations for the British financiers always "meant more than a simple vindication of property rights. It represented a unique opportunity to recoup at least part of their colonial investments".[28]

The frenzied feeding on reparation funds, as described by Draper, therefore included all parties to the crime of slave owning. The feeding fattened many and reduced the financial stress of most. In this sense, slavery was profitable to the very end. These funds were invested in the British domestic and colonial economy, and they represented a major stimulus to activity in traditional and emerging sectors. The significant growth of the British economy between 1840 and 1870 had much to do with this stimulus of reparations capital that strengthened entrepreneurship and opened up new investment opportunities.

In the Caribbean, the plantation system remained. Blacks, now freed, entered into a period of intensive policing, racial apartheid and increased hostility to their demands for justice. The West Indies planters and merchants, and their London financiers, were pleased with the reparations deal. The blacks who had been the victims of the crime received nothing. This was the greatest crime of all committed by the British state against the African people.

PART TWO

Chapter 12

The Case for Reparations

[Twenty] million pounds [that slave owners received as reparations from the British government for losing their property rights in slaves] was a huge amount; it would equate to almost 200 billion pounds today.

—*Nicholas Draper, The Price of Emancipation*

THE CASE FOR REPARATIONS SHOULD be made against the British state and a select group of its national institutions, such as merchant houses, banks, insurance companies and the Church of England. These institutions exist today. Their slave-derived wealth is not in question. From slavery to the present day, these institutions continue to accumulate wealth. The state is the recognized institution that legally and financially implemented and sustained the crimes against humanity, from which it was enriched and in other ways benefited directly and indirectly. Collaborating financial and social institutions operated the slave regimes and paid corporate taxes to the state on their slave wealth in an economy regulated by the government.

The role of the British state was not confined to the regulation and fiscal management of slavery. The state was also engaged directly in the slave system as an important investor and owner. Slaves were owned and employed by the state. In this regard the government functioned as a slave investor in much the same way as other financial institutions. The reparations claim, then, should be a government-to-government legal process in the first instance, with options to include those participating financial and social institutions that exist today as privileged beneficiaries.

SHP — Single Homeless Persons — Vauxhall   LAMBETH genocide against   Imperial War Museum

Targets Black people: British   Black British West Indians?

Representatives of Caribbean governments at the UN-sponsored World Conference against Racism provided principled leadership on the question of reparations for the crimes of chattel slavery and slave trading inflicted upon African peoples, and genocide against indigenous Caribbean peoples. Many African states, led by Nigeria, Senegal and South Africa, joined with the "West Group" and European Union nations in rejecting the legal right to reparations. Caribbean nations stood firm and refused to agree to the final declaration, which absurdly stated that chattel slavery and slave trading *should* have been crimes at that time, just as they are today. The historical evidence shows that slavery and slave trading were in fact considered as crimes *then*, as they are today.

Caribbean governments have a historic duty to take the next step and build upon this platform. They have a legal and moral responsibility to place the case of reparations for slavery before the British government. Notwithstanding the expectation of political and economic intimidation and reprisals that are perceived as likely to follow such an action, governments have an obligation to act within the context of international law and diplomatic traditions to represent the interests of their citizens.

Afro-Caribbean people suffered four hundred years of criminal racial targeting within slavery regimes. The living legacy of these crimes continues to debilitate their progeny while those who have benefited from the criminal enrichment continue to enjoy the wealth derived from the crimes. The native population of the region experienced the crime of genocide in addition to enslavement. Not to present this case constitutes an act of neglect and irresponsibility which will be judged by history as connivance and complicity.

Europe's trafficking across the Atlantic Ocean of over fifteen million enchained Africans for the purpose of chattel enslavement, and the collateral death and displacement of another thirty million on the continent, say official sources from the United Nations Educational, Scientific and Cultural Organization, represent modernity's greatest human tragedy. They were crimes against humanity that Europe has refused to accept. They constitute, furthermore, a global tragedy now described universally as the African holocaust.[1]

Britain dominated this transatlantic trade in humans at its peak in the eighteenth century. More efficiently than its European rivals, it globalized this crime and was more effective in the enrichment process. Like other principal participating European nations – Spain, Portugal, France, the Netherlands,

Germany, Russia, Sweden, Norway and Denmark – Britain has a case of reparations to answer because of these activities. The buying, selling and enslavement of African people, and the unjust enrichment that resulted from these
actions, form the basis of the case.

This charge should be answered, in the first instance, by the state as the
primary institution that framed and enforced enslavement laws, implemented
supportive fiscal measures, and invested public revenues that created and sustained the slave system. For over two hundred years, the British state, acting
on behalf of its citizens and institutions and in its own corporate interests,
legalized the non-human legal status of enslaved Africans.[2]

The British state also enforced and legitimized the use of Africans as real
estate, chattels and commercial property. These legal and economic actions,
framed by government in the national interest, were enforced violently upon
the enslaved African people in the Caribbean and elsewhere. The purpose of
these crimes was to create a massive system of wealth accumulation for the
enrichment of state and citizens.

The establishment of chattel slavery and its globalization by the British
state and commercial elites created a new and unprecedented context for
national development. The slave-based strategic initiative found support in
all branches of government – the executive, judiciary and legislature. African
enslavement became a core part of the British way of life. It fuelled the commercial engines that propelled the country into sustained development in the
eighteenth century, creating the first industrial nation.[3]

From the early seventeenth century, scholars, entrepreneurs and statesmen
were unified in recognizing slavery as the primary stimulus to the national
economy. Dozens of civil societies and corporate institutions have since told
their story, recalling their origins in the slave system. The royal family and its
ennobled elites, the established church, universities, banks and other primary
institutions that constitute the fabric of the nation accumulated wealth from
Caribbean slavery. It enlarged their operations and secured their future.

The British state participated in the process of slave-based accumulation
as a direct investor and slave owner. It bought and owned enslaved Africans
and traded on the slave market as a private agent. At the heart of these crimes
against humanity was the Caribbean – the centre of the British commercial
and investing elite in the seventeenth, eighteenth and nineteenth centuries.
Slavery in these tropical colonies enriched British families, repaired broken

fortunes and filled government treasuries. Monarchs discovered new sustainable revenue streams, companies prospered with the sale of slave-produced commodities and the British nation built its modern foundations.

Starting with a few slave ships at the end of the sixteenth century, by 1700 the English had built in the Caribbean the most profitable agricultural economies in colonial America; these were the sugar plantation enterprises of Barbados, Jamaica and the Leeward Islands. By the mid-eighteenth century, the Windward Islands were added, followed by Trinidad and Guiana by 1800.

The West Indies became the wealth-generating machine of the New World, the "hub of the British Empire". The entire colonial economic structure was built upon the enchainment and enslavement of Africans. The British made more money from slave trading and enslaving Africans than any other European nation. In the process they became the first European nation to successfully convert massive slave-based profits into domestic industrial, commercial and financial wealth.

Enrichment from slavery drove Britain's business in the eighteenth century. From the West Indies the British Empire flourished, engulfing the East Indies, Africa and Australasia. The few "scraps" of Caribbean turf that started the slave economy consumed millions of enslaved Africans who were shipped as cargo, whipped and stripped of their humanity.

These crimes against humanity have not been answered by the British state and its support institutions. They all have a reparation case to answer. The British state must take legal, political and moral ownership of these crimes as the body invested with collective, continual responsibility for the wealth of the nation.[4]

Other European states and institutions have a similar case of reparations to answer. Spain, Portugal, the Netherlands, France, Germany, Russia and the Nordic nations were the other principal investors and participants in the trafficking and enslavement of Africans. These states and citizens committed crimes against humanity in their treatment of enslaved Africans and the indigenous Caribbean people.[5]

Caribbean governments are well placed to present a collective case on behalf of the descendant citizens of enslaved Africans and native peoples. These victims have a right to justice. Caribbean states have a moral and political obligation to their citizens that must be discharged in the interest of furthering legitimate democratic governance.

Rejecting *Was*: British Refusal

Slave owners denied the criminality of genocide against native Caribbean persons, trading in enchained Africans and the enslavement of both. Private investors and the British state, which funded, legislated and enforced these practices, argued the legality of their actions. Natives were defined as savages not fit to possess the lands they inhabited, and Africans were classified as chattel property. "Savages" and "property", therefore, had no right to their lands and labour. Not only were native occupants of the land refused their right to real property, but by redefining their status and that of enslaved Africans as chattel property, they themselves became a type of property associated with the very land (real property) they occupied. Their dispossession and enslavement were considered a right and benefit of British citizenship.[6]

Few officials of the British state today would be willing to make this argument, but it remains the unstated basis of the national defence against reparations claims. The slave owners of the nineteenth century and the British state today have an umbilical link, despite the passage of time. Political continuity has forged a common understanding that the case for reparations of black people and natives must be fought fiercely.

The intention of British society is to walk away from these crimes without reparatory obligation and responsibility. State and society do not intend to be held accountable. To this end, the state has made several arguments. As discursive positions they are intended to deflect what officials understand to be a legally strong and morally compelling case that requires political resolution before it reaches international courts formulated as crimes against humanity. That is, in framing these arguments, state officials understand them to be legally weak and morally unacceptable. The politics of opposition, therefore, is where the value of these arguments is to be found.

Denial of the rightness of the reparations case has been persistent. State officials argue that if colonial governments made genocide, slave trading and slavery legal, then there is no case to answer. No crime was committed. The question of authority is important. From which source was the British state invested with the authority to impose a genocidal policy upon the native people of the Caribbean and enslave millions of Africans against their will and in the face of their persistent resistance? The natives fought back; they were crushed: the Africans rebelled and were massacred. The British state, in order to enforce native dispossession and African enslavement, committed continuous atrocities.

Recognizing the overwhelming evidence that supports the case of African popular resistance to the slave trade, the British state has adjusted its arguments. It now suggests that there was complicity and cooperation in West Africa among political elites. The intention is to argue that alleged crimes against humanity were shared and that African states should be similarly targeted. This is the classic divide-and-rule defence in which victims are blamed for their victimization. The complicity of some African leaders makes the British crime more, rather than less, heinous.

The majority of African leaders over time opposed the slave trade. For this they were destabilized and destroyed. To stand in the way of the slave trade – a business network based in European cities, sustained by massive military might and driven by large financial corporations – was to invite political annihilation. African leaders were assassinated and states destroyed; political borders were redrawn, and communities that resisted were attacked with cannon. The few states that benefited in the short term as collaborators stood against their own rebellious communities and eventually fell.[7]

There are striking similarities between the transatlantic slave trade and the international narcotics trade. African communities were overwhelmed by the superior military and financial power of the British. Some states collaborated and a few leaders reaped financial benefits, but always communities were victimized and ravished by the trade, which the British promoted. The reality of minority African collaboration, then, does not lessen British guilt or reduce its responsibility. In fact, it deepens the crime, for it used victims to facilitate the victimization of their own communities.

Many West African states today are intimidated by this official British argument and have weakened their stance on reparations. Some have abandoned support for the movement. The Caribbean world, however, is not a part of this dialogue. The importation of enchained Africans was the result of a commerce driven by British citizens and the British state.[8]

The traditional "complicity" argument used against African governments has been bolstered in recent years in the Caribbean context with the deployment of the legal concept of "remoteness". This is the notion in Common Law that seeks to "time out" wrongdoing by suggesting that there are no living defendants to answer the charge. It is an argument which says that, with the death of the defendant, the case dies too. But with crimes against humanity, the remoteness rule does not apply. International law has made provision for bringing to justice those who seek to run the time clock as a technical escape valve. In this regard, there are other issues to be addressed.[9]

First, slavery was not confined to the remote past. It is still within living memory. It was abolished in the different Caribbean islands at various times in the nineteenth century. Even when the British state abolished chattel slavery in its own colonies in 1838, its citizens continued to invest in slavery in the Spanish colonies until the 1880s. Some persons living in the Caribbean today had grandparents and great-grandparents who were enslaved. Families continue to live with the memory of slavery and to experience life as the victims of slavery. Also, the reforms to chattel slavery in 1838 led to new forms of slavery and enabled the continuation of most criminal violations against blacks.

Officials of the British state have also suggested that even if one accepts that a crime against humanity has been committed, the challenge of meeting a reparations case is impossible owing both to the enormity of the slavery system and to the impossibility of crafting a reparatory response that would be meaningful and would bring closure to the case.

This argument is self-serving and distracts from the essential validity of the case. The cases of reparations that have been settled in past decades have shown the extraordinary creativity and innovativeness of legal experts and judges. The political will to find a reparatory settlement stimulates legal ingenuity. Models can be designed and structures put in place to bring closure to these crimes. But first, there must be acknowledgement of the crime, an apology for perpetrating the crime, acceptance of responsibility, and a willingness to begin a reparatory process that is just.

The phased deployment of these arguments by the British state is an expression of the "moving goalpost" strategy. Each time an argument is defeated and set aside, a new one is invented and marshalled. The terms and conditions of the dialogue keep changing. The purpose of this approach is to play for time, where delaying a decision is an end in itself. The British state believes that the longer the reparations case is denied, the more remote it will become. These officials seem to believe that as each generation comes to maturity, the less concerned they will be with matters of history. Playing the time game is considered their best strategy. Future generations of black youth, they believe, will have less interest in the experience of their forebears and are unlikely to commit politically to matters such as reparations.

The backup tactic of the British state is political intimidation. Caribbean and African governments have been pressured by British and European states into adopting soft or reluctant positions in respect to reparations. International financial institutions, for example, such as the World Bank and the International Monetary Fund, worked with European governments to create sites of silence. Together with their development agencies, the governments of slave-owning countries have discovered instruments of intimidation. Once the word "reparations" comes up, dialogue within these environments is immediately iced and resources frozen. The fear factor continues to exist with the politics of reparations, and it acts as a barrier to the pursuit of justice. Caribbean citizens and states, then, are politically prohibited from the engagement of reparations because the climate has been designed to forestall the ability to exercise rights under law.[10]

Caribbean governments, however, have a case to present. The arguments made by British and European states cannot withstand legal and moral scrutiny. As political postures they are not sustainable. The Nuremburg Trials dealt conclusively with the principle of retroactive justice. The entire proceedings validated the legal provision that in respect of the crimes of enslavement and genocide, proceedings are not to be subverted by their historical nature. Caribbean governments have a legal, diplomatic, and ethical obligation, within the finest traditions of British jurisprudence and politics, to assist the British state in accepting responsibility for its actions and so becoming accountable.

In 2004, a team of financial analysts, historians, lawyers and actuaries was assembled by the British Broadcasting Corporation (BBC) and charged with developing a model to assess the parameters of the contribution made by Caribbean enslaved people to the British economy. The purpose of the exercise was to raise public awareness about the legitimacy of reparations claims.

Working with Robert Beckford, presenter of the British television documentary *The Empire Pays Back*, the team was asked to answer the following question: "If Britain were to pay the two million enslaved blacks in the Caribbean a wage at the lowest level of an English worker in the eighteenth and nineteenth centuries, plus damages for trauma, and loss of assets, what would the figure look like?" The group concluded that Britain would be looking at paying £7.5 trillion pounds to Caribbean blacks. When this calculation was made, the gross domestic product of Britain stood at less than half this amount. The sum reflected the considerable value of enslaved labour to British economic development. While it was not meant to be the basis of a reparations calculation, it showed the importance of the slave trade to the British economy, and the role of slavery in the national economic growth of Great Britain.

In the United States similar calculations have been made. Larry Neal, an economist, suggested that the "1983 value of the slave labor expropriated between 1620 and 1865 from Black Americans ranged from $96.3 billion to $9.7 trillion, depending on whether a 3 percent or a 6 percent rate of interest is applied".[11] The descendants of these enslaved wealth producers have a legal right to reparations from the beneficiaries of those criminally enriched. These were crimes against humanity. Their causal and immediate impact upon Caribbean persons is evident. Families in the Caribbean today have elders who knew their enslaved forebears. The mass poverty in towns and villages, widespread illiteracy, dysfunctional family structures, and rampant ill-health in the form of endemic diabetes and hypertension are contemporary expressions of the horrors of slavery that targeted black persons.[12]

The engagement of reparations begins an act of justice. It embraces a process of redemption and renewal that celebrates humanity rather than inhumanity. It shatters the silence surrounding these crimes against humanity and is, finally, about fairness, justice and closure.

Chapter 13

Anti-
Racer
John
Prescott #
Wilberforce
Tony

Blair

wicked
against Joe
most do my

"Sold in Africa"

The United Nations and Reparations in Durban

Last month in Ghana, I saw at first hand Elmina castle, which was used in this per-
nicious slave trade – a symbol of man's inhumanity to man. I saw the dungeons.
The cold, dank stench of evil remains there today.

—*Deputy Prime Minister John Prescott, Debate on the Bicentenary of the Abolition
of the Slave Trade, House of Commons, 20 March 2007*

5 Days Later

Brit govt applied to my death warrant,

CARIBBEAN DELEGATES ARRIVED IN DURBAN, South Africa, for the UN World
Conference against Racism, Discrimination, Xenophobia and Related Intolerance (WCAR) at the end of August 2001 prepared to advance the agenda
on reparations. By the time they departed, most felt disheartened by the presidents of Senegal and Nigeria, in particular, who criticized the reparations
movement, joined hands with the West and European Union groups and set
Africa adrift from its diaspora.

Some African governments, however, in a benign way, backed the reparations movement. But Africa's disunity surfaced in ways generally associated
with the expansion of the slave trade. Africans in the diaspora, as well as the
majority of African citizens at home, felt abandoned by these two leaders –
especially representing, as they did, two societies ravaged by the slave trade of
Britain. From this perspective, the Durban conference was a conceptual continuity in African fragmentation in the face of British and European organized
self-interests. Some Africans in the diaspora spoke of being "sold out" within
the context of a specific African-European political convergence.

The Caribbean governments present at Durban were Jamaica, Barbados, St Vincent and the Grenadines, Belize, Cuba, Trinidad and Tobago, Haiti, the Dominican Republic, Costa Rica, Guyana, and Suriname. The United Nations had organized an intergovernmental conference in order to address the historical crimes committed by European colonizers. Only the Cuban delegation was led by the head of state. President Castro's presence loomed large, given his enormous intellectual prestige as an analyst of racial and historical injustices in the Caribbean and beyond. Other Caribbean delegations arrived without ministerial representation, a circumstance that weakened their authority. The British delegation was led by Baroness Amos.

Considerable preparation had gone into the choice of venue by the United Nations. Expectations were raised that postcolonialism, in all its manifestations, would be publicly debated and remedies identified to make the world a safer and more tolerant place. The gathering promised to be seminal. Durban was significant in light of the post-apartheid democratic political culture established under the moral and presidential authority of Nelson Mandela. President Mbeki, his successor, sanctioned the conference. The relative success of "truth and reconciliation" approaches to building a democratic dispensation in the country from the terrible apartheid past was expected to provide the conference with an appropriate discursive tone and texture.

The WCAR was the culmination of a preparatory process in which the Caribbean had invested heavily from January 2000. Delegations participated in national and regional consultations, formal and informal meetings, three preparatory committees and two intersessional meetings. The region was also represented in a smaller working group known as the Group of 21 or G21, representatives from regional groups, mandated with the task of producing a streamlined document for negotiations over a six-week period.

The vice chancellor of the University of the West Indies (UWI), Rex Nettleford, was asked by Mia Mottley, minister of culture in Barbados, to place the university's intellectual resources at her disposal in order to shape and define a national and regional position on race and racism. To this end, a panel of UWI experts was convened and met in Barbados under the chairmanship of Minister Mottley. A paper was submitted to the minister that provided perspectives on race and racism and informed the thinking and actions of the Barbados delegation at Durban.

Leading the strategic thinking of the Barbados delegation were a pan-

African veteran, attorney-at-law David Commissiong, and UWI political scientist George Belle. Hilary Beckles chaired the Barbados delegation and served as coordinator and spokesman for the grouping of Caribbean delegations. Prior to the conference, Barbados maintained the following positions:

- The postcolonial Caribbean is a global leader in the management of race relations and a relatively successful multiracial civilization.
- Reparations for slavery should be paid and undertaken at both a national and international level.
- Colonial slavery and the European transatlantic slave trade constitute crimes against humanity.
- Reparations should begin with the establishment of an education fund.

At the conference, these positions were presented at the opening plenary by the head of delegation and argued throughout the conference. Barbados was commended for taking these positions, which were also shared by other Caribbean delegations.

The conference was scheduled to meet in formal sessions from 31 August to 7 September 2001, with a maximum of three sessions per day (10:00 a.m.–1:00 p.m.; 3:00–6:00 p.m.; 6:00–9:00 p.m.) in plenary, with parallel meetings of the two working groups for the declaration and programme of action respectively. It met in plenary on the first day to adopt the agenda and to elect the officers of the meeting. Thereafter, the plenary was used to hear statements delivered by heads of state, ministers, heads of delegation, representatives of national human rights institutions, and nongovernmental organizations. The meeting reconvened as a whole in plenary on the final day to adopt the Durban declaration and programme of action.[1]

The opening ceremony began with a cultural presentation, followed by introductory statements by the UN secretary general, Kofi Annan; the UN high commissioner for human rights, Mary Robinson; the president of South Africa, Thabo Mbeki; the president of the conference, Dr Dlamini Zuma; as well as the president of the General Assembly, Han Seung-soo.

Many of these statements addressed the need to look at the past and its connection to the present, to recognize historic injustices, to eradicate the legacies of slavery, the slave trade, and colonialism, and encouraged conference participants to unite to repair this damage. They also called for a cautious approach to the issue of reparations by suggesting that many of these injustices are of a remote historical nature and not easily amenable to acceptable recuperative strategies. These opening comments had a dampening effect on many delegates, particularly those who expected greater support for reparations. A further effect of these statements was the creation of an atmosphere at the outset that signalled the immense task ahead in achieving consensus.

The preparatory process in Geneva had been unable to agree on an agenda for the meeting and, as a result, Durban began with a draft agenda. Among the themes of the conference, the fourth theme (reparations) remained in brackets. Conference officials had considered this the day before the conference started and had reached no consensus. At the opening session, conference participants were thus faced with three options for the adoption of the agenda:

1. Adopt the agenda, without brackets, immediately. An immediate vote would have polarized the conference along north-south lines from its beginning. This was not desirable, as it would have set a divisive tone.
2. Adopt the agenda with reparations, including a footnote stating the understanding of this term for delegations. This option was not favoured, as it would involve extensive discussion that could have delayed the substantive start of the negotiations.
3. Use Article 17c of the Rules of Procedure and employ a provisional agenda until the end of the meeting. This option had not been ruled out, but it was felt that not to have an agenda from the beginning of the process would be as undesirable as voting and would postpone a discussion that would happen inevitably at the end of the conference.

Regional groups put forward their positions as follows:

• The West – made up of Canada, Japan, Australia, New Zealand, other European countries not within the European Union, and the European Union groups – stated that their position had not changed and that the adoption of the agenda with reparations could prejudice the outcome of discussions because the themes discussed would structure the final documents. On the other hand, not including reparations would not necessarily limit the discussion. Their preference was to invoke the Rules of Procedure Article 17c and utilize a provisional agenda.
• Asia wanted to adopt the agenda with reparations without brackets.
• Africa voted to adopt the agenda with reparations without brackets.

- Eastern Europe did not express an opinion but spoke of the need to be flexible.
- The Caribbean called for a full discussion of historical injustices in modernity within the context of reparations.

The president of the conference, Dlamini Zuma, South Africa's foreign affairs minister, after lengthy consultations with the European Union and the Western group, proposed a solution. The agenda was adopted with the explanatory footnote: "the use of 'compensatory' does not prejudice the outcome of deliberations". Reparations, then, could be discussed at the conference, but nothing decided would be binding on any country.

The slave-trading, slave-owning countries that had committed the crimes against humanity in empire-building won the first day at Durban. They had exercised considerable political power to marginalize the reparations movement by threatening to boycott the conference. The United States had already declared non-participation in objection to the word "reparation" appearing on the draft agenda. The European Union and "Western" countries threatened to remove themselves for the same reason. Colin Powell, the US secretary of state, and Condoleezza Rice, national security advisor, both African Americans, were bullish about the matter, stating that the world must not tell the United States how to handle its racial past and present.[2]

The European countries came to Durban united and mobilized to derail the reparations issue while maintaining support for the other items at the conference, such as the Israel-Palestine conflict. Confident in their ability to mould the conference to meet their needs, the European Union and the West bluntly issued their ultimatum: remove "reparations" from the agenda or we will remove ourselves from the conference. To save the gathering, South Africa, as host, complied, hence the compromise. Reparations would stay on the adopted agenda, but "bracketed", suggesting the non-binding status of discussions and decisions.

Pan-African Reparation: The Abuja Summit

There had been a long period of pan-African preparations for the Durban WCAR as far as the reparations issue was concerned. Critical in this regard was the First Pan-African Congress on Reparations, held in Abuja, Nigeria, *[handwritten: 1991]*   *[handwritten: Joke!]*

27 to 29 April 1993. Chief Moshood Abiola, the wealthy Nigerian businessman and ardent pan-Africanist, was the principal driving force of the congress.[3]

A seasoned campaigner of reparations, Chief Abiola used his office as chair of the Eminent Persons Group on Reparations for Africa and Africans in the Diaspora, which had been set up by the Organization of African Unity in June *[handwritten: Joke!]* 1991 to promote and finance the summit. Dudley Thompson, Jamaican high commissioner to Nigeria and stalwart of pan-Africanism, worked with the chief as rapporteur of the group.[4]

Lord Anthony Gifford, respected British jurist and campaigner for civil rights and reparations, on the invitation of Ambassador Thompson, prepared a legal submission at the conference on why Britain should pay reparations for the crimes of slave trading and slavery. Gifford reinforced the argument of Abiola with sound legal reasoning. In 1992, the chief had stated, "While we demand reparations in order to enforce justice, to feed the poor, to teach the illiterate and to house the homeless, this crusade is also important because only reparations can heal our land, comfort our souls, and restore our self-respect". Gifford was in support of this stance, as were Thompson and other leaders of the movement.[5]

Thompson was the principal Caribbean spokesman for the global reparations movement. In Britain, Bernie Grant, member of Parliament for Tottenham in North London, had been its primary advocate. As a prominent West Indian in the House of Commons, Grant's credentials in the struggle for justice for black people were well established. He was a founding member of the African Reparations Movement in Britain, an organization that predated the 1991 Committee on Reparations formed in Jamaica by George Nelson.

Abiola's group of Eminent Persons included two distinguished African scholars: Ali Mazrui of Kenya and Ade Ajayi of Nigeria. It also included Dr M'Bow, former director of UNESCO, singer Miriam Makeba and Graça Machel. The summit heard from these scholars and activists, but the rallying call came with the intervention by Lord Gifford, whose paper titled "The Legal Basis of the Claim for Reparations" held the attention of the conference. It was a well-researched document that made important statements on reparations based on international law:

1. The enslavement and trafficking of Africans was a crime against humanity.
2. International law recognizes that those who commit crimes against humanity must make reparations.

3. The reparations claim would be brought on behalf of all Africans, in Africa and the diaspora, who suffer the consequences of the crime, through the agency of an appropriate representative.
4. There is no legal barrier to prevent those who suffer the consequences of crimes against humanity from claiming reparations, even though the crimes were committed against their ancestors.
5. The claim would be brought against the governments of those countries which promoted and were enriched by the African slave trade and the institution of slavery.
6. The claim, if not settled by agreement, would be determined by a special international tribunal recognized by all parties.[6]

Although the president of Nigeria, General Ibrahim Badamasi Babangida, did not attend, he sent a clear and precise message to the conference setting out Nigeria's position on the reparations issue. He stated,

> The reparations movement seeks to preserve and forward the gains of these earlier struggles, to make Africa progress into the next century and beyond, and to make our continent and its scattered people one and whole again. Reparations combine morality with logic and historical necessity by claiming the right of the injured to compensation. If history demonstrates that Africans have been injured by slavery and colonialism, and if morality demands that injury be compensated, then the logic of the reparations movement is established alongside its morality.[7]

Chief Abiola committed to having reparations placed on the UN agenda. "It is justice we demand," he said, "and by the Grace of God, it is justice we will get." The leaders of Senegal supported the claims of the conference, as did the secretary general of the Organization of African States, Salim Ahmed Salim of Tanzania. Ambassador Thompson summed up the conference with the statement that the issue of reparations was "not a plea for charity" but that it rests "on a basic philosophy as old as justice itself".[8]

Despite its being rooted in a call for racial harmony, justice and reconciliation for a better future, the reparations dialogue at Abuja generated hostility in the capitals of Europe. Chief Abiola was targeted as "hostile to the West" even though he was a successful corporate millionaire who had worked closely with Western financial institutions. Lord Gifford summed up British hostility to the summit as follows: "I believe that what disturbs the British profoundly about the concept of reparations is that it changes the whole basis of the dialogue between Black and White, North and South, Europeans and Africans. Instead of African pleas for aid to be dispensed by a benevolent and kindly Europe, the Abuja conference demanded justice from a Europe which had committed crimes." British imperial history, Gifford continued, has

> often been characterized by hypocritical assertions of moral superiority by the colo-
> nizers. They went into Africa on a "civilising mission" and committed barbarities.
> They brought "Christian Values" to the Caribbean and allowed slaves to be whipped
> and worked to death. They portrayed emancipation in 1838 as a gift from Britannia
> to grateful slaves, forgetting that it was only through slave rebellions in the Caribbean
> and popular demonstrations in Britain that the ending of slavery was finally con-
> ceded by a ruling class which had resisted the demands for it during the previous
> forty years. They paid £20 million in compensation to the slave owners (roughly
> 40% of Britain's national budget at the time), and not a penny to the slaves.[9]

Lord Gifford's analysis served as a further launching pad for his summary of the effectiveness of the summit. The Abuja declaration, he said, passed at the end of the conference, challenged and rejected British policy thinking and the history of emancipation. It declared that the damage sustained by African peoples was "not a thing of the past, but is painfully manifested in the damaged lives of contemporary Africans everywhere". The conference, he said, urged "those countries which were enriched by slavery to give total relief from foreign debt. It called for a permanent African seat on the Security Council of the United Nations. It emphasized that what matters is not the guilt but the *responsibility* of those states and nations whose economic evolution once depended on slave labour and colonialism."[10] It called for the return to Africa of stolen artefacts and traditional treasures. It recommended the establishment of national reparations committees in Africa and the diaspora. Finally, it called upon the international community "to recognize that there is a unique and unprecedented moral debt owed to the African peoples that has yet to be paid – the debt of compensation to the Africans as the most humiliated and exploited people of the last four hundred years".

Chief Abiola was unpopular in Western political circles for bringing the reparations movement onto the global stage. In June 1993, the chief won the Nigerian presidential elections. President Babangida agreed to step down. The army, led by General Sani Abacha, declared military rule. In June 1994, Abiola was arrested and placed in military confinement until he died in prison in

June 1998. Lord Gifford examined the death of Chief Abiola and concluded, "It seemed so unnecessary and wrong. I suspected, and still suspect, that a part was played by Britain and the United States, between them the biggest outside influences on Nigeria. The coming to power of Chief Abiola was threatening to them, not because of anything in his economic or social programmes, but because of his dominant and determined role in the movement for reparations."[12]

The demand for justice, Gifford argued, which the chief had proclaimed from the podium at Abuja would have vibrated ominously through the Foreign and Commonwealth Office and the State Department. Had they persuaded General Babangida, in spite of his enthusiastic message to the conference, that Chief Abiola would not be an acceptable president of Nigeria? It would be another eight years before the issue of reparations would be mentioned at an international conference in Africa. If the motive for the removal of Chief Abiola had been to set back the cause of reparations, those who planned it had succeeded, at least for a limited time.[13]

Gorée Initiative

In June 2001, several African scholars, civil society groups, and women and youth organizations tried to prepare for the UN conference in Durban and met at Gorée Island in Senegal. The meeting was coordinated by the Inter-African Union for Human Rights. The conference noted that the

> reemerging contemporary forms of racism, racial discrimination, xenophobia and related intolerance, continue to be based on the ideology of racial and ethnic hierarchy. The principal foundation of slavery, the Slave Trade and colonialism are essentially based on supremacist claims which automatically incite the exploitation of man by man. These crimes have played a major role in consolidating racial discrimination against the African peoples and their descendants in the continent and in the Diaspora in the Americas, Europe and the Caribbean. African-Americans are prime victims of marginalization and discriminatory practice particularly by law enforcement agents and even by the penal systems.[14]

To legitimize their hegemony, the northern superpowers that support transnational corporations – the principal beneficiaries of globalization – pretended to be engaged in a process of self-criticism and to accept the principles of reparation for the victims of genocide and crimes for which they recognize responsibility. The question was asked: Does the recent recognition by the French parliament of the slave trade and the enslavement of Africans as crimes against humanity indicate a new orientation in this regard? By way of background to any possible answer, the conference also stressed that "the international community should recognize that the Slave Trade and the enslavement of Africans as well as colonialism constitute crimes against humanity and that their continuing devastating effects on the African continent are aggravated by globalization. The Slave Codes as well as present international law encourage the massive poverty that marks the African continent in the same way in which the African slaves captured, tied and forced to migrate to Europe and the Americas were marked with iron rods."[15]

Central to the conference was the presentation of a revised version of Lord Gifford's 1993 Abuja paper, "The Legal Basis for the African Claims of Reparations for the Slave Trade". Presented by Abdelbagi G. Jibril, the revised paper tackled two significant arguments presented by critics of reparations, namely, that African people were willing participants in the slave trade and that reparations is an appeal to the "conscience of the white world".[16]

The revised script noted that the argument presented to suggest that Africans themselves have participated in and benefited from the slave trade and consequently enslavement of their kin and cousins could not stand any careful scrutiny or fair judgement. Africans have always resisted their enslavement by Europeans and through all means at their disposal. It stated,

> As a matter of fact, throughout history and in all nations there have been those individuals who, for different reasons, acted against the interest of their communities. In this modern age such individuals are referred to in derogatory terms such as traitors, spies or collaborators with the enemy. If we use a rational categorization method, it will become all too graphic that those African chieftains who were accused of selling their own people to Western slave raiders do not fit under any one of these categories.[17]

In the first place, Gifford stated, the accused chieftains were forced to betray their own kin by several factors that were beyond their control. Ironically, he said "the provision of modern weapons to rival tribes and the high manipulation by slave raiders left the accused poor African chieftains in a critical position. They were practically told 'attack and enslave your neighbours or you will be attacked and enslaved'. It was also documented that on many occasions the collaborating African chieftains themselves together with their subjects were also surrounded and enslaved by the same slave raiders that cooperated with them in other raids."[18]

In respect of reparations as justice, the conference stressed the role of public activism as a necessary strategy to bring an end to illegal and immoral practices. Justice cannot wait on the inner logic and timelines of an establishment's sense of its readiness. It requires advocacy, public outrage and organized commitment. The paper also stated in this regard,

> if the reparation claim is to be merely an appeal to the conscience of the White world, it would be misconceived. For while there have been many committed individuals and movements of solidarity in the White world, its political and economic power centers have evidenced a ruthless lack of conscience when it comes to Blacks and African peoples. Yet progress has been made when the powers that rule in the White world have been compelled to recognize that the fight of non-White peoples is founded in justice. It is that form of legal redress, which may not have existed before, that has been devised.[19]

The Gorée conference went a long way towards reviving the African reparations movement as envisioned by Chief Abiola. It was a civil society gathering, outside of the specific remit of governments that remained tied to the luring of Western direct investment as a prize for turning against the policy of addressing historical crimes and injustices. The paper concludes where the Durban dialogue opened: showing that the weaknesses of West African states in respect of playing a supportive role on reparations reflect the history with which political leaders are familiar – that the "West" seeks to dispose of those who challenge their view of history by means of media demonization and, finally death. The destruction of Chief Abiola was no different fundamentally from that of other chiefs who had stood against the European slave trade centuries earlier. He died at the hands of collaborators, as did many of his predecessors.

At Gorée, then, progress was made. African civil society stood up and called upon the UN gathering at Durban to engage positively the call for reparations. The conference issued a release that became known at Durban as the Gorée Initiative. It stated,

> The co-sponsors of the Gorée Initiative are convinced that the African just demand for reparation for the grave and massive crimes committed against the continent

should solemnly be expressed and heeded in a historical moment of recognition by all those who participated in it. To escape responsibility will represent a loss of this unique opportunity that should be seized to put into practice – the human rights concepts advocated by the Western nations – and come out with concrete results that will meet the five-centuries-old aspirations of the African people for justice.[20]

Furthermore,

the principle of just and fair reparation for the Slave Trade and enslavement of Africans is the usual result of the recognition of this crime. In this specific case, it is a crime against humanity which is an imprescriptible crime. The impunity that surrounds this issue has substantially victimized and tormented Africa and it is time to put an end to this victimization. Reparation should not be considered as a sanction, but rather as a step forward in reconciling the human family.[21]

Delegates of Caribbean governments and African civil society groups arrived in Durban with deep commitment to the advancement of the reparations movement. It was anticipated that there would be splits in the positions of African governments. This had been the history.

Some African governments were expected to stand on principle, others to compromise their civil society representatives, and some to weaken the solidarity that had brought the pan-African movement to Durban. The lessons of Chief Abiola's death were expected to be played out. The reparations issue, then, was situated at the heart of the conference. It represented the most profound epistemological opportunity at the outset of the twenty-first century: Who would own and possess intellectual sovereignty over the interpretation of the past.

The truth was told. At the outset, the Caribbean group held the centre. In engaging the West and the European Union, it represented the reparations movement in a fashion consistent with the spirit of Abuja. Ambassador Thompson was there to give oversight and guidance to this continuity. It was a moment of mentoring at its best. The conference enabled a global opportunity for European states to rethink the integrity of their organized history as conceived by their "spin-doctors" from the legal, historical and philosophical fraternities.

Western myths were identified and exploded. But the European Union group especially held on to them, depreciated assets though they were. Both sides of the reparation discourse drew strength from opening remarks by Kofi Annan, secretary general of the United Nations. As a master diplomat, Annan knew how to walk between the raindrops. His remarks encouraged the reparations movement in its view that colonial slavery was a crime against humanity. He also comforted the West and the European Union in equal measure by suggesting the notions of remoteness of the crimes and the problems associated with contemporary culpability.

In effect, Annan released the trap door that enabled those who resisted reparations to escape, temporarily, the pressure of that moment. He recognized the moral correctness of the principle of reparations but queried its relevance to postmodern politics. There was no one better to pour water on the simmering coals. He did not serve the reparations movement. He stated, "Sometimes these problems [extreme human rights abuses] are in part the legacies of terrible wrongs done in the past – such as the exploitation and extermination of indigenous peoples by colonial powers, or the treatment of millions of human beings as mere merchandise to be transported and disposed of by other human beings for commercial gain. The further those events recede into the past, the harder it becomes to trace lines of accountability."[22] He was aware, however, of the incompletion and limitation of this argument and moved to the moment when the terrible truth had to be spoken:

> Yet the effects remain. The pain and anger are still felt. The dead through their descendants cry out for justice. Tracing a connection with past crimes may not always be the most constructive way to redress past inequalities, in material terms. . . . Some historical wrongs are traceable to individuals who are still alive, or corporations that are still in business. They must expect to be held to account. The societies they have wronged may forgive them, as part of the process of reconciliation, but they cannot demand forgiveness, as a right . . . a special responsibility falls on political leaders, who have accepted the task of representing a whole society. They are accountable to their fellow citizens, but also – in a sense – accountable for them, and for the actions of their predecessors.[23]

It was not difficult to gauge the impact of Annan's anti-reparations posture on the conference. It was immediate. It was equally striking how his ideas so closely resembled those expressed in Washington.

The United States had declared its hand in an official release on 4 May 2001. It stated,

Countries (and some individuals) that believe the primary issue for the Conference is some form of International Compensatory scheme for the 17th to 19th century slave trade will find no support from us. . . . We agree that slavery and the slave trade of the distant past must be acknowledged, discussed, learned from and condemned . . . however, we simply do not believe that it is appropriate to address this history, and its many vast aspects, through such measures as international compensatory measures. . . . We are not willing to agree to anything that suggests present-day liability on the part of one state to another for that historical situation.[24]

Annan's framework, then, overlapped with the position that the United States, the West and the European Union endorsed.

The anti-reparation wishes of Washington were received clearly in the capitals of Europe. The message was refined and its tone adjusted. But it was the same. It set out notions such as the historical remoteness, the unaccountability of current generations for the past, and the impracticability of any moral and material redress linked to slavery as a crime against humanity. This posture and the policy guideline represented an assertion of political power within a diplomatic context. It lacked accuracy within the context of history and law and was designed to intimidate rather than advocate.

With the United States setting preconference tones, and withdrawing within days of the official opening, Durban was thrown into difficulty. With the intergovernmental dialogue in crisis, the global nongovernmental organization (NGO) movement stepped up and provided alternative leadership. Human Rights Watch, for example, argued that slavery, the slave trade and genocide – the most severe forms of racism associated with the European colonial project, as well as subsequent racist practices of segregation and apartheid – were human rights violations of a criminal nature that should be settled by way of an effective reparations strategy.

The NGO movement rejected the notion of the historical remoteness of slavery. It argued, furthermore, that the descendants of enslaved victims of such human rights violations should be able to pursue claims of reparations, despite the fact that building such claims on behalf of descendants is very difficult and runs the risk of rejection by present-day judicial principles.

In Durban, the West and the European Union blocs, then, prompted by the United States, showed no willingness at any time to discuss reparation as a viable approach to twenty-first-century global reconciliation. At the heart of their strategy was avoidance and refusal to accept the validity of historical data. The categorization of history as "political spin" was the order of the day. For example, delegates insisted that slavery and slave trading were not crimes against humanity when they were committed, and made frequent reference to the "legal" status of these activities. That European parliaments "legalized" black enslavement against African desire seemed irrelevant.

Critically, tremendous pressure was brought to bear on some African and Asian states when the West and the European Union argued that, were such or similar slavery practices to occur today, they would undoubtedly be considered crimes against humanity and prosecuted under international law, and the victims entitled to reparations. In response, Caribbean delegates, in the vanguard of reparations for the descendants of the enslaved, drew attention to the contemporary effects of slavery as evidenced in the residual economic, social and psychological deprivation of black people. In response to this argument there was silence.

The Gorée Initiative had called for the establishment of an International Compensation Scheme for the victims of the slave trade and a Development Reparation Fund to provide resources for poverty alleviation strategies in countries affected by colonialism. The initiative stated further that the modalities of such reparation and compensation should be defined by the WCAR in a practical and result-oriented manner. As well, such reparation should be in the form of enhanced policies, programmes and measures, to be adopted by states and private companies which benefit materially from these crimes, in order to rectify, through affirmative action, the economic, cultural and political life in Africa and its diasporas.

The European Union and Western blocs presented their own draft papers on the historical past that did not mention the word "reparation", affirming their position adopted in the draft agenda. Basically, they were not prepared to accept responsibility for the crimes of slavery and other wrongs of colonialism. The plenary stage, then, was set for interventions on the subject by heads of governments.

President Mbeki of South Africa, the conference host, was first to outline a perspective which was read by most delegates as part of an attempt to promote the language and politics of compromise required to save the deliberations from implosion. He condemned slavery, genocide and apartheid, but stopped short of describing them as crimes against humanity subject to an explicit apology and reparation settlement. National concern to consolidate his government's relations with the West and European Union blocs, and policy articulations that conceived post-apartheid economic development in terms of increased Western direct foreign investment, were the compelling contexts that shaped his comments.

Next to speak was President Obasanjo of Nigeria, who questioned the relevance of reparation discussions altogether. Like South Africa, the Nigerian state was understood as reading the reparation text with eyes focused keenly on domestic and foreign policy issues. In addition to experiencing serious financial tensions with the multilateral financial institutions, Nigeria faced the additional difficulty of having to negotiate interethnic tensions in some instances as part of the politics of naming and shaming local collaborators with the Europeans in the slave trade.

A critical moment was reached with the presentation of President Wade of Senegal. He spoke against the background of strong civil-society support for reparation in his country, as indicated during both the African ministers' meeting and the Gorée summit. President Wade offered an insightful account of the evolution of pan-African dialogue but endorsed the caution on reparations expressed by presidents Mbeki and Obasanjo. But the sting in the tail, however, came with his announcement of the New African Initiative as a counter-policy to the Gorée Initiative.

Senegal, then, was split – nation versus state – as the president had opposed the Gorée Declaration, and offered an alternative framework. The New African Initiative, the president stated, would begin with the objective in mind of sponsoring an African renaissance as an expression of a mature, self-critical mentality, driven by the need to sponsor development as an indigenous process of community self-help and responsibility. The attempt to suggest that an African renaissance was hostile to reparations policy attracted contempt at the plenary, with shouts of "shame" from the audience.

The concepts and vocabulary used by President Wade offended many. Essentially the implication was that sponsorship of the New African Initiative was a break with "history" and the hegemonic development discourse of the West. He was interpreted as proposing an intellectual strategy to sideline the reparation paradigm and to promote instead the World Bank's argument that Africans should take greater responsibility for the future, beginning with a commitment to "good" governance and self-reliance.

The "black hole" thesis propagated in multilateral financial institutions circles – that the West has poured billions of aid dollars into postcolonial Africa with little identifiable result, other than the unethical and illegal enrichment of the elite – permeated the conference. The Nigerian and Senegalese leaders lacked the intellectual and moral force to weaken the evidence which showed that underdevelopment in Africa had to do with how greater sums were extracted from Africa by the West and the European Union during the five hundred years that encompassed the transatlantic slave trade and direct colonialism.

The New African Initiative, then, was promoted by South Africa, Senegal and Nigeria as an alternative argument in which Africa, the European Union and the West blocs could find cohesion and consensus. Most Caribbean and African delegates, while supportive of African self-help strategies, considered the New African Initiative as presented by President Wade to be opportunistic and subversive of the pan-African movement. There were, therefore, no surprises that Britain and the full European Union and West blocs embraced it. They declared their full support for its implementation, while Caribbean delegates experienced the cold discomfiture of the rejected.

President Wade perceived the disturbance in Caribbean minds and apologized that the New African Initiative did not include the diaspora in its conceptual planning and strategic objectives. He stated that while the idea of reparations was no longer a central concern of African governments, he understood why it was still relevant to Africans in the diaspora and, in this context, offered token support.

At this stage, what seemed clearer than ever was the depth of division between citizens (the nation) and the state in Africa. In particular, NGOs in West Africa were fully supportive of the call for reparations and provided much of the vanguard leadership for the campaign. Community and state, in the cases of Nigeria and Senegal, were clearly opposed on the subject, suggesting that, for the future, the bridge between the continent and its diaspora over which the reparation lobby should travel is that of civil society solidarity.

This realization focused and energized the Caribbean group. African Americans, well represented in the NGO forum, had no direct voice in the intergovernmental plenary. As a result, the Caribbean group considered it necessary to speak to the full "American" context of the diaspora experience, and was encouraged to hold the line on the reparation issue by the African NGO movement.

President Castro, the only head of government from the Caribbean, was first to speak from the region and set the tone and texture for a coherent diasporic response. He made the following statement: "Cuba speaks of reparations, and supports the idea as an unavoidable moral duty to the victims of racism, based on a major precedent, that is, the indemnification being paid to the descendants of the Hebrew people who in the very heart of Europe suffered the brutal and loathsome racist holocaust. However, it is not with the intent to undertake an impossible search for the direct descendants of the specific countries of the victims of actions which occurred throughout centuries."[25] Furthermore, he argued, "the irrefutable truth is that tens of millions of Africans were captured, sold like a commodity and sent beyond the Atlantic to work in slavery while seventy million indigenous people in that hemisphere perished as a result of the European conquest and colonization".[26] This contribution served to restore the relevance of the historical narrative in which reparation is conceptualized as a moral and legal project.

Importantly, the Caribbean group effectively rejected the thesis of the "historical remoteness" of slavery, and provided empirical validation for any reparations case that would seek to assure justice for all victims of crimes against humanity. In this regard, an important intervention from the Caribbean group was the call upon the European Union and West delegates to acknowledge the truth about the judicial and philosophical history of slavery in Western Europe.

The end result of these interventions was that a dialogue on reparation was forged eventually, albeit with acrimony, using language that the European Union–West alliance considered acceptable. British delegates especially feared that accepting the slave system as a crime against humanity could lead to a flood of reparation litigation. It seemed they imagined millions of black people lining up to take such legal action against their state, monarchy and commercial institutions, as well as families and individuals that were enriched by slavery. The Caribbean group called for a frank discussion of these fears with the British while urging that reparations should be accepted as a critical first step in the politics of truth and reconciliation.

The British, in particular, responded by refusing to accept that these actions were crimes against humanity at the time they were practised and argued that national and colonial law ensured their legality. At the same time they acknowledged that international law explicitly states that the use of national law to attempt validation of crimes against humanity provides no protection for the abuser. Critically, they recognized that once a human rights violation is adjudged a crime against humanity, the protective cover of the statute of limitation is removed and the reparation process kicks in as a formal procedure.

The European Union–West alliance, sensitive to contradictions and inconsistencies in their argument, prepared to rally around the idea of offering a strong "statement of regret" that condemned the tragedies inherent in the slave system. Condemnation, they were told by the Caribbean delegates, does not mean acknowledgement and acceptance of responsibility. In addition, the alliance proposed compensatory actions by way of development aid within parameters set out by the World Bank. They were not willing to accept that slavery and slave trading were a "crime against humanity" concept or to issue an explicit "apology". No consensus, then, could be reached on any of the items relevant to reparation.

On the morning of Thursday, 6 September, a full week after the formal opening, the *Conference News Daily* carried the headline "Slavery Issue: A World Divided". The subtitle to the feature story was more significant in terms of its prophecy: "Europeans and Africans still attempt to come to consensus on reparations." By the afternoon of that day, the African bloc had issued a statement that signalled its retreat to a place where the European Union and West blocs were awaiting it.[27]

The Caribbean group considered this development a forecast of an understanding forged between the African Group and the European Union–West alliance. Within the hour, it had received intelligence confirming this. A press conference was convened by the Caribbean group the following day, Friday, 7 September, reaffirming support for the reparation case. The press release called upon countries that practised and benefited from the slave system to acknowledge slavery as a crime against humanity and take responsibility for repairing the damage done to victims and their descendants.

Positions on reparations were already hardened. Acrimony, expressed in silence in some quarters and rage in others, informed the attitudes of the West and European Union delegates. African and Caribbean delegates, driving the historical and intellectual aspects of the discourse, seemed professorial in style and manner. Zimbabwe noted that while they were insistent on the need for an apology, they regarded compensation as a further affront to Africans. Senegal and Nigeria called for an apology but would only support reparations for people of African descent in the diaspora. Cuba supported reparations and urged the need to address, in addition to the legacy of slavery and the slave trade, the plight of the indigenous people of the Caribbean. Haiti supported reparations.

Pakistan recommended that the discussion of remedies and restitution be continued after the conference. They suggested the establishment of an Eminent Persons Group to continue consideration of this important issue. Jamaica spoke of the need for an apology and the recognition of slavery and the transatlantic slave trade as crimes against humanity. It also called for the payment of reparations. Barbados made its statement in the aftermath of the positions adopted by Nigeria and Senegal on reparations. This statement sought to strengthen the reparations voice by restoring prominence to issues relating to the past.

The final plenary session was nothing short of disorderly, chaotic and contentious. Delegations were prevented from making their reservations orally due to lack of time and interpretation facilities and were encouraged to submit them in writing. As such, it was difficult to know which countries made reservations on what part of the text. The Kenyan ambassador made a final statement in support of reparations that drew applause and a standing ovation. She later remarked that she had done this for Caribbean delegates who had good reason to feel let down by the outcome of negotiations among the West, the European Union and the African group.

It was clear, then, that the European Union, the West and the African group had effectively agreed to bury the reparations matter, leaving the Caribbean group feeling embattled – a sentiment shared by the African NGO movement and the African American observers present. Kofi Annan had set the tone for this outcome. The Americans had called the tune. The European Union, the West and the West Africans had danced.

The dagger in the final resolution came with the insertion of the word "should": slave trading and slavery "should" have been crimes against humanity. The African delegates agreed that it was *not* a crime at the time. They were cowed by the false notion that the involvement of some chiefs as "spies", "traitors" and "collaborators" constituted African involvement – despite the evidence presented that most of the African leaders and the majority of people resisted the trade and did their best to demonstrate that in the face of overwhelming European military power. The final declarations read as follows:

1. We acknowledge that slavery and the slave trade, including the transatlantic slave trade, were appalling tragedies in the history of humanity not only because of their abhorrent barbarism but also in terms of their magnitude, organized nature and especially their negation of the essence of the victims and further acknowledge that slavery and the slave trade are crimes against humanity and *should* always have been so.
2. The World Conference acknowledges and profoundly regrets the massive human suffering and the tragic plight of millions of men, women and children caused by slavery, transatlantic slave trade, apartheid, colonialism and genocide, and calls upon states concerned to honour the memory of the victims of past tragedies, and affirms that wherever and whenever these occurred they must be condemned and their reoccurrence prevented.
3. The World Conference further notes that some states have taken the initiative to apologize and have paid reparation, where appropriate, for grave and massive violations committed.
4. The World Conference further notes that some have taken the initiative of regretting or expressing remorse or presenting apologies, and calls on all those who have not yet contributed to restoring the dignity of the victims to find appropriate ways to do so and, to this end, we appreciate those countries that have done so.[28]

The Caribbean group stood against these declarations. It did not endorse them, as they failed to recognize slavery and slave trading as crimes against humanity at the time they were practised. The African–European Union–West alliance was rejected and formal rejections were entered into the record. By issuing an official reservation in respect of the agreement reached by the African–European Union–West group, the Durban conference did not conclude with a consensus on reparations.

Opposition to the word "should" in the final declaration was considered by the Caribbean group as critical in order to protect the future official path of the reparations movement. Reparations, then, was not set aside despite the final declarations of the conference that sought to replace it with a notion of developmental assistance consistent with the African–European Union–West Alliance. They refused to accept that the slave trade and the slave system were crimes against humanity, but the Caribbean group, and the African NGO movement, rescued the moral and political centre of Durban with its official reservation.

A statement by Geraldine Fraser-Moleketi, South Africa's minister for public administration, served as backdrop to concepts that found consensus in the final plenary. On the penultimate day of the conference she told the media, "We seek reparations as a pledge of intention, as a remedial measure, as a pledge of a developmental nature. It is important for our relationship with the developed world. We are talking of a partnership, not simply looking for handouts."[29]

There was no evidence to suggest that the United Nations, given the wording of the declaration and programme of action, intended to enable the Human Rights Commission to establish a special committee to report on reparations, as had been called for throughout the conference. Defeated but not dead, reparations remained alive as a priority issue on the international agenda. It is likely to stay there until resolved in a manner satisfactory to those populations still feeling the adverse effects of the European colonial project.

A literal reading of documents in which declarations and programmes of action are set out may suggest that reparation discourse, as opposed to compensation approaches, died at Durban, as far as the United Nations is concerned. To the extent that there was any post-Durban hope, it can be found in the Caribbean's reservation and rejection of the word "should" that sought to keep the discourse and global movement alive.

Chapter 14

British Policy

No Apology, No Reparations

William Pitt, when he was Prime Minister, said that 80 per cent of British overseas income was derived from our West Indian colonies.

—*William Hague, Member of Parliament, Debate on the Bicentenary of the Abolition of the Slave Trade, House of Commons, 20 March 2007*

TWO HUNDRED YEARS SEPARATED prime minister of Britain Tony Blair and the primary anti-slavery leader of Parliament, Thomas Buxton. But they were miles apart in their view of justice for black people. Between 2001 and 2006, Blair was blunt in his dismissal of black reparations. Buxton in the 1820s was equally firm that the enslaved blacks, rather than their enslavers, should have received reparations at emancipation. The system of slavery, Buxton insisted, was a national crime committed against Africans. Morality and legal right, he thought, dictated that they should be compensated. With these views he outraged Parliament on the eve of emancipation to the same degree that Blair has enraged the reparations movement.

The enslaved of the Caribbean, powerless to press their claim for financial compensation, could not help Buxton. Neither could Buxton help them with their desire for reparatory justice. The British Parliament, densely populated with slaveholders and other beneficiaries of slave investments, did not take Buxton's suggestion seriously. His idea died as soon as the words "slave compensation" were uttered. Parliament's position in 1834 was that blacks were property, non-humans, hence the compensation to slave owners of £20 million, paid out to meet 45,000 separate requests. The amount was "not far short of the annual cost of maintaining the army, the navy and, indeed, of running the entire country". Parliament's position in 2007 was that blacks should receive no apology and that their descendants should not receive any compensation.[1]

In the two hundred years between Buxton's call and Blair's refusal, there had been no political softening of the British parliamentary position, even though many blacks, descendants of the enslaved, came to occupy both Houses of Parliament as elected and appointed members. Blair's government maintained the "anti-slave" line, principally because British blacks have been unable, as citizens and as representatives of governments, to challenge this lineage of power and racial licence. As a result, the 1834 antipathy to the enslaved continues to be echoed in the British Parliament that continues to reject the idea of compensation for slavery. Buxton stands tall today as an historic figure for human justice, while Blair paled as a polar opposite when the matter came before his government in 2007.

Blair directed his Durban delegates to adopt a hard-line anti-reparations position. They arrived, led by Baroness Amos, an astute black politician and diplomat, to carry the policy position. As a result, the British delegation was inflexible on the issue of historical crimes and belligerent on reparations. Amos was adamant that slavery and slave trading were not crimes because the British Parliament, and its colonial machinery, had made them legal. Despite two hundred years of black resistance and rebellion, she insisted that the slave system was legal because the British Parliament deemed it to be so. Aware that national law does not legalize crimes against humanity, she did not retreat in the face of overwhelming historical arguments.

Historical truth counted for little. Amos's army of officials was silent when asked to put themselves in the position of the two million Africans that the British warehoused in West African forts and crammed into slave ships. They appeared stone-faced when asked to imagine themselves captives on the *Zong* when Captain Collingwood prepared to throw them to the sharks. It was all legal, the British argued, and the baroness defended it.

When these and similar absurdities wore thin on the consciousness of the meeting, the British backed up and charged with the argument that even if the slave system was a crime against humanity, it was all a very long time ago and therefore too remote for any recuperative legal strategy. Slavery, the British delegates implied, was a hiccup of history.

The "it was a long time ago" argument seemed strange, if not bizarre, within the context of British politics built so firmly on a celebrated historical sensibility. It is a political culture that speaks of the past in the present – the living legacy of Britannia and similar imaginings. Slavery and slave trading, all 250 years of it, were a core part of this celebrated past whose global legacies have had considerable influence on contemporary British policy.

The decades between Buxton and Blair seemed like a day in the life of the British state. Slavery was replaced in 1838 with a revised system of white supremacy that provided the blueprint for twentieth-century "apartheid" models. Blacks in the Caribbean were disenfranchised by emancipation, corralled on plantations and driven to the periphery of society. Trapped in the sustained "estate culture", and generally excluded from electoral participation for another century, they were kept as neo-slaves by their former slave owners. The British government, then, replaced slavery with apartheid, and declared its view that blacks should remain subordinate to whites as the model of post-slavery colonial reality.

This British vision of the African people was bred in the slavery period and served as the basis of the imperial project. It survived emancipation and has remained a living reality into the present. The 1930 centenary decade of emancipation was marked with anti-British riots. Workers demanded the end to the "slavery" mentality embedded in the authoritarian policy of British rule. In much the same way that enslaved blacks revolted across the Caribbean in the aftermath of Haitian independence in 1804, the 1930s witnessed the violent rejection of a century of British racist policy.

The massacre of Jamaican workers by the colonial state in 1865, which was backed by the British government, for demanding access to land as part of a post-slavery compensation package, spoke precisely the language of violence against blacks that had been endemic to British politics. Governor Eyre of Jamaica left a trail of black blood on the island as he enforced British land and labour policy. Even in the heat of the blood bath, he found strong support in parliamentary political circles. While sections of progressive public opinion condemned the massacre, he was celebrated by many prominent officials of the state as a hero of the British nation.

Those familiar with this history arrived at Durban with eyes and minds wide open. Britain remained adamant that no crimes had been committed against blacks, so there would be no apology and no reparations. Following the Durban denial, the bicentenary of the abolition of the British slave trade took centre stage. Again, the British state was presented with an opportunity to reflect with integrity upon its history. Instead, it chose to celebrate its role in the passing of legislation that illegalized its trade in African bodies in 1807. The message of the 1807 abolition was clear. It was time to move on. The criminal embarrassment of slave trading had outweighed the economic benefits; the immorality had outstripped the profitability. It was time to declare that the coffers are full, so close the vault.

It was no easy matter to shut down the shipping lanes. Trading in African bodies had become a culture – a social and economic way of life. British identity was shaped by the oppression of the black race within a global dynamic of imperial nation-building. Slave trading was a key component of the structure; it was not easy to give it up. The fingers of slave traders had to be pried from the iron collars that clenched the throats of Africans. They had to be convinced that neither the slavery world nor British global dominance would be threatened. The public had to be convinced that there was advantage in abolition and that benefits would accrue to all sectors of the economy and society.

As the Blair government rolled out its plans to celebrate William Wilberforce and his anti-slavery trade colleagues as heroes of British "goodness", reparations advocates prepared to foreground the call for an official apology for crimes against humanity. The prime minister, the queen and the government were called upon by persons and organizations in Britain, the Caribbean, Africa and the world at large to apologize for British slave trading and slavery. They were urged, as the nation that benefited most, to become a global example for racial atonement in order to set the racial consciousness of the world at peace.

Blair refused. He gathered the "black troops" of the Labour Party to his side. Baroness Amos, Diane Abbott, David Lammy and Lord Morris of Handsworth all lined up behind their party leader. The queen remained silent. Critics of New Labour said it was a shameful sight to see and hear descendants of enslaved blacks singing the Blair song in and out of Parliament. What was clear, however, was that the black group in the British Parliament did not support, not even moderately, the notion of reparations as reconciliation. Bernie Grant's legacy in Parliament was brushed aside by those black members who followed him.[2]

Believing his primary task was to barricade Britain behind a reparations wall, Blair positioned Deputy Prime Minister John Prescott, a man from Hull who does not view British politics through a Wilberforce window, to set the tone. Baroness Amos joined with Prescott to communicate the government's policy that slavery and slave trading were legal.[3]

There was considerable fanfare as Blair broadcast the British historic refusal. Arrangements were made for a West African video message to be streamed to the Elmina Slave Fort in Ghana. It was also relayed through parts of Britain on enormous screens. Downing Street had crafted the prime minister's statement with lawyers at hand. Blair issued another of the British "statements of regret" – an expression of "deep sorrow" – all rhetorical, political pacifiers designed to get over anniversary anger bred by denial and refusal.[4]

The "statement of regret" was consistent with the "deep sorrow" position first expressed at Durban. Then, it was issued in anger as officials believed it was extracted by delegates who had exposed the sham of the Labour politics. Blair met with President Kufuor of Ghana, a well-known ally in the anti-reparations group. Together they shaped the political reception of the "deep sorrow" statement, which was carried in full as an 850-word article in the *New Nation* newspaper. Blair had also invited groups of eminent persons to a reception at Downing Street in order to domesticate his denial that slavery was a crime against humanity.

Blair was soft-spoken while making his "deep sorrow" statement that cut through the hearts of reparations advocates. His lawyers inserted the following legal missile within the text: "It is hard to believe what would now be a crime against humanity was legal at the time." This is the political pathway down which Blair led his party, his black parliamentary posse, and the British nation. "It was legal at the time", he said, a statement that connects to postures adopted in Durban six years earlier. There, it was argued that slavery "should" have been illegal, but it was not.

Some argued that the Jewish holocaust was "legal at the time". The genocidal actions were approved by the German state. The judicial and legislative institutions of the Third Reich had allowed the mass murder of Jews, blacks and gypsies in Germany. Blair, of course, knew this. His delegates at Durban would have briefed him on the dialogue that revealed the historical inaccuracy of their statement. Blair ended his "regret" statement with an acknowledgement that slaving and slavery were "profoundly shameful" acts, but all "legal" and officially approved by the British state "at the time".[5]

Deputy Prime Minister Prescott and David Lammy, the young black minister for culture, engaged the press on the prime minister's statement. Prescott made it clear, in his usual assertive tone, that the notion of an apology was out of the question since the British state was not going to open itself to any reparations claims. Lammy, speaking for his leader, stated that he did not wish to get involved in a "blame fest" about slavery and that his prime minister had "gone further than any other leader of western democracy" in offering his "statement of regret". The prime minister, he said, "has struck the right balance between providing for the future, commemorating the past, and moving forward as a multiethnic nation".

Baroness Amos was dispatched to Ghana to read the Blair message before an audience primed by the supportive President Kufuor but that excluded the civil society organizations that had pushed for an apology and reparations long before the Durban debacle. The use of Ghana's Elmina Slave Fort for this purpose did not go down well in Ghana, government endorsement notwithstanding. For many, the baroness's presence was unwelcome, even though Prescott reported that while in Ghana a minister of government had told him that his nation did not need any apology from Britain.

The Tories and New Labour agreed. Blair had apologized to the Irish in 1997 for Britain's role in the potato famine in nineteenth-century Ireland and said that Britain could have done more to alleviate the pain and suffering of the Irish people. The queen was asked to apologize on behalf of the British state to the Maori people of New Zealand, who in the 1860s were massacred, had their land stolen and saw the labour of their children exploited by British settlers. The queen had also apologized to the Indian people for the massacre of up to 1,200 people at Amritsar in the Punjab by the British in 1919. The monarch and prime minister rolled out apologies for crimes committed by their citizens. But the apologies stopped when it came to the African people. Blacks were not entitled; they were not in the same category, since neither the Maori nor the Indians were classified by British settlers and British law as "nonhuman". No other race was subject to the extremes of British racism and inhumanity in the colonial period.

Black people continue to experience the intensity of racism on a global scale, an enduring legacy of the enormity of the crime of slavery. The Tory shadow secretary of foreign affairs, William Hague, spoke for the Conservative Party, a political organization with eighteenth-century social and ideological roots buried deep in the profits of slavery and slave trading. Hague told *Sky News* that an apology for the actions of previous generations sounded "rather hollow and meaningless". Why, then, did he not offer this response when the prime minister and the queen had apologized to the Indians, the Maori and the Irish? He went on to state, "I think that the prime minister got it right, saying that we should regret . . . the terrible crimes of the slave trade." The best we can do, he concluded, "is to learn the lesson of the slave trade and slavery for modern times".[6]

New Labour and Old Tories, then, were united in their handling of the historical crimes against humanity as far as black people are concerned. The right and the left flanks of British politics were united. Such solidarity was consistent with the political approach that had allowed Britain to enter and dominate the slave trade and colonial slavery. It was this cohesion that kept the crime out of serious consideration in Parliament for over one hundred years.

The true lesson was not to be found in the ideas expressed by Secretary Hague, but in the realization that black people, seeking justice for the crimes committed against them, unlike other ethnicities, can reasonably expect to find in Britain a wall of political solidarity. The presence on the progressive side of powerful white voices like Lord Gifford's, and on the reactionary side, black empowered voices like Baroness Amos's, demonstrates the infinite capacity of humanity to fracture in the face of injustice.

The black community in Britain that received these rehearsed reports, and in Africa where official allies were once again pressed into coalition for imagined gains, were far from amused by Amos and lamented the litany of Lammy. Blair should not be blamed nor the queen be questioned. They did what they had to do in their view to defend Crown and state. As prisoners to this past, they spoke from the cells of their consciousness in which black people, once chattels and now like ghosts, remained ghastly creatures they wished would go away and take their history with them.

The press reported having a glimpse at the partially exposed cabinet notes of the baroness during a media briefing, revealing Blair's desire to get the repa-

rations issue out of the way before the end of the year. There was no surprise
that the government wanted to get through the bicentenary year with as little
controversy as possible and without being pushed to offer an apology for slavery. If the year could come and go, and the mission of "no apologies: no reparations" could be achieved, then Labour would have won a major policy battle
over the blacks. And so they did.[7]

An effort was made to divert attention from the truth and legal implications
of British slavery. Oona King, the former member of Parliament for Bethnal
Green and Bow, confessed that Blair feared black reparations under his watch.
In rejecting Blair's brazenness, Esther Stanford of the Pan-African Reparations
Coalition told the British Broadcasting Corporation that black people were
"talking about an apology of substance which would then be followed by various reparative measures including financial compensation".[8]

Blair's statement, Stanford said, was meaningless, empty words, which said
"you can commit crimes against humanity, against African people and get
away with it". In this regard she was supported by Kofi Mawuli Klu of
the British rights group Rendezvous of Victory. Blair's statement, Mawuli
Klu said, "has heightened feelings among people in the African community.
We want an apology of substance that addresses the demands for African
reparations".[9]

The queen had seen the outrage on the faces of persons who considered
demeaning the legally crafted, and crafty, "deep sorrow" statement from her
first minister. She came face to face with the fallout from the fallacious content
of Blair's attempt to get through 2007 without a hiccup. A commemorative
church service was held at Westminster Abbey. Queen Elizabeth, the Duke
of Edinburgh, Prime Minister Blair and dozens of religious leaders filled the
abbey.

The archbishop of Canterbury, Rowan Williams, dug deep beneath Blair's
surface with a sermon that ended thus: "We, who are the heirs of the slave-
owning and slave-trading nations of the past, have to face the fact that our
historic prosperity was built in large part on this atrocity." And furthermore,
that "those who are the heirs of the communities ravaged by the slave trade
know very well that much of their present suffering and struggling is the result
of centuries of abuse".[10]

However, the service was not intended to press the case for an apology from
Blair or his queen but rather to celebrate and glorify William Wilberforce,

who had done the best he could to end the British slave trade. The Church of England had apologized for its role as a slave owner. Linda Ali of the United Society for the Propagation of the Gospel expressed her disappointment with the British government and Blair in particular. "I don't see what is so very difficult about apologizing for what is such a great crime against humanity", Ali said.

Lady Kat Davson, the great-great-great-granddaughter of William Wilberforce, commenting on Blair's statement, noted that "slavery is one of the largest pieces of our wounded history, our world-wide wounded history, and has to be confronted in order to get peace in our world". Such prominent voices were raised against slavery and slave trading in the seventeenth, eighteenth and nineteenth centuries but were brushed aside by more powerful messages that framed the "national interest". In 2007, as in the two hundred years before 1807, such voices of humanity were staged and then silenced when the curtain came down.

Like the Africans who jumped from slave ships into a sea of greater trouble, one man, a Nigerian, Toyin Agbetu, a member of a human rights group, interrupted the service and demanded an apology from the queen and prime minister. Agbetu sprang from his seat during the service, ran to the front of the altar and, within ten feet of the queen, shouted at her, "You should be ashamed. This is an insult to us!" The proceedings came to an abrupt halt as the thirty-nine-year-old remonstrated with the queen while security guards restrained him.[11]

While under physical control, Agbetu shouted, "You don't have no decency, Mr Blair, to make an apology and the word sorry, and you, the Queen. . . . This is a disgrace to our ancestors", he bellowed, pointing his finger at the queen. "Millions of our ancestors are in the Atlantic," he said, and staring at Blair, "Sorry is so hard for you, sir! . . . This is an insult! . . . We should not be here. All you Christians who are Africans should walk out of here."[12]

Outside the abbey, meanwhile, protestors were not aware of what was going on inside. They kept up the chant: "1807 to 2007, nothing's changed". Shortly after Agbetu was evicted, an African journalist stood up and, while looking at the queen, was wrestled to the ground by security guards. "These things run very deep", said Saphie Clarkson, descendant of Thomas Clarkson. As the queen made her way out, clearly shaken by the event, Leo Muhamad of the Nation of Islam said to a small group of onlookers: "Crocodile tears. The

Queen is complicit, the monarchy is complicit." Looking around at the build-ings in the area, he continued, "All this you see was built on slavery."

Arrested and handcuffed, Agbetu was escorted from the abbey and taken to the Charing Cross police station where he was charged under section 5 of the Public Order Act. The service resumed. One member of the congregation, Henry Bonsu, said, "The Queen was unruffled but looked interested."[13]

Parliamentary Postures

Parliament did all it could to ensure that reparations did not feature as a core part of the national bicentenary discussion. It was a complex, well-crafted year of activities, designed, as Baroness Amos inadvertently implied, to "get it over with". A week before the service at the abbey, the House of Commons had engaged in an important discussion on the vital importance of slave trading and slavery to the British economy and society in the eighteenth and nine-teenth centuries and the role of slave-produced wealth in the development of Britain as the first industrial nation.

Deputy Prime Minister John Prescott introduced the bicentenary debate on the floor at 3:44 p.m. It was 20 March 2007. He began by thanking mem-bers of the bicentenary advisory group, as well as his "ministerial colleagues, the leader of the other place, Baroness Amos, and the Under-secretary of State for Culture, Media, and Sport, his Hon. friend, the Member for Tottenham [Mr Lammy]". What followed was an impressive ventilation of the evidence of Britain's crime against humanity. All that needed to be said should be said, Prescott concluded.[14]

But there was no admission of responsibility for the crimes described or reflection on the need of black people for compensation for the illegal enrich-ment and inhumane exploitation. The crime was described in detail by parliamentarians, but none was prepared to take the next step of ownership, apology and commitment to repair.

It was a bizarre political discourse – intelligent in content, powerful in form, but empty in logical meaning and political implication. Parliament refused to apologize or take responsibility. Prescott began with the admonition that "everyone, and I mean everyone, should feel the sorrow, the pain and the regret – yes, the regret" for what had happened to the African people –

evidence, he said, of "man's inhumanity to men, women and children". Parliament then got down to the matter of discussing "slavery and capitalism" and paying tribute to Eric Williams's classic work. Wayne David, Labour member of Parliament for Caerphilly, asked of Hague if he was willing "to acknowledge how fundamental the slave trade was to the economy of Britain at that time" and whether he was "aware that much of the capital for the early industrialization of South Wales came from slave trade based in Bristol".

Hague replied that while he had risen to speak on the politics of abolition, he could admit that the slave trade "was clearly profitable enough for a lot of people in Liverpool and Bristol to engage in it" and that "through the existence of slavery, the plantations were clearly enormously profitable, at times, because of the immense European demand for sugar in the eighteenth century". William Pitt, prime minister, had "said that 80 per cent of Britain's overseas income was derived from [the] West Indian colonies". Hague indicated, unlike some historians, that while he was not prepared to haggle over the degree of profitability of the slave trade, there was no doubt that the British system of black enslavement was enormously profitable for the county.

Not to be outdone, the Liberal Democrats, led in the debate by Dr Vincent Cable, member of Parliament for Twickenham, thought it important to inform the house that "slavery was not peripheral; it was at the heart of the British economy for well over a century". "It was something in which all parts of British society were implicated . . . and it was the basis of the prosperity of the church, and, one should add, of the royal family".

The honourable member had clearly prepared for the debate. He went on to inform the house that in 1720 some 420 "members of the House of Commons invested in the South Sea Company, which was the main financial vehicle for investment in the slave trade". Commenting on his own "liberal" political tradition, he spoke of Prime Minister William Gladstone, whose father John Gladstone "owned hundreds of slaves and acres of plantations in Guiana". When William entered Parliament, he said, his "maiden speech" was "a passionate defence of slavery" because most people in the house were of the view that while "the slave trade was sordid . . . there was nothing inherently wrong in owning slaves and profiting from them".

Then came Jeremy Corbyn, Labour member of Parliament for Islington North, who spoke about the extent to which "members of Parliament were deeply involved in the slave trade", which he said "was a central core of British life". After describing the many place names about British cities that celebrate the trade, he told the House that "the profits from the slave trade were astronomical" and that many British financial institutions to this day began in the engagement with the slave trade. After being interrupted and contradicted by Stephen Williams, Liberal Democrat for Bristol West, Corbyn continued:

> I was talking about the amounts of money made from the slave trade by some of the richest people in Britain. For example, Sir Francis Baring was a Member of Parliament for 18 years and died leaving a legacy of £1 million, which was a heck of a lot of money in the 18th century. William Beckford became the first English millionaire MP. . . . If we look at the planters who made money from the West Indian plantations, particularly in Jamaica, we see that the Beckford family included several Members of Parliament.

Corbyn spoke of the role played by enslaved black people in opposing the slave trade and slavery. He told the house that "the profits made by the sugar industry and many others led to the British banking system, to Barclays, the Midland, and many other banks in this country". Furthermore, he said, "such interests are still around . . . and making a great deal of money".

In addition, Corbyn drew support from Dawn Butler, member of Parliament for Brent South, on the premise that "the banks were directly linked to the slave trade". For those who did not know, Barclays, she said, was established by "two plantation owners who traded in slaves; also that Lloyds began as a centre where runaway slaves were collected before establishing itself in 1692 as an insurance business covering slaves, slave ships, and plantations".

The Scottish parliamentary group also took the opportunity to admit to the enrichment of their country from the crimes of slavery. Malcolm Bruce, Liberal Democrat, told members that "in 1796, 30 per cent of the estates in Jamaica were owned by the Scots". Furthermore, he said, "in 1817, 10 years after the abolition of the trade, 32 per cent of the slaves in Jamaica were owned by Scots". He told colleagues that he lived briefly in a tobacco baron's house in Glasgow and represented a constituency in Aberdeenshire from which "some of the richest plantation owners originated". But critically, he noted, "on the back of that trade, Glasgow claimed to be the second city of the Empire", always ready to compete for status with Liverpool.

Diane Abbott, Labour member of Parliament for Hackney North and Stoke Newington, spoke of the role of London in driving slave trading and slavery for over three hundred years, along with other cities such as Liverpool, Bristol, Glasgow, Barnstaple, Bideford, Dartmouth, Exeter, Plymouth, Poole, Portsmouth and Whitehaven. "Huge fortunes which were made from the slave trade by banks and manufacturers", she said.

Abbott mentioned the "Heywood brothers, Arthur and Benjamin, who made their fortune in the slave trade". "Arthur Heywood", Abbott stated, "went on to found a bank, which became the Bank of Liverpool, then Martin's Bank and eventually Barclays Bank". "Thomas Leyland," she said, "another huge slave trader from Liverpool, served four terms as the city's mayor. He set up Leyland's Bank, which became Bullins Bank, and eventually the Midland Bank."

The debate was rich in historical detail and focused on the many issues raised by the bicentenary. But there was a significant matter that everyone seemed unwilling to acknowledge. Finally, Dawn Butler, Labour member of Parliament for Brent South, a black woman, broke the silence. She was the first member of the Commons who used the word "reparations". Butler was the nineteenth speaker. She had abruptly interrupted Abbott who, as the senior black member of the house, was determined not to address the issue of compensation.

But Butler's rupture was not due to the debate on reparations. Rather, it had to do with setting forth the Haitian case for historic debt repayment to France. Many historians, she said, feel that the reparations paid to the French government by Haiti between 1825 and 1922, amounting to the equivalent of about £105 million today and which contributed significantly to Haiti's status as one of the poorest nations in the Western Hemisphere, should be repaid. Abbot was asked to comment.

Persistent in her refusal to comment on any reparations issue, Abbott replied with a ten-minute tangential speech. She did not connect to the question, and at no time did she ever mention the words "Haiti" or "reparations". It was rather a blunt refusal to comment on the concept raised by the question and a naked parade of the party line in Parliament.

The absence of the word "reparations" from Abbott's attempt at sidestepping Butler, however, ended tragically when she said in summary, "I applaud the government for the action that they have taken to celebrate this important bicentenary, but there are lessons to learn in this day and age. If my slave ancestors could look down from the gallery and hear this debate, they would be happy and proud." "Unlikely", someone said from the gallery, "very unlikely".

Dr Vincent Cable, Liberal Democrat, was first to put the issue squarely before the house after Abbott's detour from Butler's line. "A formal apology of the type that is often sought is not quite right", he said, "but we have to go a long way to acknowledge that the slave trade was not some distant event from which we are entirely disconnected". The best way that "we can honour the past and pay reparations to it", he said, "if that is what is sought, is by ensuring that contemporary slavery is properly and decisively dealt with". Reparations, possibly, but compensation? Impossible. "Once we understand the history," said Jeremy Corbyn, "we must go forward." Reparation, in this exchange, was cast as backward looking and not consistent with the national interest.

How then, asked Claire Curtis-Thomas, Labour member of Parliament for Crosby, "does a nation repay that debt?" In 1994, she said, the City Council of Liverpool passed a motion "formally apologizing" for its participation in the slave trade. It entered a process of reparations by building "a museum and study centre dedicated to the subject of slave trading and slavery". This, she said, has gone "some way towards acknowledging the part that it played in the slave trade". But if the city of Liverpool led the way in this regard, followed by London, why then not the British government – especially, as Curtis-Thomas concluded, since "the victims and the criminals of that trade will never see justice"?

The answers to this question, however, can be found in the House of Lords debate that took place two months later on 10 May 2007. Unlike those in the House of Commons, the Lords were less concerned with the details of Britain's criminal enrichment and more committed to a frank discussion of the principle and policy of reparations. It was more of an academic discussion and less of a political parade.[15]

The opening salvo came from Baroness Howells, who commended the prime minister for his "expression of regret". She quickly acknowledged that "Britain was very good at slavery", and that slavery meant a great deal to the British way of life. She also commended the prime minister for his admission that "the wealth so created laid the foundation of the Industrial Revolution, culminating in Britain's imperial zenith in the late nineteenth and early twentieth centuries".

Baroness Howells also called for an end to attempts by historians to justify the British imperial history of "conquest", "occupation of others' lands", and slavery and urged that the time had come to "avoid inserting qualified approval" of history, and the "post-imperial justifications" of national history. Concluding the debate on 7 June 2007, she asked the "noble Lords" to "look long and hard, with a spirit of empathy and understanding at the debris which is the hangover of that historical era". It was an intriguing, intelligent beginning.

Lord Lester of Herne Hill wasted no time as the second speaker in delving to the heart of the matter. He made reference to an earlier debate on 14 March 1996 on a question by Lord Gifford, asking whether the government would make appropriate reparation to African nations, and to the descendants of Africans, for the damage caused by the slave trade and the practice of slavery. The House, led by the influential opposition voice of Lord Wilberforce, the great-great-grandson of the celebrated William Wilberforce, had rejected the proposal.[16]

Lord Wilberforce indicated his acceptance in principle of the idea of reparations for enslavement but could not agree in this case since, in his judgement, he could find no "unquestionable responsibility" or "unquestioned guilt" among British people today for what had happened. He suggested that slavery was too remote to hold legal sway over the British public and government today. The guilty party, he said, could not be identified nor were the beneficiaries evident. Reparations, he said, for this reason would have to proceed from a moral case, not a legal case.

On the 1996 occasion, Lord Willoughby de Broke had argued that reparations "breed envy and distrust and stir up hatred", while Lord Gisborough stated that the idea of reparations was absurd. "Where would it stop?" Gisborough asked. The Viscount of Falkland added that "the African people are immensely forgiving. To encourage the kind of attitude of fervent desire for reparation suggested here would go against the grain, certainly among Africans, because it is not in their nature".[17]

Speaking on behalf of the Conservative Party in 1996, Lord Chesham opposed the proposal on six counts:

1. Slavery was practised by the Africans.
2. African leaders were partners to the European traders.

3. Private traders and companies, not the British government, ran the slave trade.
4. No residual effects of slavery could be found among Africans or their diaspora descendants.
5. Racism was a global phenomenon, not just between blacks and whites.
6. The task of knowing which blacks should receive reparation was impossible.[18]

The law lords did their best to discredit Gifford's proposal. They denied the evidence of slave trading and slavery and sought to extricate the British from responsibility by blaming others. Lord Gifford, it has been said, was not as prepared as he could have been, both empirically and conceptually, and consequently his reply to Chesham's inaccurate assertions could have been more effective.

The lords, then, in 2007, were at it for the second time. This time around, Lord Lester's reiteration of Lord Wilberforce's position was designed to set the bicentenary stage for a sound rejection of any reparations proposal. His opening comments did just that. Wilberforce, after all, carried considerable moral authority in the house on all matters material to slavery.

The Lord Bishop of Ripon and Leeds countered in part by drawing reference to the formal apology given by the general synod of the Church of England "for the ownership of plantations and slaves" and reiterated that apology. He welcomed the "effort made by Harewood House in Leeds to encourage visitors . . . to reflect on how it is the product of slavery profits made by the Lascelles family". Reparations, however, was not mentioned by the Lord Bishop as a legal consequence of the formal apology given by the synod, although, in his opinion, the country should begin a process of reconciliation and healing by simply recognizing "the extent to which our (national) cultural heritage is based around the profits of slavery".

Jamaican-born Lord Morris of Handsworth was first, however, to call for an apology that would attract no reparations in the form of monetary compensation. After making reference to his slave ancestry, as Diane Abbott had done in the Commons debate, he went a step further: "The nation must start by fully acknowledging that some of its institutions and companies were involved in this heinous crime against humanity."

In an effort to "tackle the legacy", Lord Morris said, "we must start by saying 'sorry'". Recognizing that most of his colleagues in the House were not prepared to say sorry, he refrained, "If we cannot find it in our humanity to say sorry to the slaves, let us at least say sorry for the trade in which we were engaged." Moving on the question of financial compensation, he then fell into line with the government position: "A case has been made for reparation. As a nation we have a massive propensity to devalue the victim but comfort the perpetrator. The church and other slave owners received compensation for losing their slave labour. Surely, it is morally right that the descendants of the enslaved deserve some consideration. However, we all recognize that the difficulties involved would be insurmountable, so we must find other imaginative and creative ways to atone for these crimes against humanity." He called upon financial institutions that were enriched by the slave system to contribute to a "legacy fund" which could be used to drive public education, especially in schools, and to create economic opportunities for communities and countries that have been disadvantaged by their slavery background.

Before Lord Morris's ideas settled in the minds of members, Lord Selsdon rose to debunk his suggestions. He stated, quite stridently, "I do not really believe that one should apologize for the past, or that you can live with the sins of your fathers." Considering himself a "practical man, not influenced by intellectual arguments", he challenged the house to set aside any notion of apology or reparation, since "we cannot do anything to change the past".

In this regard, he was supported by the Earl of Sandwich, whose ancestors were slave owners and received compensation money in 1834. He, too, was rather blunt: "I do not understand the logic of reparations," he said, "because . . . there can be no present moral or legal government responsibility for these actions; apology and atonement can only be symbolic." He was supportive, however, of proposals such as educational interventions and of "an annual day being set aside".

The debate ended with an expected extirpation of the reparations case. This came in the form of Baroness Amos's reiteration of Prime Minister Blair's statement that "it is hard to believe that what would now be a crime against humanity was legal at the time". She expressed her "deep sorrow" and promptly wound up the debate. It was then left to Baroness Howells, who had introduced the discussion, to say that her "slave ancestors" would be "very pleased with today's debate".

Chapter 15

The Caribbean Reparations Movement

I am happy that we are having this debate: we must not forget that the British economy was built on the backs of those who suffered in slavery.

—*Dawn Butler, Member of Parliament, Debate on the Bicentenary of the Abolition of the Slave Trade, House of Commons, 20 March 2007*

THE CARIBBEAN REPARATIONS MOVEMENT IS a moral, legal and political response to the crimes against humanity committed during the European imperial project – specifically the genocide against the native population and the trading and enslavement of enchained bodies of Africans. In the Caribbean context, the British were the quintessential enslavers. During the bicentennial debate in the House of Commons in 2007, one member of Parliament told the Speaker the poignant truth: "The slave trade was . . . at the centre, not at the periphery of the British economy. It was something in which all parts of British society were implicated . . . and it was the basis of the prosperity of the Church and, and one should add, of the royal family."[1]

Both the indigenous community and the enslaved Africans understood the genocidal and enslaving actions of the British and other Europeans to be criminal and immoral. They resented and resisted their captivity and enslavement, demanded the restoration of their lands and liberty and insisted on social justice. It is against this historical background and within this political context that the Caribbean reparations movement has been conceived and its praxis promoted.

The British colonizing enterprise in the Caribbean was predicated on the racial profiling and targeting of Caribbean natives and enslaved Africans. The former were earmarked for genocide, the latter for chattel enslavement. Both were subject to specific race-based, social, legal and military actions. As socially targeted and militarily defeated ethnic groups, they were stripped of their right to freedom and of recognition of their humanity and given a servile role to play in exchange for their lives. An overpowering mercantile and military force descended upon them for four hundred years.

British modernity first practised its brand of totalitarianism within this colonial context. Natives and Africans were deemed disposable. The blood of the enslaved and colonized flowed freely within the new social construct. Labour and race suppression were the two sides of the imperial coin. Slavery was big business; it ensured Britain's biggest, global bonanza.

Enslaving Africans became a kind of popular culture in Britain during the eighteenth century. It was the only way of life in the Caribbean. It was practised on plantations, taken to towns and visited upon villages. The institutionalization of this culture promoted the notion that blacks were beasts of burden. This value system led inexorably to an emancipation programme in which slave owners received a £20 million package, while the enslaved blacks were sent back to work without reparations and respect.

The racist underpinning of emancipation legislation served to promote the political and ethical principles that reside at the core of the Caribbean Reparations Movement. Malcolm Moss, a member of the British Parliament, reminded the House of Commons on 20 March 2007 that Thomas Clarkson had asked in 1785 the critical question: "Is it lawful to make slaves of others against their will?" He knew the answer, as did his colleague William Wilberforce, who, according to Martin Linton, member of Parliament for Battersea, had recorded "his disgust at the fact that £20 million . . . were paid in compensation to slave-owners".[2]

At the centre of the Caribbean reparations movement resides this extraordinary human injustice. From the moment of emancipation, a momentum began building in the Caribbean for correcting this outrage that followed criminal enslavement. Slave owners were compensated, and the enslaved further exploited; this injustice engendered a campaign for the atonement of reparations.

Caribbean hearts and minds were never far apart on this injustice imposed by British economic power and political might. They knew it to be a racist action cloaked in compassion. As a result, wherever the injustice of a racist emancipation was perpetrated within European colonial empires, the spirit of reparation has galvanized generations to this day. Only the form and functions of the movement have changed since 1838. The feelings have become entrenched.

The Haitian reparation experience served as an intimidating action by the West to other Caribbean governments. At the centre of the crime of enslavement and the injustice of non-repaired emancipation was the terrorizing of Haiti. While Buxton had rejected in 1825 the idea of reparations for British slave owners and suggested compensation of the enslaved, the French government had set out to bring the fledgling Haitian state to its knees.

As Haitians in 1825 celebrated their twenty-first anniversary of nationhood, France and Britain demanded reparations for former slave owners in exchange for the official recognition of the state. The British slave owners extracted £20 million from their government, and the French slave owners received 90 million gold francs from Haiti. Both were massive amounts which contributed enormously to the national debt of Britain and Haiti.

The self-liberated community of Haiti paid for the international recognition of their government. They signed the treaty to pay while French gun boats patrolled their harbours. In both the British and Haitian cases, the enslaved were defeated on the reparations issue by the slave owners. The slave owners held considerable political power in the British Parliament, and the French military complex, still smarting over its defeat in the revolutionary war for freedom, was only too keen to intimidate the Haitian government.

The World Conference against Racism, Discrimination, Xenophobia and Related Intolerance in Durban provided a challenging context within which the Caribbean reparations movement gained momentum and conceptual focus. While generally Caribbean citizens were supportive of the need for reparations, however defined and imagined, at least until Durban, the active support for the movement had remained with the radical left. The disaster in Durban enabled the reparations issue to move centre stage in Caribbean politics, creating a bridge between left and right in the party political spectrum. The gathering of support in mainstream politics was possible because the manner of British rejection disturbed the majority public opinion and engendered a new level of determination.

Significantly, then, Durban was the moment that moved the reparations discourse from rhetoric to reality. The cards were now on the table; players adopted positions and ground tactics were exposed. But Durban was more. It was the great decider; the place where the Caribbean and African America found themselves sandwiched between colluding Europe and Africa. This geopolitics resurrected diasporic unity and re-centred the movement.

The intensity of Anglo-American opposition to reparations infiltrated official thinking in the Caribbean. The context was created within which the first regional formal request to a European government for reparations was treated and trampled upon. It was the case placed before the French government by Haitian president Bertrand Aristide in 2004. France, unlike Britain, had made a formal apology for its criminal engagement in slave trading and slavery.

Reparations payments to France, finally fixed at 90 million gold francs, crippled the fledgling Haitian state for the remainder of the century. The Haitians knew it to be a criminal imposition. At Durban there was a formal call for the repayment of these extorted sums, estimated at US$21,685,135,571.48 in present value. It was a central theme in caucus deliberations.

The Caribbean group insisted that such an action by France was consistent with their claim to global diplomatic leadership. Certainly, the casting of Haiti as the poorest country in the Western Hemisphere has now been understood as a consequence of this financial strangulation. The global publication of these hitherto buried historical facts had an immediate impact on world opinion. There was enormous global support for Haiti's cause.

President Aristide acted immediately after Durban to facilitate the dialogue. As the 2004 bicentenary of independence approached, he made a formal request to the French government for the repatriation of US$21 billion: "We are asking for the money that belongs to us." This was the first time that a postcolonial Caribbean government had made an official request for reparations to a European government. Strictly speaking, it was not a request for reparations for slavery as a crime against humanity, but a demand for public funds extracted by criminal means by one state from another.[3]

The Haitian declaration of independence on 1 January 1804 had formally ended French rule in the country. It also represented a blistering blow to all the remaining slave-based colonies in the Caribbean and wider Americas. The United States, fearful of black liberation spreading from the Caribbean, moved to join France in isolating the Haitian state politically. The US Congress banned trade relations with the regime. Spain and Britain were keen to show solidarity with France and joined the anti-Haitian alliance. In 1806, the United States had imposed trade embargos, which were renewed in 1807 and 1809. Trade prohibition was bolstered with frequent aggressive threats of military invasion and re-enslavement of Haitians if they did not pay compensation to France.

The amount imposed upon Haiti by France, and backed by Britain, was "twice the value of the entire country's net worth". In calling for the repayment of this sum, Aristide said that France should "hand over the dollars so the country can celebrate its 200th Independence". In a special commemoration of the Battle of Vertieres, where enslaved blacks defeated French imperial troops to complete the revolutionary war for freedom in 1803, Aristide told citizens that "today, tomorrow, we will win the battle of restitution". In the months building up to the bicentennial celebrations, Aristide repeated his call throughout the country and finally made the formal request to the French government for the repayment of the US$21 billion "ransom".[4]

French political reactions were swift and predictable. First, there was a blunt refusal to contemplate seriously an official dialogue. This was followed by a diplomatic initiative to remove the item from the agenda, which was followed by veiled threats and subversion. Regis Debray, respected socialist French intellectual, was dispatched to Port-au-Prince to discuss the matter with the government. The prime minister established within the Ministry of Foreign Affairs a Committee on Reflection of Haiti that would deliberate on the Debray reports.

Meanwhile, French foreign minister Dominique de Villepin was outlining to the media a proposal he intended to submit to the United Nations on 26 February 2004, calling for the removal of Aristide from office and the sending of an international security force to Haiti. The foreign minister unleashed his opposition to Aristide within the context of growing civil unrest in the county.

It was expected that the response from France, Britain and the United States would be aggressive. Once again the West, the former slave-owning nations, politically surrounded the Haitian state and demanded a policy reversal. This had been the nature of the historic relations between the United States and Europe on anti-slavery politics in Haiti from the outset. Two hundred years later, these nations remained locked into the same frozen postures on the question of the legacies of enslavement.

News of the destabilization of Aristide's regime dominated the media waves. Reports of anti-government NGOs being funded by France and the United States in order to create civil unrest were rampant. An article was circulated in the regional media in which Cikiah Thomas, interim chairman of Global Afrikan Congress, stated, "We do have information from our intelligence that once the demand was put on the table to the government of France, they in collaboration with the United States financed a nongovernmental organization which articulated the legitimate grievances of students and sections when they stated that the president bears heavy responsibility for the current situation." "A new page must be opened in Haiti's history", stated French foreign minister de Villepin.[5]

His comments had already been echoed by the French president, Jacques Chirac. When asked by the press to comment on Aristide's remarks, Chirac said that France had already done much to support Haiti with millions of francs in aid. He went on to warn the Haitian government to be very reflective "before bringing up claims of this nature". He further threatened, "I cannot stress enough to the authorities in Haiti the need to be very vigilant about, how should I say, the nature of their actions and their regime."[6]

Late in the evening on 28 February 2004, two days after Foreign Minister de Villepin spoke about the need for a "new page in Haiti's history", a joint French-US military force invaded Haiti and removed Aristide from office. He found himself in the Central African Republic, a dictatorship government backed by France, after a twenty-hour flight in American custody, ignorant of where he was heading. Regis Debray had done his deed for his government. He reported to France that Aristide's reparations claim had "no legal basis" and that there was no popular support in the government and country for the claim.[7]

Aristide's departure was reported as a "resignation". He said, however, that US officials and military forces in Haiti had made it clear that he should leave in order to save his life and that of his family. He considered the American action as a betrayal of trust to accommodate the French. The removal of Aristide was the final stage in a long drawn-out drama. One scholar noted that efforts were being made since the beginning of 2003 to drive a wedge between his government and the international community: "Grants, loans, and aid were indeed suspended by the US, the EU, Canada and others to the tune of $1 billion."[8] Planning the fall of Aristide, he said, was on the agenda the moment the leader turned his attention to the US$21 billion owed his country by France, and if Aristide had stayed and refrained from making a demand for reparations nothing would have happened.

Aristide stated that his "kidnapping" was violent in that he was apprehended and flown to unknown destinations. Disoriented in space, his fate was uncertain, though it was made clear to him that his days in office as president of Haiti were over, and he would never return. The French government's kidnapping of the first Caribbean head of government, Toussaint L'Ouverture, two hundred years earlier (he later died in a French dungeon) echoed through the Aristide affair. France has never been anything other than violently aggressive to liberation movements in its colonies. Aristide attracted the military and political wrath of Paris and was removed from office. He was fortunate to have remained alive.

Haiti is a member of Caribbean Community (CARICOM), the regional political grouping which at the time of Aristide's removal was headed by P.J. Patterson, prime minister of Jamaica. Powerless to act, CARICOM called an emergency meeting of regional heads of government in Montego Bay to discuss Aristide's overthrow.

The media reported different accounts of the circumstances of Aristide's arrest. Prime Minister Keith Mitchell of Grenada stated that there was "an unsettling feeling among leaders as to what 'really occurred'". He called upon the United States and "some of the bigger countries whose names have been called in this matter" to tell the world what really happened in Haiti. The press also reported CARICOM's desire to make a formal request to the UN secretary general, Kofi Annan, to "launch a probe into the circumstances of the dramatic loss of power" by Aristide.[9]

Patterson, in his role as chairman of CARICOM, told the press that "he could not properly discuss at this time the strategy of this initiative to involve the UN", but indicated that "regional foreign and legal affairs officials were advising on the matter", which he stressed remained of "grave importance" to the community. Within a short time, this matter was purged from the Caribbean press, and it has subsequently remained peripheral.[10]

Within a few hours of Aristide's kidnapping and exile, more than one thousand US troops landed in Haiti. On 5 March, CARICOM officials asked the Bush government for an explanation of events. The reply could be no clearer: "There was nothing to investigate or discuss."[11] Feeling deceived by the United

States, CARICOM countries were receiving a lesson in big-power politics in Caribbean history. The message was unequivocal. Any Caribbean government that makes an official request for reparations would be deemed an aggressive nation and treated accordingly. Caribbean governments understood the message and, appropriately chastised, recoiled and made only rhetorical statements on the subject henceforth.

The final irony was Aristide's arrival in Jamaica on 14 March 2004, where he would begin the second phase of his exile. Just a slither of sea away from his homeland, Aristide held audience with regional and international visitors in his secured hideout. It was in Montego Bay that he had first declared his intention to seek repayment from France.

Randall Robinson, founder of TransAfrica and author of *The Debt: What America Owes to Blacks*, a seminal work in the American reparations discourse, reported that he had heard from a "White House source" that Condoleezza Rice, in her role as presidential advisor to George W. Bush, had "threatened the Jamaican government, telling it to expel President Aristide or face the consequences".[12]

Aristide entered the third phase of his exile in South Africa. African governments had been more vocal in response to his overthrow than his fellow Caribbean heads of state. The African Union, a group of fifty countries formed in 2002, described his removal from office as "unconstitutional". It stated further that his overthrow "set a dangerous precedent for a duly elected person". The union called for the non-recognition of the French-backed rebel forces that had destabilized his regime. The French deputy foreign minister, Guy Moskit, responded that "constitutional legality was respected" since Aristide had signed a letter of resignation before his departure from Haiti.[13]

Myrtha Desulme, chairman of the Haiti–Jamaica Exchange Committee, told the Inter Press Service News Agency (IPS) that the call for reparations had deeply disturbed French politics and that many hostile official comments were still coming out of Paris. However, Dr J. Michael Dash of New York University, a highly respected expert on Haitian society, noted that the US–French alliance which toppled the Caribbean president was connected to the forging of a renewed friendship between the two nations that had soured after disagreements over the invasion of Iraq. "The French do not like to face up to their slave-owning colonial past", he said; but we live in an age, when reparations of all kinds are being asked for "and this one is a documented sum of money paid to a colonial power to compensate for loss of property, and which plunged Haiti into decades of debt".[14]

The plot unfolded predictably. France and the United States selected a leader in Haiti who was willing to carry out their bidding. On 16 March 2004, Gérard Latortue, hand-picked and repackaged, was installed as interim prime minister. He was described as titular leader of "a unity government" that had no role or place for any member of Aristide's party, the Fanmi Lavalas. James Foley, ambassador to Haiti, stated to the press that Latortue was well chosen and that he would help the situation in the country to stabilize, and "significant US and international aid" could be expected. The same day, the Jamaican government announced that it did not recognize the interim government and would not do so until the CARICOM summit ruled on the matter on 25 March.[15]

The final twist in the tale of the plot was also predictable. It could be seen on its way from Paris and Washington. The first significant public declaration made by Latortue was to officially withdraw the reparations request made to France by Aristide. He did so aggressively, to orchestrated French fanfare. "This claim was illegal", he said, "ridiculous", in fact, and "was made only for political reasons. Haiti wants to have good relations with France", he added, and as far as his government was concerned "the matter is closed". He went on to add that what "we need now is increased cooperation with France that could help us build roads, hospitals, schools, and other infrastructures".[16]

Latortue might have forgotten that he had told the *Miami Herald* from his home in Boca Raton, Florida, in December of the previous year that, while he did not believe France was legally obligated to repay the debt, "it's the moral and politically responsible thing to do". Times had changed, and so had Latortue.[17] Meanwhile, the French defence minister, Michele Alliot-Marie, on a tour of Haiti, denied that any of these developments were connected to the restitution demand and insisted that France was motivated solely by a desire to assist the Haitian people.

At the same time, Barbados was leveraging its Durban leadership and reputation to host a follow-up conference in October 2002. Billed as the reconvening of the Durban dialogue by its organizers, the Pan-African Commission, a government institution, the objective was to reassemble global reparations groups, particularly from the NGO community. The conference was officially titled "African and African Descendants World Conference against Racism". It was held at the Sherbourne Conference Centre, 1 to 5 October 2003.[18]

Headed by David Commissiong, the prominent lawyer and pan-Africanist who had been a leading voice in the Durban conference, this conference was rocked to its core on day one. A motion from members of the fifty-strong British delegation proposed and received majority support for the removal of all "white people" from the plenary. Suggesting that the conference was billed as a meeting of "Africans and African descendants only", Kwaku Bonsu, a black London activist, stated, "We told the [organizers] emphatically that we don't want to be sitting down with no Europeans or Asians . . . and they assured us that is an African and African only event and that is why we came here."

The motion passed by majority vote: "All non-Africans were asked to leave quietly." "White" journalists, translators and civil-rights leaders from Cuba, the United Kingdom and the United States removed themselves. Tears were shed by some expelled delegates, and all expressed sadness and frustration at the development. A tearful white mother, Martine Pilé, who was born in Luxembourg, and her mixed-race daughter, Shamkoe Pilé, born in Barbados to a black father, remarked that their expulsion meant for them that "apartheid was reborn in Barbados". Her daughter was invited to stay; she was not. "It hurts so much", she said. "I am married to a black Barbadian, and have been told on other occasions that I am a no-good white woman because I am married to a black man. I was proud to be a part of young country, and proud to have my children here because I thought I could hope for a better world. Now I find what happened to me today very hard to swallow."[19] Other persons, such as Dr Lily Golden, a white Russian civil-rights scholar, spoke of the shock of expulsion and the role of her country in assisting the black liberation struggles in Africa when the West was opposed to their independence and decolonization.[20]

For many in the reparations movement, the Sherbourne summit was a decisive setback. Doudou Diène, who attended as a UN special rapporteur against racism and xenophobia, railed against the resolution as a "move to derail Durban gains". He told the press, "There is a strong, organized and deliberate campaign to weaken the final document of Durban. The campaign is really powerful, not only to wipe out the memory of Durban, but also to stop any kind of follow-up, so that the best thing for us to do in trying to give ammunition to the campaign to weaken Durban is to approve this matter."[21] Diène seemed unaware that for many persons within the conference, the Durban declaration, as far as it relates to reparations, was a betrayal of the diaspora movement, and a triumph for African leaders who had rallied with the West and European Union to smash the reparations agenda.

It was against the backdrop of the Durban dismissal of the African diaspora that tempers were raised around the emotions of distrust. Commissiong called for calm and understanding. He was not at the conference when the motion was passed, and on his return described the action as regrettable though understandable. He used his office, furthermore, to assure the wider community that the reintegration of the delegation would occur. He also distanced the Pan-African Commission from the resolution, noting that he could "speak for at least one of the Caucasian persons that were there, whom I know was a very strong supporter of the pan-African movement and black issues".[22]

It was not surprising that the lead group behind the motion heralded out of Britain. Blacks there have had a horrid experience with white supremacy racism at all levels of society and had reacted very emotionally at their country's opposition to the reparations discourse at Durban. Scarred by decades of institutional racism, black Britons have developed a cerebral distrust of official British society. Barbados was the site of this ventilation, and fittingly so, since this is the place where Britain had built the Caribbean's first slave society.

The Government of Barbados moved swiftly to express its disapproval of these developments and to condemn all forms of racial profiling, while declaring continued support for the reparation movement and the overall agenda of black empowerment as a philosophy of postcolonial governance. Attorney general Mia Mottley, who had assembled the Barbados delegation to Durban in her then role of culture minister, issued a statement: "We are compelled to make it absolutely clear that this government does not support segregation in any form or racism in any guise. We are unequivocally opposed to any resolution seeking to separate persons on the basis of race or ethnic origins. We have fought too long as a nation against this type of injustice."[23] In the end, arrangements were made for "white" delegates to continue their scheduled participation.

Prime Minister Blair's response to the Caribbean leadership at Durban was a highly organized, well-dressed public-relations drive designed to show that Britain cared about postcolonial Africa while rejecting the Caribbean's need for an apology for slavery. On 4 May 2004, he announced an intention to forge a new global consensus to tackle "Africa's woes". The Commission for Africa, he said, would be a powerful agitator for change in a continent plagued by poverty, conflict and HIV/AIDS. Its purpose, furthermore, he said at the Downing Street launch, would be to get an agenda of change that is internationally agreed upon.[24]

Blair launched the Commission for Africa in February 2004 to honour the British deal struck with those African governments at Durban who had rejected the reparations agenda. He described Africa during the launch as "the scar on the conscience of the world". He pledged as a counterpoint to reparations that Britain would make African issues the focal point of the country's presidency of the Group of Eight the following year.[25] The commission included African politicians and civil society leaders in its membership of fourteen, and it was mandated to present its report to the G8 Summit in July 2005. Once again, Blair's Britain had window-dressed the issue, leaving the African members of the commission to explain why it had been a dismal failure.[26]

Meanwhile, however, another commission had been hard at work. The National Commission on Law and Order was established by the government of Barbados to research and report on matters pertaining to public governance, particularly in reference to the marginalization of working-class black communities that saw their alienation in terms of the legacies of slavery and apartheid.

The commission submitted its report in August 2004. It declared outright the need for the government and society to "resolve the issue of reparations" by deepening the dialogue with "the European powers which benefited from the transatlantic slave trade and the institution of slavery". The report stated, furthermore, that, at emancipation, blacks in Barbados did not enter a new era on a "level playing field", and that the "descendants of slave owners inherited a system of privileges, which they have been tenacious in protecting: property, wealth, access to education, to health care, to social standing, to credit, and to opportunity and advancement".[27]

The establishment of post-slavery apartheid, the report noted, preserved white minority economic and social domination into the twentieth century. This legacy of slavery was considered to be the primary source of national social and economic conflict. The commission called for "the government of Barbados to take an active interest in the campaign to put the issue of reparations on the international agenda in the interest of the people".[28] In the months ahead, the Caribbean reparations movement shifted its focus to Suriname, where delegates at a conference on racism resolved on 6 October 2004 to unite efforts across the world to seek reparations from corporations and countries that were involved in and enriched by slavery.

The six-day Global African Conference adopted a constitution that called for the creation of a committee to oversee various lawsuits demanding reparations for the descendants of enslaved Africans. "Never before have Africans been so united on one issue", said Ray Winbush, a psychologist from Morgan State University in Baltimore and author of the text *Should America Pay? Slavery and the Raging Debate on Reparations*. More than two hundred delegates gathered in Paramaribo for the Second Global African Conference, which was also billed as a follow-up to the 2001 Durban conference.

The Bicentenary

As 2007 approached, the bicentennial year of the abolition of the British transatlantic slave trade, the global reparations movement gained intensity in terms of recognition ceremonies, public education media programmes and statements from political leaders. Within the NGO community, the reparations movement focused more on legal and political procedures to advance the cause. In some respects, the idealism of a moral crusade for justice had been shattered at Durban, leaving the movement to inhabit a real political environment typified by combative and acrimonious relations.

Caribbean governments were taken unaware by the aggressiveness of the Durban anti-reparations agenda. They used the bicentennial build-up to make public declarations – some sincere, others to placate the growing public support for the reparations movement. Most governments set out national agendas to mark the moment; some linked these formal programmes to calls for reparations; others took more serious steps and moved to establish initiatives to strengthen the movement. Collectively, the Caribbean in 2007 was informed by the politics of reparations, though the massive impact of hosting the Cricket World Cup transcended all other considerations in the public imagination.

The Government of Trinidad and Tobago announced a six-month bicentenary calendar of events, with a budget of TT$3.6 million. It entailed a national public education campaign about slavery and slave trading but was not accompanied by a commitment to reparations from the British state. The Barbados government moved a step further. Dame Billie Miller, minister of foreign affairs, gave addresses in Barbados and at the United Nations in which she linked the atrocities of slavery to ongoing Caribbean problems and asked for a formal reparations discourse that would merge the two in a constructive fashion.[29]

In delivering the 2007 Wilberforce Lecture in Hull, Prime Minister Owen Arthur of Barbados also called for a sincere reparations dialogue. He stated, "I am aware that the issue of reparations, at least for the victims of the transatlantic slave trade and their descendants, has been a controversial one and it need not be so. It is not a matter of retribution, but one of morality. We need to bring equity to the emancipation process and closure to the criminal activity that was racial chattel slavery."[30] The reparations cause being fought for, he said, was not a mission of mendicancy. He described it as a dialogue of understanding, reconciliation, healing and social justice. There is a need for several reparations projects to assist in clearing away the debris of slavery and colonialism. One practical step, he said, in the area of education, could be the setting up of a Wilberforce Education Fund to achieve the following:

1. Finance, by means of scholarships and concessionary conditions, the education of hundreds of students from CARICOM at British universities on an annual basis
2. Finance dozens of visiting British lectureships at the campuses of the University of the West Indies, in areas to be agreed on
3. Finance student and teacher exchanges between African universities and the University of the West Indies
4. Fund the establishment for decades of a joint British-Caribbean Centre for Multiracial Studies and Policy Development at the University of the West Indies[31]

Such a fund, Arthur said, "would become the centrepiece of a new programme for British-Caribbean cooperation that would go beyond economic and financial issues, that goes beyond security issues, that speaks to a social development that places a supreme value on cultural diversity and harmonious relations between people of different ethnic origins".

Many of these initiatives had been presented to the Durban conference by the Barbados delegation, both in plenary and in bilateral discussion with the British. They would therefore not have surprised the Hull gathering, which was represented heavily by government officials.

On 27 March 2007, to mark the bicentenary of the abolition of the British transatlantic slave trade, the Caribbean region observed a moment of silence at 12:00 p.m., which was followed by a series of activities. Prime Minister Ralph Gonsalves of St Vincent and the Grenadines, speaking at a rally in Dominica, reiterated that slavery was a "criminal activity" and should not go without redress. Other speakers called for CARICOM's support for reparations. Prime Minister Roosevelt Skerritt, the host, supported the reparations call and reminded the rally that "we are in a world where the developed countries are enriching themselves with the toil of people in developing countries".[32]

Kingston Harbour, Jamaica, was the site of a major ceremony that symbolically reenacted the trauma of the arrival and sale of enslaved Africans. The programme of activities, organized by Verene Shepherd, historian at the University of the West Indies, was initially sponsored in 2005 by the government of P.J. Patterson. Prime Minister Portia Simpson-Miller, who had succeeded Patterson, gave the feature address and joined with the Rastafarian representatives who had advocated for reparations for many years.

President Bharrat Jagdeo of Guyana made the strongest demand by a Caribbean head of state. European nations must atone for the horrors of the slave trade; the statements of regret coming out of Blair's British government constituted mere lip service and more was required. Addressing a commemorative ceremony in his country, he stated that "now some members of the international community have recognised their active role in this despicable system, they need to go one step further and support reparations".[33]

Speaking to an audience that included diplomatic envoys from Britain, the European Union and the United States, Jagdeo stressed that "the international community was quick to recognize the Jewish holocaust and rightly so. They must also now recognize that there was an African holocaust".[34] The president added that failure to act would reveal that statements of regret coming out of European governments were "meaningless and platitudinous". He was clear that the ceremony was not a celebration of Britain's anti–slave trade legislation, but a memorial to the enslaved who had fought to end slavery and their allies in British politics.[35]

The minister of culture, youth and sport, Dr Frank Anthony, intensified his president's position. Speaking in parliament, he stated, "We are saying that slavery was a crime against humanity and we want that to be acknowledged." Parliament passed a motion to this effect and reiterated that reparatory action is required to redeem the crime. "It is very difficult to get retributive justice, and therefore, we are asking for reparation justice", said Anthony. The government, he confirmed "has been making this call for the [European] governments which have benefited from slavery to pay reparation. They should make an apology."[36]

While Caribbean governments acted out their divisions, the deputy prime minister of Britain, John Prescott, was making a tour of the region. Prescott's agenda was to affirm Blair's strategy of "no apology". Read as blasphemy in some quarters, the Blair tirade generated considerable turmoil within circles supportive of reparations. Prescott arrived in Jamaica, where the government had already declared its intention to establish a reparation commission to research the issues and make recommendations for consideration by Parliament.

An open forum was held at the Mona campus of the University of the West Indies on 22 May 2007, which Minister Prescott addressed. There had already been rumblings in the country about statements made by Prescott on behalf of his government, and the environment was heavily charged. As the meeting progressed, Mike Henry, a Jamaica Labour Party member of parliament, erupted and stormed out, stating that Prescott's refusal to entertain an apology from the British government for the crime of slavery "was disrespectful of the feelings of the descendants of slaves in the Caribbean".[37]

Henry considered Prescott's approach to Jamaican people "patronizing" and stated that his unwillingness to make a "courtesy call on the House of Representatives where the issue was being debated" was offensive. The meeting at the university was described by the media as "stormy". Henry asked Prescott, "How is it that you are prepared to pay the slave owners but not willing to compensate the slaves?"[38]

Later in the summer these sentiments were echoed by Prime Minister Gonsalves, who made the case for reparations while addressing the African Union Bicentennial Global Dialogue in Barbados. He described the brutality of the British transatlantic slave trade and the enslavement of Africans as "the most monumental crime ever for a free people to have endured". Yet, he said, "no person, no company, no nation which operated and profited handsomely from the slave trade and slavery has ever paid any reparation or any proper recompense".[39]

"The case for reparations is unanswerably strong", Gonsalves told the gathering, which he then urged to realize how it is being "sharply resisted by European nations". Indeed, he said, "Europe's resistance is bolstered by the arrogance, folly, and ignorance of fifth columnists in Africa and its diaspora, including the Caribbean, who insist on trotting out the absurd position that the trade in African slaves was facilitated by some African collaborators, and thus African countries should pay reparations."

The UN special sitting on the bicentenary in March also presented Caribbean heads of governments with a global opportunity to declare official support for the reparations movement. Prime Minister Denzil Douglas of St Kitts and Nevis, addressing the special session of the General Assembly on 26 March 2007, insisted that the European countries that enriched themselves from the crimes of slave trading and slavery must apologize formally and prepare to pay reparations: "It is undisputed that such nations were developed on the blood, sweat and tears of our enslaved forefathers, and it is only right, and the decent thing to do, to make amends and extend their apologies into the realm of atonement for the legal and economic support and for the activities that were the norm of the slave trade and slavery." Reparations, he said, "is the only circumstance that will allow for true forgiveness and forward movement in the world".[40]

These ideas were reinforced by Dame Billie Miller, Barbados's senior minister of foreign affairs and foreign trade, when she addressed the general debate of the sixty-second session of the UN General Assembly on 3 October 2007. Describing the slave trade as "one of the earliest crimes against humanity", Dame Billie noted that European slave owners had made effective use of reparations as a legal instrument in the nineteenth-century emancipation process and that it was consistent for descendants of the enslaved to do likewise in this time in the search for "equity in the emancipation process".[41]

Jamaica established a Reparations Commission on 14 May 2009. Chaired by Barry Chevannes, noted Jamaican sociologist, it held its first meeting on 15 October that year. Its remit was to "receive submissions, hear testimonies, evaluate research and studies, engage in dialogue with relevant interest groups in the society" – its greatest proponents being the Rastafarian community that has consistently promoted and brought the issue to the forefront of their arguments. Given eighteen months to submit its deliberations and recommendations, the commission is one of a kind in the Caribbean. Established by the Jamaica Labour Party, its agenda picks up from the work done earlier by the Peoples National Party, whose reparations thrust was driven by Verene Shepherd.

While Prime Minister Bruce Golding of Jamaica did not affirm support for the reparations movement, powerful elements within his government and party took strong and consistent leadership roles within the movement. In general, however, the core of the movement in Jamaica, as elsewhere within the Caribbean, is to be found within civil society organizations and the consciousness of the social majority. The relationship between society and state on the issue remains cautious, though it is evident that it is only a matter of time before an active official agenda takes shape.

The masses clearly support a constructive strategy to move forward with the reparations issues, but to date opposition forces have been effective in confusing and fragmenting the critical arguments endemic to the discourse. The Rastafarians of the region have remained consistent in their leadership with respect to raising consciousness about the historical crimes of slavery and colonialism. Over time, they have increased their effectiveness in promoting their views across a wider spectrum of society, especially among youth. They represent a significant pillar in the movement and have used the creative and performing arts as a primary vehicle of communication and advocacy with considerable effect.

Caribbean states and citizens, then, are gradually working their way to a general consensus on how best to proceed with the legal and political steps which must be taken to place an official reparations claim before the British and European governments. Best thinking at this time is that each country should seek to establish a national reparations commission which would enable the formation of a Caribbean reparations commission as the regional negotiating machinery. The University of the West Indies, Cave Hill campus, has been asked by the national Pan-African Commission, which is spearheading the establishment of a national commission, to convene a conference on reparations with a view to establishing the regional body. The university has agreed to do so with a view to moving the process. The plan of action, therefore, is for the region as a whole to present officially reparation claims to British and

European governments thereby validating the rightness of President Aristide's 2004 initiative.

The electoral defeat of the Jamaica Labour Party government in the December 2011 general election led to the return of Portia Simpson-Miller as prime minister. As a veteran politician with strong grassroots credentials, she was expected by the reparations movement to offer strong support. Instead, Simpson-Miller made a public declaration on 5 March 2012 that sent shock waves through the movement. She stated that slavery was "wicked and brutal" but "whether Britain will be able to pay compensation I don't know. We have heard the call, but I'm not making any calls on the British government." Furthermore, she added: "If Britain wishes to apologise, fine with us, no problem at all."[42] Against the background of these statements, her government proceeded to re-establish the National Commission on Reparations under the chair of Professor Verene Shepherd, with Lord Gifford serving as a director. Jamaica, then, the largest receiving market for enslaved Africans in the British Caribbean, joined with Nigeria and Senegal, the largest suppliers, in opposing the reparations movement.[43]

While the English trade in enslaved Africans had begun on a large scale in 1672 under the corporate management and leadership of the Duke of York (who later became King James II), it seemed a striking coincidence that Simpson-Miller's comments were made during a visit to the island by Prince Harry, the younger son of Charles, Prince of Wales. Simpson-Miller's remarks resonated beyond Jamaica and the Caribbean, and they were a talking point in pro-reparations circles throughout West Africa. Coming a decade after the Durban declaration, they have served to galvanize grassroots support for the reparations movement while simultaneously deepening the already Balkanized official regional positions.[44]

Notes

Black Manifesto

Chapter 1

1. See Gert Oostindie, ed., *Facing Up to the Past: Perspectives on the Commemoration of Slavery from Africa, the Americas, and Europe* (Kingston: Ian Randle, 2001); see also Mari J. Matsuda, "Looking to the Bottom: Critical Legal Studies and Reparations", *Harvard Civil Rights–Civil Liberties Law Review* 22, no. 323 (1987): 362–97.
2. Sandra Jamison, "A Permanent International Criminal Court: A Proposal That Overcomes Past Objections", *Denver Journal of International Law and Policy* 23 (1995): 419. See also Boris I. Bittker, *The Case for Black Reparations* (New York: Random House, 1973); and Roy L. Brooks "Not Even an Apology", in *When Sorry Isn't Enough: The Controversy over Apologies and Reparations for Human Injustice*, ed. Roy L. Brooks (New York: New York University Press, 1999) , 309–14.
3. See Clarence J. Munford, *Race and Reparations: A Black Perspective for the Twenty-first Century* (Trenton, NJ: Africa World Press, 1996). See also Jared Taylor, *Paved with Good Intentions: The Failure of Race Relations in Contemporary America* (New York: Carroll and Graf, 1992); Robert S. Lecky and H. Elliott Wright, eds., *The Black Manifesto: Religion, Racism and Reparations* (New York: Sheed and Ward, 1969); and Manning Marable, *Speaking Truth to Power: Essays on Race, Resistance, and Radicalism* (Boulder: Westview Press, 1996).
4. See Anthony Gifford, *The Passionate Advocate* (Kingston: Arawak, 2007), 243–44. See also Manning Marable, *How Capitalism Underdeveloped Black America* (Washington, DC: Howard University Press, 1981); and Walter Rodney, *How Europe Underdeveloped Africa* (London: Bogle L'Ouverture, 1972).
5. See Michael T. Martin and Marilyn Yaquinto, eds., *Redress for Historical Injustices in the United States: On Reparations for Slavery, Jim Crow, and Their Legacies* (Durham, NC: Duke University Press, 2007).
6. See Matsuda, "Looking to the Bottom".
7. See Gifford, *Passionate Advocate*, 243–44.
8. Ibid.

Reparation *Jews* *Blocking Jws*

9. See Richard F. America, "Reparations and Public Policy", *Review of Black Political Economy* 26, no. 3 (1999): 77–83; Amiri Baraka, *The Essence of Reparations* (Philipsburg, St Martin: House of Nehesi, 2003); Watson Branch, "Reparations for Slavery: A Dream Deferred", *San Diego International Law Journal* 3 (2002): 177–206; Roy L. Brooks, *Atonement and Forgiveness: A New Model for Black Reparations* (Berkeley: University of California Press, 2004).

10. See Neal Boudette, "Seeking Reparations: A Holocaust Claim Cuts to the Heart of the New Germany", *Wall Street Journal*, 29 March 2004, A1.

11. J. Angelo Corlett, *Race, Racism, and Reparations* (Ithaca: Cornell University Press, 2003); William Darity Jr and Dania Frank, "The Economics of Reparations", *American Economic Review* 93, no. 2 (2003): 326–29.

12. See Henry Louis Gates Jr, "The Future of Slavery's Past", *New York Times*, 29 July 2001; Jeffrey Ghannam, "Repairing the Past: Demands Are Growing for Reparations for the Descendants of African Slaves in America", *American Bar Association Journal* 86 (November 2000): 39–43. *Bussy Land*

13. See Hilary Beckles, "The Concept of 'White Slavery' in the English Caribbean during the Early Seventeenth Century", in *Early Modern Conceptions of Property*, ed. John Brewer and Susan Staves (New York: Routledge, 1995), 572–85.

14. See Robin Blackburn, *The Making of New World Slavery: From the Baroque to the Modern, 1492–1800* (London: Verso, 1997), 255, 263–65.

15. See G.K. Lewis, *Main Currents in Caribbean Thought: The Historical Evolution of Caribbean Society in Its Ideological Aspects* (London: Heinemann, 1983), 207–8.

Chapter 2

1. See Hilary Beckles, "The Genocide Policy in English–Karifuna Relations in the Seventeenth Century", in *Empire and Others: British Encounters with Indigenous People, 1600–1850*, ed. Martin Daunton and Rick Halpern (London: UCL Press, 1999), 280–302 ; see also Beckles, "Kalinago (Carib) Resistance to European Colonisation of the Caribbean", *Caribbean Quarterly* 21, no. 1 (1987): 55–77.

2. J. Paul Thomas, "The Caribs of St Vincent: A Study in Imperial Maladministration, 1763–1773", *Journal of Caribbean History* 18, no. 2 (1984): 60–73.

3. Jalil Sued-Badillo, "Ethnohistorical Research in the Hispanic Caribbean", in *General History of the Caribbean*, vol. 1, *Autochthonous Societies*, ed. Jalil Sued-Badillo (London: UNESCO, 2003), 8–29. See also Michael Craton, *Testing the Chains: Resistance to Slavery in the British West Indies* (Ithaca: Cornell University Press, 1982), 23.

4. William Stapleton to Lords of Trade and Plantations, 6 August 1681, *Calendar of State Papers, Colonial Series* (*CSPC*), 1681–1685, no. 304.

5. Bernard Marshall, *Slavery, Law, and Society in the British Windward Islands, 1763–1823* (Kingston: Arawak, 2007), 21.

6. Ibid., 24.

7. Ibid., 22.

8. G.K. Lewis, *Main Currents in Caribbean Thought: The Historical Evolution of Caribbean Society in Its Ideological Aspects* (London: Heinemann, 1983), 104.

9. Ibid., 105.

10. Ibid.

11. Ibid.

12. Richard S. Dunn, *Sugar and Slaves: The Rise of the Planter Class in the English West Indies, 1624–1713* (New York: Norton, 1973), 7, 15.

13. Carl Ortwin Sauer, *The Early Spanish Main* (Berkeley: University of California Press, 1966), 58, 193.

14. Troy S. Floyd, *The Columbian Dynasty in the Caribbean, 1492–1526* (Albuquerque: University of New Mexico Press, 1973), 97; see also Kenneth R. Andrews, *Trade, Plunder and Settlement: Maritime Enterprises and the Genesis of the British Empire, 1480–1630* (Cambridge: Cambridge University Press, 1984), 282; and Craton, *Testing the Chains*, 22.

15. See Sauer, *Early Spanish Main*, 35; Lewis, *Main Currents*, 64; Dunn, *Sugar and Slaves*, 24; John Eaden, ed. and trans., *The Memoirs of Père Labat, 1693–1705* (London: Frank Cass, 1970), 75–76.

16. Eaden, *Memoirs*, 83, 98, 104, 109.

17. Dunn, *Sugar and Slaves*, 8; Lewis, *Main Currents*, 104.

18. Lewis, *Main Currents*, 105.

19. Eaden, *Memoirs*, 137.

20. Ibid.

21. Governor Stapleton of the Leewards to the Lords of Trade and Plantations, 22 November 1676, *CSPC* 1676, no. 499.

22. C. Gullick, "Black Caribes Origins and Early Society", in *Transactions of the Seventh International Congress on Pre-Columbian Cultures of the Lesser Antilles* (Montreal: Centre de Recherches Caraïbes, 1978), 283–87; William Young, *An Account of the Black Caribs in the Island of St Vincent's* (London, 1795; repr., London: Frank Cass, 1971), 5–8; see also Nancy Gonzalez, *Sojourners of the Caribbean: Ethnogenesis and Ethnohistory of the Garifunas* (Urbana: University of Illinois Press, 1988).

23. "The State of the Case concerning our Title to St Lucia", n.d. 1664, *CSPC* 1661–68, no. 887; Rev. C. Jesse, "Barbadians Buy St Lucia from Caribs", *Journal of the Barbados Museum and Historical Society* 32 (1968): 180–82.

24. Governor Sir Thomas Modyford to the Duke of Albemarle, 16 March 1668, *CSPC* 1661–68, no. 1714.

25. Petition of Major John Scott to the King, n.d. 1667, *CSPC* 1661–68, no. 1525; Governor Lord William Willoughby to the King, 11 February 1668, *CSPC* 1661–68, no. 547; Henry Willoughby to William Willoughby, 15 June 1667, *CSPC* 1661–68,

no. 1498; Craton, *Testing the Chains*, 22–23; Governor William Lord Willoughby to the King, 9 July 1668, *CSPC* 1661–68, no. 1788.

26. Copy of a Treaty between William Lord Willoughby and several of the chief captains of Caribs, 23 March 1668, *CSPC* 1661–68, no. 1717.
27. Lord Willoughby to the King, 13 March 1668, *CSPC* 1661–68, no. 1714.
28. Governor Sir Thomas Modyford to the Duke of Albemarle, 16 March 1668, *CSPC* 1661–68, no. 1714.
29. Governor Stapleton to the Lords of Trade and Plantations, 27 May 1672, *CSPC* 1669–72, nos. 46, 61.
30. Governor Atkinson to Lord of Trade and Plantations, 4 July 1676, *CSPC* 1676, no. 37; Governor Stapleton to Council of Trade and Plantations, December 1676, *CSPC* 1676, no. 43; Petition of Several Merchants of London on Adventures to the Caribbean Islands to the Lords of Trade and Plantations, 10 January 1676, *CSPC* 1676, no. 36.
31. Governor Stapleton to the Council of Trade and Plantations, 8 February 1675, *CSPC* 1675–76, no. 428; Governor Atkins to Secretary for Colonies, 17 February 1675, *CSPC* 1675–76, no. 439.
32. Petition of Several Merchants of London on Adventures, 10 January 1676, *CSPC* 1676, no. 36.
33. Governor Stapleton to Lords of Trade and Plantations, 16 August 1681, *CSPC* 1681–85, no. 410–11.
34. Governor Stapleton to Lords of Trade and Plantations, 3 January 1682, *CSPC* 1681–85, no. 204; Journal of Lords of Trade, 18 October 1681, no. 259.
35. King to Stapleton, February 1682, *CSPC* 1681–85, no. 411; Sir Richard Dutton to Lords of Trade, 3 January 1682, *CSPC* 1681–85, no. 181; Journal of the Assembly of Nevis, 14 June 1682, ibid.
36. Eaden, *Memoirs*, 110–11.
37. Craton, *Testing the Chains*.
38. Ibid.
39. Ibid., 149
40. Ibid., 206–7.

Chapter 3

1. John C. Appleby, "War, Politics, and Colonisation, 1558–1625", in *The Origins of Empire*, ed. Nicholas Canny (London: Oxford University Press, 1998), 59.
2. Ibid.
3. Hugh Thomas, *The Slave Trade: The History of the Atlantic Slave Trade, 1440–1870* (London: Papermac, 1997), 156.

4. P.E.H. Hair and Robin Law, "The English in West Africa", in Canny, *Origins of Empire*, 246.
5. Thomas, *Slave Trade*, 156–57.
6. Hair and Law, "English", 261–62.
7. Moira Ferguson, *Subject to Others: British Women Writers and Colonial Slavery, 1670–1834* (New York: Routledge, 1992), 11.
8. For summaries of this literature, see Winthrop D. Jordan, *White over Black: American Attitudes towards the Negro, 1550–1812* (Chapel Hill: University of North Carolina Press, 1968); and David Brion Davis, *Inhuman Bondage: The Rise and Fall of Slavery in the New World* (Oxford: Oxford University Press, 2006).
9. Robin Blackburn, *The Making of New World Slavery: From the Baroque to the Modern, 1492–1800* (London: Verso, 1997), 329.
10. Ibid.
11. Ibid., 328; see also Hair and Law, "English", 254.
12. Blackburn, *Making of New World Slavery*, 328.
13. Hair and Law, "English", 255; see also *Calendar of State Papers Colonial, America and West Indies 1574–1660*, vol. 1.
14. George Zook, *The Company of Royal Adventurers Trading into Africa* (Lancaster, PA: New Era, 1919), 13, 16, 72.
15. Ibid., 74
16. Ibid., 82
17. Thomas, *Slave Trade*, 394; Hair and Law, "English", 257.
18. Hair and Law, "English", 259.
19. Christopher L. Brown, "The British Government and the Slave Trade: Early Parliamentary Enquiries, 1713–83", in *The British Slave Trade: Abolition, Parliament and People*, ed. Stephen Farrell, Melanie Unwin and James Walvin (Edinburgh: Edinburgh University Press, 2007), 26, 27, 28.
20. Ibid., 29.
21. Ibid., 30.
22. Martin Daunton and Rick Halpern, eds., *Empire and Others: British Encounters with Indigenous People, 1600–1850* (London: UCL Press, 1999), 12.
23. Brown, "British Government", 30.
24. Ibid., 30–31
25. Ibid., 32
26. Ibid., 33
27. Ibid., 34
28. Daunton and Halpern, *Empire and Others*, 12.
29. James Walvin, *Black Ivory: A History of British Slavery* (London: Fontana Press, 1993), 30.
30. See Thomas, *Slave Trade*. See also Hilary Beckles, "The Wilberforce Song: How

Black resistance

Enslaved Caribbean Blacks Heard British Abolitionists", in Farrell, Unwin and Walvin, eds., *British Slave Trade*, 120–21.

31. See Winston McGowan, "African Resistance to the Atlantic Slave Trade in West Africa", *Slavery and Abolition* 11, no. 1 (May 1990): 5–29.

32. See Thomas, *Slave Trade*, 402–4; "An Account of the Voyage of the Hannibal, 1693/94", in *Documents Illustrative of the History of the Slave Trade to America*, ed. Elizabeth Donnan (1930; New York: Octagon, 1969), 1:395–96, 401–3, 407–8.

33. Marcus Rediker, *The Slave Ship: A Human History* (New York: Viking, 2007), 40.

34. Ibid.

35. Ibid.

36. See Thomas, *Slave Trade*, 422; Hilary Beckles and Verene Shepherd, *Saving Souls: The Struggle to End the Transatlantic Slave Trade* (Kingston: Ian Randle, 2007), 12–13.

37. Paul E. Lovejoy, "The Volume of the Atlantic Slave Trade: A Synthesis", *Journal of African History* 23 (1982): 474–501. See also Joseph E. Inikori, *Africans and the Industrial Revolution in England: A Study in International and Economic Development* (Cambridge: Cambridge University Press, 2002); David Eltis, *The Rise of African Slavery in the Americas* (Cambridge: Cambridge University Press, 2000); Philip D. Curtin, *The Atlantic Slave Trade: A Census* (Madison: University of Wisconsin Press, 1969); Beckles, "The Wilberforce Song", 114–15.

38. Herbert S. Klein, *The Middle Passage: Comparative Studies in the Atlantic Slave Trade* (Princeton, NJ: Princeton University Press, 1978).

39. Hilary McD Beckles and Verene A. Shepherd, *Trading Souls: Europe's Transatlantic Trade in Africans* (Kingston: Ian Randle, 2007), 62.

40. Joseph C. Miller, "The Significance of Drought, Disease, and Famine in the Agriculturally Marginal Zones of West-Central Africa", *Journal of African History* 23 (1982): 17–61; Joseph C. Miller, "Capitalism and Slaving: The Financial and Commercial Organisation of the Angolan Slave Trade", *International Journal of African Historical Studies* 17 (1984): 1–52; Joseph C. Miller, *Way of Death: Merchant Capitalism and the Angolan Slave Trade, 1730–1830* (Madison: University of Wisconsin Press, 1988).

41. Patrick Manning, "The Slave Trade in the Bight of Benin, 1640–1890", in *The Uncommon Market: Essays in the Economic History of the Transatlantic Slave Trade*, ed. Henry Gemery and Jan Hogendorn (New York: Academic Press, 1979), 104–40; Patrick Manning, *Slavery and African Life: Occidental, Oriental, and African Slave Trades* (New York and Cambridge: Cambridge University Press, 1990).

42. Walvin, *Black Ivory*.

43. David Richardson, "Profits in the Liverpool Slave Trade: The Accounts of William Davenport, 1757–1784", in *Liverpool, the African Slave Trade and Abolition*, ed. Roger Anstey and P.E.H. Hair; Occasional Series (Bristol: Historical Society of Lancashire and Cheshire, 1976), 2:69–90.

Chapter 4

1. Richard S. Dunn, *Sugar and Slaves: The Rise of the Planter Class in the English West Indies, 1624–1713* (New York: Norton, 1973), 71, 227–28, 238–46; Winthrop Jordan, *White over Black: American Attitudes towards the Negro, 1550–1812* (Chapel Hill: University of North Carolina Press, 1968), ch. 1. Dunn noted that "the most tragic thing about Afro-American slavery is that all of the black man's admirable human qualities – his sociability, adaptability, endurance, loving kindness, and domesticated, disciplined culture – earned him nothing but debasement in the New World" (Dunn, *Sugar and Slaves*, 74).

2. See Hilary Beckles, "Social and Political Control in the Slave Society", in *General History of the Caribbean*, vol. 3, *The Slave Societies of the Caribbean*, Franklin W. Knight (London: UNESCO, 1997), 194–221.

3. "Voyage of the Hannibal, 1693–94", in *Documents Illustrative of the History of the Slave Trade to America*, ed. Elizabeth Donnan (New York: Octagon, 1969), 1:395–96, 401–3, 407–8.

4. See Hugh Thomas, *The Slave Trade: The History of the Atlantic Slave Trade, 1440–1870* (London: Papermac, 1997), 395.

5. Colin A. Palmer, "The Slave Trade, African Slavers and the Demography of the Caribbean to 1750", in Knight, *General History*, 12.

6. Ibid., 13.

7. Robin Blackburn, *The Making of New World Slavery: From the Baroque to the Modern, 1492–1800* (London: Verso, 1997), 259.

8. Ibid., 260.

9. Dunn, *Sugar and Slaves*, 228.

10. *An Account of His Majesty's Island of Barbados and the Government Thereof* (1683), Sloane MS 2441, British Library, London. See also Hilary Beckles, *Black Rebellion in Barbados: The Struggle against Slavery, 1627–1838* (Bridgetown, Barbados: Antilles, 1987), 23.

11. Richard B. Sheridan, *Sugar and Slavery: An Economic History of the British West Indies, 1623–1775* (Bridgetown, Barbados: Caribbean Universities Press, 1974), 67–69.

12. Acts of Barbados, 1645–1680, CO 30/2; 1682–1692, CO 30/5, PRO London.

13. Dunn, *Sugar and Slaves*, 246.

14. Richard Hall, *Acts Passed in the Island of Barbados, 1643–1762* (London, 1764), no. 42.

15. Dunn, *Sugar and Slaves*, 240.

16. Ibid.

17. Hall, *Acts Passed*, no. 42

18. Ibid., ff. 112–13.

19. Ibid.

20. Ibid.

21. Beckles, "Social and Political Control", 198.

22. *House of Commons Accounts and Papers*, vol. 26, 1789, no. 646a, pt. iii.

23. [John Poyer], "A letter to His Excellency the Right Honourable Francis Lord Seaforth by a Barbadian", 22 June 1801. (Reprinted in *Journal of the Barbados Museum and Historical Society* 8, no. 4 [1941]: 150–65.) See also Beckles, *Black Rebellion*, 82.

24. The Petition of Foyle and Rivers can be found in Thomas Burton, *Diary of Thomas Burton, Esq., . . . from 1656 to 1659* (London: Henry Colburn, 1828), 4:252–307; also in Leo Stock, ed., *Proceedings and Debates in the British Parliament Respecting North America* (Washington, DC: Carnegie Institute, 1924–41), 1:247–73.

25. Burton, *Diary*, 4:254.

26. Ibid., 4:355.

27. Ibid., 4:257.

28. Ibid., 4:256.

29. Ibid., 4:257.

Chapter 5

1. See Elsa V. Goveia, *West Indian Slave Laws of the 18th Century* (St Lawrence, Barbados: Caribbean Universities Press, 1970), 36; also published in *Revisita de Ciencias Sociales* 4, no. 1 (1960): 75–106.

2. Hilary Beckles, "Social and Political Control in the Slave Society", in *General History of the Caribbean*, vol. 3, *The Slave Societies of the Caribbean*, ed. Franklin W. Knight (London: UNESCO, 1997), 214–15.

3. Lowther Plantation Papers, Add. MS 43507, British Library, London.

4. Seymour Dresher, "Public Opinion and Parliament in the Abolition of the British Slave Trade", in *The British Slave Trade: Abolition, Parliament and People*, ed. Stephen Farrell, Melanie Unwin and James Walvin (Edinburgh: Edinburgh University Press, 2007), 43–44.

5. James Walvin, *Black Ivory: A History of British Slavery* (London: Fontana Press, 1993), 15.

6. Ibid.

7. Ibid., 16.

8. John Weskett, *A Complete Digest of the Laws, Theory and Practice of Insurance* (London, 1781), 525. See also Walvin, *Black Ivory*, 17.

9. See "The *Zong*, 1781", at http://www.umich.edu/~ece/student_projects/slavery/the_zong.html.

10. Walvin, *Black Ivory*, 17. In his book *The Zong: A Massacre, the Law, and the End of*

Slavery (New Haven: Yale University Press, 2011), Walvin discusses the confusion over the numbers but consistently uses 132.

11. Ibid., 19.
12. Ibid.
13. Ibid.
14. Ibid., 20; emphasis added.
15. Ibid.
16. Ibid., 20–21.

Chapter 6

1. See Hilary Beckles, *Centering Woman: Gender Discourses in Caribbean Slave Society* (Kingston: Ian Randle, 1999), 22–30.
2. Orlando Patterson, *The Sociology of Slavery: An Analysis of the Origins, Development, and Structure of Negro Slave Society in Jamaica* (London: MacGibbon and Kee, 1967), 160; see also B.W. Higman, *Slave Population and Economy in Jamaica, 1807–1834* (Cambridge: Cambridge University Press, 1976), 42.
3. Richard S. Dunn, *Sugar and Slaves: The Rise of the Planter Class in the English West Indies, 1624–1713* (New York: Norton, 1973), 253.
4. John Oldmixon, *The British Empire in America* (London: Mapp, 1708), 2:129.
5. Colonel Hilton to Reverend John Snow, 16 August 1816, Codrington MSS, Barbados Accounts, 1721–1838, Lambeth Palace Library, London.
6. F.W.N. Bayley, *Four Years' Residence in the West Indies* (London: William Kidd, 1830), 497.
7. See the letters of Elizabeth Fenwick, in *The Fate of the Fenwicks: Letters to Mary Hays, 1798–1828*, ed. A.F. Wedd (London: Methuen, 1927), 163–207.
8. See Hilary Beckles, *Natural Rebels: A Social History of Enslaved Black Women in Barbados* (London: Zed Books, 1989). Chapter 7 explores the roles of enslaved women as prostitutes and mistresses.
9. Claude Levy, *Emancipation, Sugar and Federalism: Barbados and the West Indies, 1833–1876* (Gainesville: University of Florida Press, 1980), 30; see also B.W. Higman, *Slave Populations of the British Caribbean, 1807–1834* (Baltimore: Johns Hopkins University Press, 1984), 231.
10. Fenwick, *Fate of the Fenwicks*, 169.
11. Report on the Negroes at Newton Plantation, 1796, Newton Papers, M523/288, ff. 1–20, Senate House Library, University of London.
12. Evidence of William Sharpe, in *A Report of a Committee of the Council of Barbados, Appointed to Inquire into the Actual Conditions of the Slaves of this Island* (Bridgetown, Barbados: W. Walker, 1822), 5–6; see also Evidence of Nicholas Brathwaite, British Sessional Papers, House of Commons, 1791 (34) vol. 42, p. 183.

13. See Thomas Cooper, *Facts Illustrative of the Condition of the Negro Slaves in Jamaica* (London: Hatchard, 1824), 42; J.B. Moreton, *Manners and Customs in the West India Islands* (London: W. Richardson, 1790), 132.

14. See *A Report of a Committee of the Council of Barbados*, 4–10; see also Edward Long, *The History of Jamaica*, 3 vols. (London, 1774).

15. Testimony of Captain Cook, British Sessional Papers: House of Commons, 1791 (34), vol. 42, p. 202.

16. Ibid.

17. Major Wyvill, "Memoirs of an Old Officer, 1776–1807", MSS Div., Library of Congress, Washington, DC, 386.

18. John Augustine Waller, *A Voyage in the West Indies* (London: Richard Phillips, 1820), 20–21.

19. George Pinckard, *Notes on the West Indies* (London: Longman, 1806), 1:245–46.

20. J. Sturge and T. Harvey, *The West Indies in 1837* (London: Hamilton and Adams, 1837), 1; Wyvill, "Memoirs", 383.

Chapter 7

1. See R. Anstey, "The British Slave Trade, 1761–1807: A Comment", *Journal of African History* 17 (1976): 606–7; Richard N. Bean, *The British Transatlantic Slave Trade, 1650–1775* (New York: Ayer, 1975); William Darity Jr, "The Numbers Game and the Profitability of the British Trade in Slaves", *Journal of Economic History* 45 (1985): 693–703.

2. Patrick O'Brien, "European Economic Development: The Contribution of the Periphery", *Economic History Review* 35 (1982): 1–18; Patrick Karl O'Brien and Louis Prados de la Escosura, "The Costs and Benefits for Europeans from Their Empires Overseas", *Revista de Historia Economica* 16 (1988): 29–89; Cedric J. Robinson, "Capitalism, Slavery, and Bourgeois Historiography", *History Workshop: A Journal of Socialist and Feminist Historians* 23 (1987): 122–40; Richard B. Sheridan, "The Plantation Revolution and the Industrial Revolution, 1625–1775", *Caribbean Studies* 9 (1969): 5–25.

3. Kenneth Morgan, *Slavery, Atlantic Trade and the British Economy, 1660–1800* (Cambridge: Cambridge University Press, 2000), 10.

4. See Richard B. Sheridan, "The Wealth of Jamaica in the Eighteenth Century", *Economic History Review*, n.s., 18, no. 2 (1965): 292–311; Barbara L. Solow, "Caribbean Slavery and British Growth: The Eric Williams Hypothesis", *Journal of Development Economics* 17 (1985): 99–115; J.R. Ward, *British West Indian Slavery: The Process of Amelioration, 1750–1834* (Oxford: Clarendon Press, 1988).

5. Eric Williams, *Capitalism and Slavery* (Chapel Hill: University of North Carolina

Press, 1944), 52; Adam Smith, *The Wealth of Nations*, ed. Edwin Cannan (1776; New York: Modern Library, 1937 ed.), 538; Arthur Young, "An Inquiry into the Situation of the Kingdom on the Conclusion of the Late Treaty", in *Annals of Agriculture and Other Useful Arts* (London, 1784), 1:13; John J. McCusker and Russell R. Menard, *The Economy of British America, 1607–1789* (Chapel Hill: University of North Carolina Press, 1985), 144–45; Hilary Beckles, "The 'Hub of Empire': The Caribbean and Britain in the Seventeenth Century", in *The Oxford History of the British Empire*, vol. 1, *The Origins of Empire*, ed. Nicholas Canny (Oxford: Oxford University Press, 1998), 218–19.

6. K.G. Davies, *The North Atlantic World in the Seventeenth Century*, vol. 4, *Europe and the World in the Age of Expansionism* (Minneapolis: University of Minnesota Press, 1974), 60.

7. McCusker and Menard, *Economy of British America*, 147; Nuala Zehedieh, "Trade, Plunder, and Economic Development in Early English Jamaica", *Economic History Review* 38 (1986): 205–22; Robert M. Bliss, *Revolution and Empire: English Politics and the American Colonies in the Seventeenth Century* (Manchester: Manchester University Press, 1990), 9.

8. Beckles, "Hub of Empire", 219.

9. Davies, *North Atlantic World*, 4:60–61; McCusker and Menard, *Economy of British America*, 148.

10. John H. Parry, "The English in the New World", in *The Westward Enterprise: English Activities in Ireland, the Atlantic and America, 1480–1650*, ed. K.R. Andrews, N.P. Canny, P.E.H. Hair and D.B. Quinn (Liverpool: Liverpool University Press, 1978), 2; Jack P. Greene, *The Intellectual Construction of America: Exceptionalism and Identity from 1492 to 1800* (Chapel Hill: University of North Carolina Press, 1993), 55; Karen Ordahl Kupperman, *Providence Island, 1630–1641: The Other Puritan Colony* (Cambridge: Cambridge University Press, 1993), ch. 7–8.

11. Davies, *North Atlantic*, 72–96; Henry A. Gemery, "Emigration from the British Isles to the New World", *Research in Economic History* 5 (1989): 179–23; Nicholas Canny, "English Emigration into and across the Atlantic during the Seventeenth and Eighteenth Centuries", in *Europeans on the Move: Studies on European Migration 1550–1800*, ed. Nicholas Canny (Oxford: Oxford University Press, 1994), 39–75.

12. Winthrop Jordan, "Unthinking Decision: Enslavement of Negroes in America", in *Shaping Southern Society: The Colonial Experience*, ed. T.H. Breen (New York: Oxford University Press, 1976), 100. See also Edmund S. Morgan, "The First American Boom: Virginia, 1618 to 1630", *William and Mary Quarterly* 28 (1971): 178–79.

13. David Galenson, *White Servitude in Colonial America: An Economic Analysis* (Cambridge: Cambridge University Press, 1981), 3–19; and *Traders, Planters, and Slaves: Market Behavior in Early English America* (New York: Cambridge University Press, 1986), 137. See also Abbot Emerson Smith, *Colonists in Bondage: White Servitude*

and Convict Labor in America 1607–1776 (Chapel Hill: University of North Carolina Press, 1947), 5.

14. See Richard S. Dunn, *Sugar and Slaves: The Rise of the Planter Class in the English West Indies, 1624–1713* (New York: Norton, 1973), 44–116; William Cronon, *Changes in the Land: Indians, Colonists, and the Ecology of New England* (New York: Hill and Wang, 1983).

15. Dunn, *Sugar and Slaves*, 188–223.

16. See E. Lipson, *The Economic History of England* (London: A. and C. Black, 1943), 3:184; see also Edgar S. Furniss, *The Position of the Laborer in a System of Nationalism* (New York: Augustus M. Kelley, 1957), 15–40; Josiah Child, *A New Discourse on Trade* (London, 1692); Sir Dalby Thomas, *An Historical Account of the Rise and Growth of the West India Colonies* (London, 1690).

17. Child, *A New Discourse*, 121, 163.

18. James A. Rawley, *The Transatlantic Slave Trade: A History* (New York: Norton, 1981), 129.

19. Ibid., 133.

20. Ibid., 135.

21. Ibid., 138.

22. Ibid., 143.

23. Ibid.

24. Ibid., 146.

25. Ibid.

26. Ibid.; see also C.L.R. James, *The Black Jacobins: Toussaint L'Ouverture and the San Domingo Revolution* (New York: Vintage, 1963).

27. Rawley, *Transatlantic Slave Trade*, 147.

28. Ibid.

29. Ibid., 168.

30. Ibid., 179.

31. Ibid., 171.

32. Ibid., 169.

33. Ibid.

34. Ibid., 177.

35. Ibid., 193.

36. Robin Blackburn, *The Making of New World Slavery: From the Baroque to the Modern, 1492–1800* (London: Verso, 1997), 514.

37. Ibid., 517.

38. Ibid.

39. David Richardson, "The Slave Trade, Sugar, and British Economic Growth, 1748–1776", in *British Capitalism and Caribbean Slavery: The Legacy of Eric Williams*, ed. Barbara L. Solow and Stanley L. Engerman (Cambridge: Cambridge University Press, 1987), 107.

40. Kenneth Morgan, *Slavery, Atlantic Trade and the British Economy, 1660–1800* (Cambridge: Cambridge University Press, 2000), 33.
41. Blackburn, *Making of New World Slavery*, 511, 516.
42. Ibid., 517.
43. Ibid., 519.
44. Ibid., 522.
45. Ibid., 533, 535, 536.
46. Ibid., 542.
47. Ibid., 543.
48. Ibid., 376, 378, 385, 395.
49. Ibid., 403, 404.
50. Ibid., 423.
51. Ibid., 421.
52. Ibid., 422.
53. Ibid.
54. Richardson, "Slave Trade", 105.
55. Ibid. 132
56. Morgan, *Slavery*, 33.
57. Ibid., 97, 98.
58. See Barbara L. Solow, "Capitalism and Slavery in the Exceedingly Long Run", in Solow and Engerman, *British Capitalism*, 51–77.
59. Ibid., 52, 55.
60. Ibid., 55, 57.
61. Ibid., 70.
62. Ibid., 71, 72.
63. Ibid., 75.
64. Ibid.

Chapter 8

1. See Edward Long, *The History of Jamaica* (London, 1774), 2:378–79; Bryan Edwards, *The History, Civil and Commercial of the British Colonies of the West Indies* (London: Stockdale, 1793), 2:92–94; Elsa V. Goveia, *Slave Society in the British Leeward Islands at the End of the Eighteenth Century* (New Haven: Yale University Press, 1965), 290–92.
2. Mary Turner, *Slaves and Missionaries: The Disintegration of Jamaican Slave Society, 1787–1834* (Urbana: University of Illinois Press, 1982).
3. Nicholas Draper, *The Price of Emancipation: Slave-Ownership, Compensation and British Society at the End of Slavery* (Cambridge: Cambridge University Press, 2010), 314–16.

4. Draper, *Price of Emancipation*, 160. See also Frank J. Klingberg, ed., *Codrington Chronicle: An Experiment in Anglican Altruism on a Barbados Plantation, 1710–1834* (Berkeley: University of California Press, 1949); Vincent T. Harlow, *Christopher Codrington, 1668–1710* (London: Oxford University Press, 1928).

5. J. Harry Bennett, *Bondsmen and Bishops: Slavery and Apprenticeship on the Codrington Plantations of Barbados, 1710–1838* (Berkeley: University of California Press, 1958), 1.

6. Ibid., viii.

7. Ibid., 10.

8. Ibid., 27.

9. Ibid., 44.

10. Ibid.

11. Ibid., 22, 44, 45, 46.

12. Ibid., 48.

13. Ibid., 52.

14. Ibid.

15. Ibid., 26, 27, 29, 30.

16. Ibid., 77.

17. Ibid., 77, 78, 80, 81.

18. Ibid., 72.

19. Ibid., 87, 88.

20. Ibid., 89.

21. Ibid., 90.

22. Ibid., 90, 91.

23. Ibid., 94.

24. Ibid., 116.

25. Ibid., 119.

26. Ibid.

Chapter 9

1. See Kathleen Mary Butler, *The Economics of Emancipation: Jamaica and Barbados, 1823–1843* (Chapel Hill: University of North Carolina Press, 1995); Kathleen Mary Butler, "'Fair and Equitable Consideration': The Distribution of Slave Compensation in Jamaica and Barbados", *Journal of Caribbean History* 22 (1988): 138–62.

2. Richard Pares, *A West-India Fortune* (London: Longman, 1950); Richard Pares, "Merchants and Planters", *Economic History Review*, supp. 4 (1960): 1–13, 26–33; S.G. Checkland, *The Gladstones: A Family Biography, 1764–1851* (Cambridge: Cambridge University Press, 1971); S.G. Checkland, "John Gladstone as Trader and Planter", *Economic History Review*, n.s., 7, no. 2 (1954): 216–29; S.G. Checkland,

"Finance for the West Indies, 1780–1815", *Economic History Review*, n.s., 10, no. 3 (1958): 461–69; V.E. Chancellor, "Slave-Owner and Anti-Slaver: Henry Richard Vassall Fox, 3rd Lord Holland, 1800–1840", *Slavery and Abolition* 1, no. 3 (1980): 263–75.

3.   S.D. Smith, *Slavery, Family, and Gentry Capitalism in the British Atlantic: The World of the Lascelles, 1648–1834* (Cambridge: Cambridge University Press, 2006); S.D. Smith, "Merchants and Planters Revisited", *Economic History Review*, n.s., 55, no. 3 (2002): 434–65.

4.   Nicholas Draper, *The Price of Emancipation: Slave-Ownership, Compensation and British Society at the End of Slavery* (Cambridge: Cambridge University Press, 2010), 9.

5.   See Smith, *Slavery, Family, and Gentry*, 6.

6.   Ibid., 48.

7.   Ibid.

8.   Ibid., 86.

9.   Ibid., 87.

10.   Ibid., 138.

11.   Ibid., 186.

12.   Ibid.

13.   Edwin Lascelles, James Colleton, Edwin Drax, Francis Ford, Reverend John Brathwaite, John Walter, William Holder, James Holder, Philip Gibbes and John Barney, *The Following Instructions are offered for the consideration of Proprietors and Managers of a Plantation in Barbados and for the Treatment of Negroes* (London, 1786). Reprinted in *Journal of Barbados Museum and Historical Society* 11, no. 1 (1934): 23–31.

14.   Ibid.

15.   Ibid., 25.

16.   Ibid., 27.

17.   Draper, *Price of Emancipation*, 320.

18.   Ibid., 313.

19.   Ibid., 313–14.

20.   Ibid., 315.

Chapter 10

1.   Eric Williams, *Capitalism and Slavery* (Chapel Hill: University of North Carolina Press, 1944), 154–78; see also Nicholas Draper, *The Price of Emancipation: Slave-Ownership, Compensation and British Society at the End of Slavery* (Cambridge: Cambridge University Press, 2010), 87, 93; Christopher L. Brown, *Moral Capital:*

Foundations of British Abolitionism (Chapel Hill: University of North Carolina Press, 2006); P.J. Cain and A.G. Hopkins, "Gentlemanly Capitalism and British Overseas Expansion, I: The Old Colonial System, 1688–1850", *Economic History Review*, n.s., 39, no. 4 (1986): 501–25; T.M. Devine, "An 18th Century Business Elite: Glasgow–West India Merchants, 1750–1815", *Scottish Historical Review* 57, no. 1 (1978): 40–67; Nicholas Draper, "The City of London and Slavery: Evidence from the First Dock Companies, 1785–1800", *Economic History Review* 61, no. 2 (2008): 432–66; Douglas Hamilton, *Scotland, the Caribbean and the Atlantic World, 1750–1820* (Manchester: Manchester University Press, 2005).

2. Draper, *Price of Emancipation*, 90–91

3. Ibid., 156.

4. Ibid., 157.

5. Ibid.

6. Ibid., 168.

7. Ibid.

8. Ibid., 176.

9. Ibid., 178.

10. Ibid., 250.

11. Ibid., 140.

12. Ibid., 212.

13. Ibid., 242.

14. Ibid.

15. Williams, *Capitalism and Slavery*, 101.

16. Draper, *Price of Emancipation*, 243.

17. Ibid., 244.

18. Ibid., 245. *Jews*

19. Ibid., 246. See "Lehman Brothers Admits Profits from Slavery; Makes Insensitive Comments", *Chicago Sun Times*, 25 November 2003; James Cox, "Corporations Challenged by Reparations Activists", *USA Today*, 21 February 2002; "Lehman Bros; 1 Brother Owned 7 Slaves in 1860", *USA Today*, 21 February 2002.

20. Draper, *Price of Emancipation*, 246. *Rothschilds Papers.*

21. Ibid., 248–49.

22. Ibid., 249.

23. Kenneth Morgan, *Slavery, Atlantic Trade and the British Economy, 1660–1800* (Cambridge: Cambridge University Press, 2000), 77.

24. Ibid.

Chapter 11

1. See Kathleen Mary Butler, *The Economics of Emancipation: Jamaica and Barbados, 1823–1843* (Chapel Hill: University of North Carolina Press, 1995), 1–5; Thomas Bender, ed., *The Anti-Slavery Debate: Capitalism and Abolitionism as a Problem of Historical Interpretation* (Berkeley: University of California Press, 1992); Dalton Conley, "Calculating Slavery Reparations: Theory, Numbers, and Implications", in *Politics and the Past: On Repairing Historical Injustices*, ed. John Torpey (Lanham, MD: Rowman and Littlefield, 2003), 117–25; Ben Dalbey, "Slavery and the Question of Reparations", *International Socialist Review* 26 (2002): 74–80.

2. See B.W. Higman, "The West India 'Interest' in Parliament, 1807–1833", *Historical Studies* 13, no. 49 (1967): 1–19; Peter Marshall, *Bristol and the Abolition of Slavery: The Politics of Emancipation* (Bristol: Bristol Historical Association, 1975); Michael Moohr, "The Economic Impact of Slave Emancipation in British Guiana, 1832–1852", *Economic History Review* 25, no. 4 (1972): 588–607; A.C. Pigou, "The Problem of Compensation", *Economic Journal* 35, no. 140 (1925): 568–82.

3. Nicholas Draper, *The Price of Emancipation: Slave-Ownership, Compensation and British Society at the End of Slavery* (Cambridge: Cambridge University Press, 2010), 106–7.

4. Ibid., 74.

5. Ibid., 72, 90–93.

6. Ibid., 79.

7. Ibid., 81.

8. Ibid., 82.

9. Ibid., 85.

10. Ibid., 87.

11. Ibid., 89.

12. Butler, *Economics of Emancipation*, 8.

13. Ibid., 9.

14. Ibid.

15. Ibid., 35.

16. Ibid., 19, 21.

17. Ibid., 23, 24.

18. Ibid., 27.

19. B.W. Higman, *Slave Populations of the British Caribbean, 1807–1834* (Baltimore: Johns Hopkins University Press, 1984), 80.

20. Draper, *Price of Emancipation*, 191–203.

21. Ibid., 4.

22. Ibid., 115.

23. Draper, *Price of Emancipation*, appendix 16.

24. Ibid., 16.
25. Ibid., 244.
26. Butler, *Economics of Emancipation*, xvi.
27. Ibid., 71.
28. Ibid., 44.

Chapter 12

1. See foreword by Frederico Mayor, director general of United Nations Educational, Scientific and Cultural Organization (UNESCO), and introduction by Doudou Diène, director of intercultural projects, UNESCO, in "The Slave Route", http://unesdoc.unesco.org/images/0011/001144/114427eo.pdf. See also Nicholas Canny, ed., *The Origins of Empire*, vol. 1 of *The Oxford History of the British Empire* (Oxford: Oxford University Press, 1998).
2. See Eric Williams, *Capitalism and Slavery* (Chapel Hill: University of North Carolina Press, 1944); Hilary Beckles, "Capitalism and Slavery: The Debate over the Williams Thesis", *Social and Economic Studies* 33 (1984), 171–90.
3. G.K. Lewis, *Main Currents in Caribbean Thought: The Historical Evolution of Caribbean Society in Its Ideological Aspects* (London: Heinemann, 1983); Denis M. Benn, "The Theory of Plantation Economy and Society: A Methodological Critique", *Journal of Commonwealth and Comparative Politics* 12 (1974): 249–60.
4. See Hilary Beckles and Verene Shepherd, eds., *Caribbean Slavery in the Atlantic World* (Kingston: Ian Randle, 2000).
5. See Anthony Gifford, *The Passionate Advocate* (Kingston: Arawak, 2007).
6. See Hilary Beckles, "The Genocide Policy in English–Karifuna Relations in the Seventeenth Century", in *Empire and Others: British Encounters with Indigenous People, 1680–1850*, ed. Martin Daunton and Rick Halpern (London: UCL Press, 1999), 280–302.
7. See Hugh Thomas, *The Slave Trade: The History of the Atlantic Slave Trade, 1440–1870* (London: Papermac, 1997).
8. See Barbara L. Solow and Stanley L. Engerman, eds., *British Capitalism and Caribbean Slavery: The Legacy of Eric Williams* (New York: Cambridge University Press, 1987).
9. See Gert Oostindie, ed., *Facing Up to the Past: Perspectives on the Commemoration of Slavery from Africa, the Americas, and Europe* (Kingston: Ian Randle, 2001).
10. Randall Robinson, *The Debt: What America Owes to Blacks* (New York: Dutton, 2000); Rhoda E. Howard-Hassmann and Anthony P. Lombardo, "Framing Reparations Claims: Differences between the African and Jewish Social Movements for Reparations", *African Studies Review* 50, no. 1 (2007): 27–48; Ricardo Laremont,

Murdered Famous — killed for being
½ caste Sian Blake
Arthur Kent SIMPSON. Black British ed

"Political versus Legal Strategies for the African Slavery and Reparations Movement", *African Studies Quarterly* 2, no. 4 (1999): 13–17.

11. Cited in Clarence Munford, *Race and Reparations: A Black Perspective for the Twenty-first Century* (Trenton, NJ: Africa World Press, 1996), 428–29.

12. Ali Mazrui and Alamin Mazrui, *Black Reparations in the Era of Globalization* (Binghamton, NY: Institute of Global Cultural Studies, 2002).

Chapter 13

1. See Hilary Beckles, "Report of the World Conference against Racism, Racial Discrimination, Xenophobia and Related Intolerance, Durban, South Africa, 31 August–8 September, 2001", http://www.un.org/WCAR/aconf189_12.pdf; see also the United Nations Human Rights Commission's report on the World Conference against Racism, Racial Discrimination, Xenophobia and Related Intolerance, http://www.un.org/WCAR/durban.pdf.

2. See "Rice Says US Blacks Should Not Be Paid for Slavery", *Daily Observer*, Monday, 10 September 2001.

3. See Anthony Gifford, *The Passionate Advocate* (Kingston: Arawak, 2007), 243–54; "The Legal Basis for the African Claims of Reparations for the Slave Trade" (typescript, 1993).

4. Gifford, *Passionate Advocate*, 243–44.   typed White Racist!

5. Ibid., 245.

6. Ibid., 246–51.

7. Ibid., 251.

8. Ibid., 252.

9. Ibid., 252–53.

10. Ibid., 253.

11. Ibid.

12. Ibid.

13. Ibid.

14. *Slave Trade and Reparations: Gorèe Initiative* (pamphlet, Geneva, 2001).

15. Ibid.

16. Abdelbagi G. Jibril, "The Legal Basis for the African Claim of Reparation for the Slave Trade" [amended version of Lord Anthony Gifford's paper of the same title], International Seminar on Reparation (Gorèe Island), 26 June 2001.   There is None!

17. Ibid., 1.

18. Ibid.

19. Ibid., 2.

20. *Slave Trade and Reparations: Gorèe Initiative.*   They hate black people!

What is Gifford's' Interest?
Not in Black Britain.

21. Ibid.   *hates Blacks – wants a white zone*
22. Kofi Annan, plenary presentation to the UN World Conference against Racism, Discrimination, Xenophobia and Related Intolerance, Durban, South Africa, 31 August 2001.
23. Ibid.
24. Government of the United States, official press release, UN World Conference against Racism, Discrimination, Xenophobia and Related Intolerance, 4 May 2001, http://lists.topica.com/lists/TheBlackList/read/message.html?sort=d&mid=9000 57969.
25. Fidel Castro, plenary presentation, UN World Conference against Racism, Discrimination, Xenophobia and Related Intolerance, Durban, South Africa, 31 August 2001.
26. Ibid.
27. "Slavery Issue: A World Divided", *Conference News Daily*, 6 September 2001.
28. See also Gifford, *Passionate Advocate*, 264–65.
29. Robert E. Sullivan, *Conference News Daily*, 6 September 2001.

Chapter 14

1. "Thomas Fowell Buxton: The Fight for Abolition", British Broadcasting Corporation (BBC) Norfolk, Abolition of the Slave Trade, http://www.bbc.co.uk/Norfolk, last updated 9 April 2008.
   See Nicholas Draper, *The Price of Emancipation: Slave-Ownership, Compensation and British Society at the End of Slavery* (Cambridge: Cambridge University Press, 2010), 106–7; see also R.E.P. Wastell, "The History of Slave Compensation, 1833 to 1845" (MA thesis, London University, 1932), 233–34.
2. Colin Brown, "Blair Admits to 'Deep Sorrow' Over Slavery – But No Apology", *Independent*, 27 November 2006, http://news.bbc.co.uk/2/hi/6185176.stm.
3. Ibid.
4. See Anthony Gifford, "Reparations and the Bicentennial of the Abolition of Slave Trade", posted 3 July 2008, http://ijchr.org.archives/23.
5. Joe Churcher and Ben Padley, "Blair Refuses to Bow to Slave Trade Apology", *Independent*, 26 March 2007, 1–3.
6. See Joe Churcher and Ben Padley, "Blair Refuses".
7. Quotes in respect of Baroness Amos, in Brown, "Blair Admits".
8. "Blair 'Sorrow' over Slave Trade", BBC News, 27 November 2006, http://news .bbc.co.uk/2/hi/6185176.stm.
9. "Blair's Slavery Sorrow Not Enough, Say Activists", *Gleaner*, 28 November 2006, http://www.jamaica-gleaner.com/gleaner/20061128/news/news2.html.

10. "Church Considers Slavery Payments", BBC News, posted 26 March 2007, http://news.bbc.co.uk/2/hi/uk_news/6494243.stm.

11. "Protester Demands an Apology from Queen over Slavery", 28 March 2007, http://www.scotsman.com/news/uk/protester-demands-an-apology-from-queen-over-slavery-1-692628.

12. Royson James, "This Is a Disgrace", 28 March 2007, http://www.thestar.com/article/196773.

13. Ibid.

14. All subsequent quotations in the debate are from the House of Commons Official Report, Parliament 2007, *Hansard*, 20 March 2007, vol. 458, no. 64, http://www.publications.parliament.uk/pa/cm200607/cmhansrd/cmo70320/debtext/70320-0007.htm.

15. House of Lords, *Hansard*, 10 May 2007, http://www.publications.parliament.uk/pa/ld200607/ldhansrd/text/70510-0003.htm. Subsequent quotations from the debate are taken from this source.

16. See Anthony Gifford, *The Passionate Advocate* (Kingston: Arawak, 2007), 258.

17. Ibid., 259.

18. Ibid.

Chapter 15

1. Vincent Cable, member of Parliament, speaking in Parliament on 20 March 2007. Cited in House of Commons Official Report, Parliamentary Debates, *Hansard*, 20 March 2007, vol. 458, no. 64, 708–9, http://www.publications.parliament.uk/pa/cm200607/cmhansrd/cmo703 20/debtext/70320-0007.htm. All references cited in this chapter to the House of Commons debate are from this volume.

2. Debates, 738, 770.

3. President Aristide, press briefing, Montego Bay, Twenty-fourth CARICOM Summit, Jamaica, July 2003, *Asia Africa Intelligence Wire*, 5 July 2003, http://www.accessmylibrary.com/coms2/Summary_0286-23721073_ITM; see also "Crisis Linked to Reparations", *Sunday Sun*, 7 March 2004, 12A.

4. See Jacqueline Charles, "Aristide Pushes for Restitution from France", http://www.latinamericanstudies.org/haiti/haiti-restitution.htm.

5. Paul Farmer, "Who Removed Aristide?", *London Review of Books* 26, no. 8 (15 April 2004): 28–29.

6. Charles, "Aristide Pushes for Restitution".

7. Peter Hallward, to the editor, *London Review of Books* 26, no. 9 (6 May 2004), http://www.lrb.co.uk/v26/n08/paul-farmer/who-removed-aristide.

8. Anthony Fenton, letter to the editor, *London Review of Books* 26, no. 11 (3 June 2004), http://www.lrb.co.uk/v26/n08/paul-farmer/who-removed-aristide.

Caricom a Joke!

9.   "Mitchell: Haiti Needs International Intervention", *Sunday Sun*, 7 March 2004; "Caricom Calls for UN Probe", *Sunday Sun*, 7 March 2004.

10. Ibid.

11. Sourcewatch, "Haiti's Thirty-third Coup?", http://Sourcewatch.org/index.php?title =International_Politics_and _Haiti in_ 2004, 2.

12. Ibid.; see also "International Politics in Haiti in 2004", http://www.sourcewatch .org/index.php?title=International_Politics_and_Haiti_in_2004.

13. Agence France Presse, "Aristide's 'Removal' from Haiti Unconstitutional: African Union", Common Dreams website, 9 March 2004, http://www.commondreams .org/headlines04/0309-06.htm.

14. Dione Miller, "Aristide's Call for Reparations from France Unlikely to Die", Inter Press Service, 12 March 2004, http://ipsnews.net/news.asp?idnews=22828.

15. Sourcewatch, "Haiti's Thirty-third Coup".

16. Joseph Guyler Delva, "Haiti Drops 'Ridiculous' $22 Billion Claim (of Money Owed by France)", *Reuters*, 18 April 2004, http://www.democraticunderground.com/ discuss/duboard.php

17. Charles, "Aristide Pushes for Restitution".

18. "British Delegates: We Were Misled", *Daily Nation*, 3 October 2002.

19. Ibid.

20. Ibid.

21. "Move to Derail Durban Gains", *Daily Nation*, 4 October 2002.

22. "Commissiong: Issue Should Not Have Arisen", *Daily Nation*, 3 October 2002; "Commissiong Not Involved in Passing Resolution", *Advocate News*, 3 October 2002.

23. "Mottley Knocks 'Banning' Resolution", *Daily Nation*, 4 October 2002; see also "Whites Not to Be Left Out: Mottley Knocks 'Banning' Resolution", *Barbados Advocate*, 4 October 2002.

24. See Commission for Africa, http://www.commissionforafrica.info.

25. http://www.news.bbc.co.uk/2/hi/Africa/1575428.stm.

26. "Commission for Africa Holds 1st Meeting", *Advocate News*, 5 May 2004.

27. "Focus on Reparations", *Advocate News*, 18 August 2004.

28. Ibid.

29. "Statement by the Hon. Dame Billie A. Miller, M.P; Senior Minister and Minister of Foreign Affairs and Foreign Trade of Barbados to the General Debate of the 62nd Session of the UN General Assembly, Oct. 3, 2007", http://www.un.org/webcast /ga/62/2007/pdfs/barbados.

30. "Arthur: Give Back to Slave Children", *Daily Nation*, 27 March 2007.

31. Ibid.

32. "Caribbean Marks 200th Anniversary of End of Britain's Transatlantic Slave Trade", *Advocate News*, 27 March 2007.

33. "Guyana Calls for Reparations", BBCCaribbean.com, 27 March 2007, http://www .bbc.co.uk/caribbean/news/story/2007/03/070327_jagdeore parations.shtml.

34. Ibid.

35. Ibid.

36. "Guyana's Government Calls for Reparatory Justice for African Slavery", *Advocate News*, 8 February 2007.

37. "MP Walks Out on Blair's No. 2", *Sun on Saturday*, 26 May 2007.

38. Ibid.

39. "Gonsalves Puts Case for Reparations", *Daily Nation*, 30 August 2007.

40. "Apology for Slavery Not Enough", *Daily Nation*, 27 March 2007.

41. Statement by Dame Billie Miller, United Nations General Assembly, 3 October 2007.

42. Gordon Rayner, "Jamaican PM: It Would Be 'Fine with Us' if Britain Apologised for 'Wicked and Brutal' Slavery", Telegraph, 6 March 2012, http://www.telegraph .co.uk/news/uknews/prince-harry/9125124/Jamaican-PM-it-would-be-fine-with-us -if-Britain-apologised-for-wicked-and-brutal-slavery.html.

43. "Jamaica Will Seek No Reparation from Britain", *Gleaner*, 7 March 2012.

44. "Henry Bashes Simpson Miller for Reparation Comments", *Gleaner*, 8 March 2012.

Selected Bibliography

America, Richard F. "Reparations and Public Policy". *Review of Black Political Economy* 26, no. 3 (1999): 77–83.

Andréadès, A. *History of the Bank of England, 1640–1903*. London: P.S. King and Son, 1909.

Andrews, Kenneth R. *Trade, Plunder and Settlement: Maritime Enterprises and the Genesis of the British Empire, 1480–1630*. Cambridge: Cambridge University Press, 1984.

Anstey, Roger. *The Atlantic Slave Trade and British Abolition, 1760–1810*. London: Macmillan, 1975.

———. "The British Slave Trade, 1761–1807: A Comment". *Journal of African History* 17 (1976): 606–7.

Asante, Molefi Kete. *Afrocentricity*. Trenton, NJ: Africa World Press, 1988.

Aufhauser, Keith. "Profitability of Slavery in the British Caribbean". *Journal of Interdisciplinary History* 5, no. 1 (1974): 45–67.

Austen, Ralph A. "The Slave Trade as History and Memory: Confrontations of Slaving Voyage Documents and Communal Traditions". *William and Mary Quarterly* 58 (2001): 229–44.

Azeez, James. *The Compensation Controversy*. History Gazette, no. 12. Georgetown: History Society, University of Guyana, 1989.

Baraka, Amiri. *The Essence of Reparations*. Philipsburg, St Martin: House of Nehesi, 2003.

Barbour, Violet. "Marine Risk and Insurance in the 17th Century". *Journal of Economic and Business History* 1 (1929): 561–96.

Barclay, Alexander. *A Practical View of the Present State of Slavery in the West Indies*. London: Smith, Elder and Co., 1826.

Bayley, F.W.N. *Four Years' Residence in the West Indies*. London: William Kidd, 1830.

Bean, Richard N. *The British Transatlantic Slave Trade, 1650–1775*. New York: Ayer, 1975.

———. "A Note on the Relative Importance of Slaves and Gold in West African Exports". *Journal of African History* 15 (1974): 351–96.

256   Selected Bibliography

Beckles, Hilary. *Black Rebellion in Barbados: The Struggle against Slavery, 1627–1838*. Bridgetown, Barbados: Antilles, 1987.

———. "Capitalism and Slavery: The Debate over the Williams Thesis". *Social and Economic Studies* 33 (1984): 171–90.

———. *Centering Woman: Gender Discourses in Caribbean Slave Societies*. Kingston: Ian Randle, 1999.

———. "The Concept of 'White Slavery' in the English Caribbean during the Early Seventeenth Century". In *Early Modern Conceptions of Property*, edited by John Brewer and Susan Staves, 572–85. New York: Routledge, 1995.

———. "An Economic Life of Their Own: Slaves as Commodity Producers and Distributors in Barbados". In *The Slaves' Economy: Independent Production by Slaves in the Americas*, edited by Ira Berlin and Philip Morgan, 31–47. London: Frank Cass, 1991.

———. "The Genocide Policy in English–Karifuna Relations in the Seventeenth Century". In *Empire and Others: British Encounters with Indigenous People, 1600–1850*, edited by Martin Daunton and Rick Halpern, 280–302. London: UCL Press, 1999.

———. "The 'Hub of Empire': The Caribbean and Britain in the Seventeenth Century". In *The Oxford History of the British Empire*. Vol. 1, *The Origins of Empire: British Overseas Enterprise to the Close of the Seventeenth Century*, edited by Nicholas Canny, 218–40. Oxford: Oxford University Press, 1998.

———. "Kalinago (Carib) Resistance to European Colonisation of the Caribbean". *Caribbean Quarterly* 21, no. 1 (1987): 55–77.

———. *Natural Rebels: A Social History of Enslaved Black Women in Barbados*. London: Zed Books, 1989.

———. "Property Rights in Pleasure: The Marketing of Enslaved Women's Sexuality". In *West Indies Accounts: Essays on the History of the British Caribbean and the Atlantic*, edited by Roderick A. McDonald, 169–87. Kingston: University of the West Indies Press, 1996.

———. "A 'Riotous and Unruly Lot': Irish Indentured Servants and Freemen in the English West Indies, 1644–1713". *William and Mary Quarterly* 47 (1990): 503–22.

———. "Social and Political Control in the Slave Society". In *General History of the Caribbean*. Vol. 3, *The Slave Societies of the Caribbean*, edited by Franklin W. Knight, 194–221. London: UNESCO, 1997.

———. "The 200 Years War: Slave Resistance in the British West Indies: An Overview of the Historiography". *Jamaican Historical Review* 14 (1982): 1–10.

———. *White Servitude and Black Slavery in Barbados*. Knoxville: University of Tennessee Press, 1989.

———. "The Wilberforce Song: How Enslaved Caribbean Blacks Heard British Abolitionists". In *The British Slave Trade: Abolition, Parliament and People*, edited by Stephen Farrell, Melanie Unwin and James Walvin, 113–127. Edinburgh: Edinburgh University Press, 2007.

Beckles, Hilary, and Andrew Downes. "The Economic Transition to the Black Labour System in Barbados, 1630–1680". *Journal of Interdisciplinary History* 18 (1987): 225–47.

Beckles, Hilary, and Verene Shepherd, eds. *Caribbean Slavery in the Atlantic World.* Kingston: Ian Randle, 2000.

———. *Saving Souls: The Struggle to End the Transatlantic Slave Trade.* Kingston: Ian Randle, 2007.

———. *Trading Souls: Europe's Transatlantic Trade in Africans.* Kingston: Ian Randle, 2007.

Bender, Thomas, ed. *The Anti-Slavery Debate: Capitalism and Abolitionism as a Problem of Historical Interpretation.* Berkeley: University of California Press, 1992.

Benn, Denis M. "The Theory of Plantation Economy and Society: A Methodological Critique". *Journal of Commonwealth and Comparative Politics* 12 (1974): 249–60.

Bennett, J. Harry. *Bondsmen and Bishops: Slavery and Apprenticeship on the Codrington Plantations in Barbados, 1710–1838.* Berkeley: University of California Press, 1958.

Berlin, Ira. "American Slavery in History and Memory and the Search for Social Justice". *Journal of American History* 90, no. 4 (2004): 1251–68.

Bickell, Rev. R. *The West Indies as They Are: or A Real Picture of Slavery.* London: Hatchard, 1825.

Billingsley, Andrew. *Climbing Jacob's Ladder: The Enduring Legacy of African-American Families.* New York: Simon and Schuster, 1992.

Bittker, Boris I. *The Case for Black Reparations.* New York: Random House, 1973.

Blackburn, Robin. *The Making of New World Slavery: From the Baroque to the Modern, 1492–1800.* London: Verso, 1997.

———. *The Overthrow of Colonial Slavery, 1776–1848.* London: Verso, 1999.

Blake Hannah, Barbara, et al. Jamaica Reparations document, Jamaica Reparations Committee. Kingston, 2003.

Bliss, Robert M. *Revolution and Empire: English Politics and the American Colonies in the Seventeenth Century.* Manchester: Manchester University Press, 1990.

Bollard, O. Nigel. *The Formation of a Colonial Society: Belize from Conquest to Crown Colony.* Baltimore: Johns Hopkins University Press, 1977.

Branch, Watson. "Reparations for Slavery: A Dream Deferred". *San Diego International Law Journal* 3 (2002): 177–206.

Brathwaite, C.K. "London Bourne of Barbados, 1793–1869". *Slavery and Abolition* 28, no. 1 (2007): 23–40.

Brathwaite, Edward Kamau. *The Development of Creole Society in Jamaica, 1770–1820.* Oxford: Clarendon Press, 1971.

———. "The Slave Rebellion in the Great River Valley of St James, 1831/32". *Jamaican Historical Review* 13 (1982): 11–30.

Brewer, John, and Susan Staves, eds. *Early Modern Conceptions of Property.* New York: Routledge, 1995.

Brooks, Roy L. *Atonement and Forgiveness: A New Model for Black Reparations.* Berkeley: University of California Press, 2004.

———, ed. *When Sorry Isn't Enough: The Controversy over Apologies and Reparations for Human Injustice.* New York: New York University Press, 1999.

Brophy, Alfred L. "Some Conceptual and Legal Problems in Reparations for Slavery". *Annual Survey of American Law* 58 (2003): 497–558.

Brown, Christopher L. "The British Government and the Slave Trade: Early Parliamentary Enquiries, 1713–83". In *The British Slave Trade: Abolition, Parliament and People,* edited by Stephen Farrell, Melanie Unwin and James Walvin, 27–41. Edinburgh: Edinburgh University Press, 2007.

———. *Moral Capital: Foundations of British Abolitionism.* Chapel Hill: University of North Carolina Press, 2006.

Brown, David. *Race, Class, Politics and the Struggle for Empowerment in Barbados, 1914–1937.* Kingston: Ian Randle, 2012.

Brown, Elaine. *A Taste of Power: A Black Woman's Story.* New York: Pantheon, 1992.

Browne, Robert. "The Economic Basis for Reparations to Black America". *Review of Black Political Economy* 21, no. 3 (1993): 99–110.

Burn, W.L. *Emancipation and Apprenticeship in the British West Indies.* London: Jonathan Cape, 1937.

Burnard, Trevor. "European Migration to Jamaica, 1655–1780". *William and Mary Quarterly* 53 (1996): 769–96.

———. "Passengers Only: The Extent and Significance of Absenteeism in Eighteenth-Century Jamaica". *Atlantic Studies* 1, no. 2 (2004): 178–95.

———. "Prodigious Riches: The Wealth of Jamaica Before the American Revolution". *Economic History Review* 54 (2001): 514–16.

———. "Who Bought Slaves in America? Purchasers of Slaves from the Royal African Company in Jamaica, 1674–1709". *Slavery and Abolition* 17 (1996): 68–92.

Burnley, William H. *Opinions on Slavery and Emancipation in 1823.* London: James Ridgway, 1833.

Burton, Thomas. *Diary of Thomas Burton, Esq., . . . from 1656 to 1659.* London: Henry Colburn, 1828.

Bush, Barbara. "White 'Ladies', Coloured 'Favourites', and Black 'Wenches': Some Considerations on Sex, Race, and Class Factors in Social Relations in White Creole Society in the British Caribbean". *Slavery and Abolition* 2 (1981): 245–62.

Butler, Kathleen Mary. *The Economics of Emancipation: Jamaica and Barbados, 1823–1843.* Chapel Hill: University of North Carolina Press, 1995.

———. "Fair and Equitable Consideration: The Distribution of Slave Compensation in Jamaica and Barbados". *Journal of Caribbean History* 22, nos. 1–2 (1988): 138–62.

Cain, P.J., and A.G. Hopkins. "Gentlemanly Capitalism and British Overseas Expansion, I: The Old Colonial System, 1688–1850". *Economic History Review,* n.s., 39, no. 4 (1986): 501–25.

Racist, Anti-Black 'colonial'
Beckles + Shephard
= "Tag Team" Commonwealth,

———. "Gentlemanly Capitalism and British Overseas Expansion, II: New Imperialism, 1850–1945". *Economic History Review*, n.s., 40, no. 1 (1987): 1–26.

Cannadine, David: "Aristocratic Indebtedness in the Nineteenth Century: The Case Re-opened". *Economic History Review*, n.s., 30, no. 4 (1977): 624–50. *Nobles Debts*

Canny, Nicholas, ed. *The Origins of Empire: The Oxford History of the British Empire*. Oxford: Oxford University Press, 1998.

Canny, Nicholas, and Anthony Pagden, eds. *Colonial Identity in the Atlantic World, 1500–1800*. Princeton, NJ: Princeton University Press, 1992.

Carmichael, A.C. *Domestic Manners and Social Condition of the White, Coloured, and Negro Population of the West Indies*. 2 vols. London: Whittacker, 1833. *Manners*

Carrington, Selwyn. "Management of Sugar Estates in the British West Indies at the End of the Eighteenth Century". *Journal of Caribbean History* 33 (1999): 27–53. *Sugar*

———. "The State of the Debate on the Role of Capitalism in the Ending of the Slave System". In *Caribbean Slave Society and Economy: A Student Reader*, edited by Hilary Beckles and Verene Shepherd, 435–46. New York: The New Press, 1991.

Carmichael, Stokely, and Charles V. Hamilton. *Black Power: The Politics of Liberation*. New York: Penguin Books, 1967. *Black Power*

Carter, Henderson. *Labour Pains: Resistance and Protest in Barbados, 1838–1904*. Kingston: Ian Randle, 2012.

Chancellor, V.E. "Slave-Owner and Anti-Slaver: Henry Richard Vassall Fox, 3rd Lord Holland, 1800–1840". *Slavery and Abolition* 1, no. 3 (1980): 263–75. *Noble*

Checkland, S.G. "American versus West Indian Traders in Liverpool, 1793–1815". *Journal of Economic History* 18, no. 2 (1958): 141–60.

———. "Finance for the West Indies, 1780–1815". *Economic History Review*, n.s., 10, no. 3 (1958): 461–69.

———. *The Gladstones: A Family Biography, 1764–1851*. Cambridge: Cambridge University Press, 1971. *PM*

———. "John Gladstone as Trader and Planter". *Economic History Review*, n.s., 7, no. 2 (1954): 216–29.

Child, Josiah. *A New Discourse on Trade*. London, 1692.

Cohen, William B. *The French Encounter with Africans: White Responses to Blacks, 1530–1880*. Bloomington: Indiana University Press, 1980.

Coleridge, Henry. *Six Months in the West Indies in 1825*. London: John Murray, 1832. *Where?*

Collins, D.R. *Practical Rules for the Management and Medical Treatment of Negro Slaves in the Sugar Colonies*. London: J. Barfield, 1803. *Medical Doctors*

Colthurst, John Bowen. *The Colthurst Journal: Journal of a Special Magistrate in the Islands of Barbados and St Vincent, July, 1835–September, 1838*, edited by Woodville Marshall. Millwood: KTO Press, 1977. *Bergy*

Conley, Dalton. "Calculating Slavery Reparations: Theory, Numbers, and Implications". In *Politics and The Past: On Repairing Historical Injustices*, edited by John Torpey, 117–25. Lanham, MD: Rowman and Littlefield, 2003. *Rep*

Jam Cooper, Thomas. *Facts Illustrative of the Condition of the Negro Slaves in Jamaica*. London: Hatchard, 1824.

Corlett, J.Angelo. *Race, Racism, and Reparations*. Ithaca: Cornell University Press, 2003.

Red Indians Costo, Rupert, and Jeannette Costo. *Indian Treatises: Two Centuries of Dishonor*. San Francisco: Indian Historical Press, 1977.

bargys Cracknell, Everill, ed. *The Barbadian Diary of General Robert Haynes, 1787–1836*. Medstead, Hampshire: Azania Press, 1934.

Craton, Michael. "Property and Propriety: Land Tenure and Slave Property in the Creation of a British West Indian Plantocracy, 1612–1740". In *Early Modern Conceptions of Property*, edited by John Brewer and Susan Staves, 497–529. New York: Routledge, 1995.

———. *Sinews of Empire: A Short History of British Slavery*. New York: Anchor Books, 1974.

———. *Testing the Chains: Resistance to Slavery in the British West Indies*. Ithaca: Cornell University Press, 1982.

Craton, Michael, and James Walvin. *A Jamaican Plantation: A History of Worthy Park, 1670–1970*. London: Allen, 1970.

Cress-Welsing, Francis. *The Isis Papers: The Keys to Colors*. Chicago: Third World Press, 1991.   I'm bored!

Cronon, William. *Changes in the Land: Indians, Colonists, and the Ecology of New England*. New York: Hill and Wang, 1983.

Curtin, Philip D. *The Atlantic Slave Trade: A Census*. Madison: University of Wisconsin Press, 1969.

———. "The British Sugar Duties and West Indian Prosperity". *Journal of Economic History* 14 (1954): 157–73.

———. *Economic Change in Pre-Colonial Africa: Supplementary Evidence*. Madison: University of Wisconsin Press, 1975.

———. "Epidemiology and the Slave Trade". *Political Science Quarterly* 83 (1968): 190–216.

Daget, Serge. "The Abolition of the Slave Trade by France: The Decisive Years, 1826–1831". In *Abolition and Its Aftermath: The Historical Context, 1790–1916*, edited by David Richardson. London: Frank Cass, 1985.

———. "France, Repression of the Illegal Slave Trade, and England, 1817–1850". In *The Abolition of the Atlantic Slave Trade: Origins and Effects in Europe, Africa, and the Americas*, edited by David Eltis and James Walvin, 193–217. Madison: University of Wisconsin Press, 1982.

Rep Dalbey, Ben. "Slavery and the Question of Reparations". *International Socialist Review* 26 (2002): 74–80.

Darity, William, Jr. "British Industry and the West Indies Plantations". In *The Atlantic Slave Trade: Effects on Economies, Societies, and Peoples in Africa, the Americas, and*

See Wilber Jwee + the 'academic' Racists

Europe, edited by Joseph E. Inikori and Stanley L. Engerman, 247–79. Durham, NC: Duke University Press, 1992.

———. "The Numbers Game and the Profitability of the British Trade in Slaves". *Journal of Economic History* 45 (1985): 693–703.

Darity, William, Jr, and Dania Frank. "The Economics of Reparations". *American Economic Review* 93, no. 2 (2003): 326–29.

Daunton, Martin. "Gentlemanly Capitalism and British Industry, 1820–1914". *Past and Present* 122 (1989): 119–58.

Daunton, Martin, and Rick Halpern, eds. *Empire and Others: British Encounters with Indigenous Peoples, 1600–1850*. London: University College of London Press, 1999.

Davidoff, Leonore, and Catherine Hall. *Family Fortunes: Men and Women of the English Middle Class, 1780–1850*. London: Hutchinson, 1991.

Davidson, Basil. *The African Slave Trade*. Boston: Atlantic, Little and Brown, 1961.

Davies, K.G. "Joint-Stock Investment in the Later Seventeenth Century". *Economic History Review* 4, no. 3 (1952): 283–301.

———. *The North Atlantic World in the Seventeenth Century*. Vol. 4, *Europe and the World in the Age of Expansionism*. Minneapolis: University of Minnesota Press, 1974.

———. *The Royal African Company*. Atheneum, NY: Holiday House, 1970.

Davis, David Brion. *Inhuman Bondage: The Rise and Fall of Slavery in the New World*. Oxford: Oxford University Press, 2006.

———. *The Problem of Slavery in an Age of Revolution, 1770–1823*. Ithaca: Cornell University Press, 1975.

Davis, Ralph. *The Industrial Revolution and British Overseas Trade*. Leicester: Leicester University Press, 1979.

Dean, Warren. *Rio Claro: A Brazilian Plantation System, 1820–1920*. Palo Alto, CA: Stanford University Press, 1976.

Delgado, Richard. *The Coming Race War? And Other Apocalyptic Tales of America after Affirmative Action*. New York: New York University Press, 1996.

Devine, Thomas M. "An Eighteenth Century Business Elite: Glasgow–West India Merchants, 1795–1800". *Scottish Historical Review* 57, no. 1 (1978): 40–67.

Dickson, William. *Mitigation of Slavery*. London: Longman, 1814.

Diop, Cheikh. *The Cultural Unity of Black Africa*. Chicago: Third World Press, 1978.

Donnan, Elizabeth, ed. *Documents Illustrative of the History of the Slave Trade to America*. 4 vols. 1930; repr. New York: Octagon, 1969.

Draper, Nicholas. "The City of London and Slavery: Evidence from the First Dock Companies, 1795–1800". *Economic History Review* 61, no. 2 (2008): 432–66.

———. " 'Possessing Slaves': Ownership, Compensation, and Metropolitan Society in Britain at the Time of Emancipation, 1834–40". *History Workshop: A Journal of Socialist and Feminist Historians* 64 (2007): 74–102.

*Catherine Hall, Nick Draper — all Jews Whites
No West-Indians*

——. *The Price of Emancipation: Slave-Ownership, Compensation and British Society at the End of Slavery.* Cambridge: Cambridge University Press, 2010.

Drescher, Seymour. *Capitalism and Anti-Slavery: British Popular Mobilization in Comparative Perspective.* New York: Oxford University Press, 1987.

——. *Econocide: British Slavery in the Era of Abolition.* Pittsburgh, PA: Pittsburgh University Press, 1977.

——. *The Mighty Experiment: Free Labour versus Slavery in British Emancipation.* Oxford: Oxford University Press, 2002.

——. "Public Opinion and Parliament in the Abolition of the British Slave Trade". In *The British Slave Trade: Abolition, Parliament and People*, edited by Stephen Farrell, Melanie Unwin and James Walvin, 42–65. Edinburgh: Edinburgh University Press, 2007.

Dresser, Madge. *Slavery Obscured: The Social History of the Slave Trade in an English Provincial Port.* New York: Continuum, 2001.

Du Bois, William E.B. *The World and Africa.* New York: International Publishers, 1965.

Dunn, Richard S. *Sugar and Slaves: The Rise of the Planter Class in the English West Indies, 1624–1713.* New York: Norton, 1973.

Eaden, John, ed. and trans. *The Memoirs of Père Labat, 1693–1705.* London: Frank Cass, 1970.

Edwards, Bryan. *The History, Civil and Commercial, of the British Colonies in the West Indies.* 5 vols. London: Stockdale, 1793–1819.

Elbl, Ivana. "The Volume of the Early Atlantic Slave Trade". *Journal of African History* 38 (1997): 31–75.

Elder, Melinda. *The Slave Trade and the Economic Development of Eighteenth-Century Lancaster.* Halifax: Ryburn, 1992.

Eltis, David. "The British Contribution to the Transatlantic Slave Trade". *Economic History Review* 32 (1979): 211–27.

——. *Economic Growth and the Ending of the Transatlantic Slave Trade.* New York: Oxford University Press, 1987.

——. "Europeans and the Rise and Fall of African Slavery in the Americas". *American Historical Review* 98 (1993): 1399–423.

——. *The Rise of African Slavery in the Americas.* Cambridge: Cambridge University Press, 2000.

——. "The Traffic in Slaves between the British West Indian Colonies, 1807–1833". *Economic History Review* 25 (1972): 55–64.

——. "The Volume and African Origins of the Seventeenth Century English Transatlantic Trade: A Comparative Assessment". *Cahiers d'Etudes d'Africanes* 138 (1995): 617–27.

Eltis, David, Stephen D. Behrendt, David Richardson and Herbert S. Klein, eds. *The Transatlantic Slave Trade: A Database on CD-ROM.* Cambridge: Cambridge University Press, 1999.

Eltis, David, and James Walvin, eds. *The Abolition of the Atlantic Slave Trade: Origins and Effects in Europe, Africa and the Americas*. Madison: University of Wisconsin Press, 1981.

Engerman, Stanley L. "The Atlantic Economy of the Eighteenth Century: Some Speculations on Economic Development in Britain, America, Africa, and Elsewhere". *Journal of European Economic History* 24 (1995): 145–75.

———. "The Realities of Slavery: A Review of Recent Evidence". *International Journal of Comparative Sociology* 20 (1979): 44–66.

———. "Economic Change and Contract Labour in the British Caribbean: The End of Slavery and the Adjustment to Emancipation". *Explorations in Economic History* 21 (1984): 133–50.

———. "Coerced and Free Labour: Property Rights and the Development of the Labour Force". *Explorations in Entrepreneurial History* 29 (1992): 1–29.

———. "Some Considerations Relating to the Property Rights in Man". *Journal of Economic History* 33 (1973): 43–65.

Engerman, Stanley L., and Eugene D. Genovese, eds. *Race and Slavery in the Western Hemisphere*. Princeton, NJ: Princeton University Press, 1975.

Fackenheim, Emil. *The Jewish Return into History: Reflections in the Age of Auschwitz and a New Jerusalem*. New York: Schocken, 1978.

Farrell, Stephen, Melanie Unwin and James Walvin, eds. *The British Slave Trade: Abolition, Parliament and People*. Edinburgh: Edinburgh University Press, 2007.

Ferguson, Moira. *Subject to Others: British Women Writers and Colonial Slavery, 1670–1834*. New York: Routledge, 1992.

Fick, Carolyn. *The Making of Haiti: The San Dominique Resolution from Below*. Knoxville: University of Tennessee Press, 1990.

Fiskus, Ronald J. *The Constitutional Logic of Affirmative Action*. Durham, NC: Duke University Press, 1992.

Flaherty, Peter, and John Carlisle. *The Case against Slave Reparations*. Falls Church, VA: National Legal and Policy Centre, 2004. http://nlpc.org/sites/default/files/Reparationsbook.pdf.

Floyd, Troy S. *The Columbian Dynasty in the Caribbean, 1492–1526*. Albuquerque, NM: University of New Mexico Press, 1973.

Fogel, Robert William, and Stanley L. Engerman. "Philanthropy at Bargain Prices: Notes on the Economics of Gradual Emancipation". *Journal of Legal History* 3, no. 2 (1974): 377–401.

Fortune, Stephen. *Merchants and Jews: The Struggle for British West Indian Commerce, 1650–1750*. Gainesville: University of Florida Press, 1984.

Foyle, Oxenbridge, and Marcellus Rivers. "England's Slaves or Barbados' Merchandise?" Represented in a Petition to the High and Honourable Court of Parliament, London, 1659. Reproduced in *Gentleman's Magazine* 43, 1773.

Brixton's homosexual + White Jew premacy,

Color

Franklin, John Hope. *The Color Line: Legacy for the Twenty-first Century*. Columbia: University of Missouri Press, 1993.

Jew

Frederickson, George M. *White Supremacy: A Comparative Study in American and South African History*. Oxford: Oxford University Press, 1981.

Friedlander, Henry. *The Origins of Nazi Genocide: From Euthanasia to the Final Solution*. Chapel Hill: University of North Carolina Press, 1995.

Furniss, Edgar S. *The Position of the Laborer in a System of Nationalism*. New York: Augustus M. Kelley, 1957.

Galenson, David. *Traders, Planters and Slaves: Market Behaviour in Early English America*. Cambridge: Cambridge University Press, 1986.

———. *White Servitude in Colonial America: An Economic Analysis*. Cambridge: Cambridge University Press, 1981.

Gaspar, David Barry. *Bondmen and Rebels: A Study of Master-Slave Relations in Antigua*. Baltimore: Johns Hopkins University Press, 1985.

Gates, Henry Louis, Jr. "The Future of Slavery's Past". *New York Times*, 29 July 2001.

Geggus, David Patrick. *Slavery, War, and Revolution: The British Occupation of Saint Dominique, 1793–1798*. Oxford: Clarendon Press, 1982.

Gemery, Henry A., and Jan S. Hogendorn. "The Atlantic Slave Trade: A Tentative Economic Model". *Journal of African History* 15 (1974): 223–46.

Gemery, Henry A., and Jan S. Hogendorn, eds. "Assessing Productivity in Pre-Colonial African Agriculture and Industry, 1500–1800". *African Economic History* 19 (1990–91): 31–35.

———. "Comparative Disadvantage: The Case for Sugar Cultivation in West Africa". *Journal of Interdisciplinary History* 9 (1979): 429–49.

———. *The Uncommon Market: Essays in the Economic History of the Transatlantic Slave Trade*. New York: Academic Press, 1979.

Genovese, Eugene D. *From Rebellion to Revolution: Afro-American Slave Revolts in the Making of the Modern World*. Baton Rouge: Louisiana State University Press, 1979.

Ghannam, Jeffrey. "Repairing the Past: Demands Are Growing for Reparations for the Descendants of African Slaves in America". *American Bar Association Journal* 86 (November 2000): 38–43, 70.

Gifford, Anthony. *The Passionate Advocate*. Kingston: Arawak, 2007.

Gilmore, John. "The Rev. William Harte and Attitudes to Slavery in Early Nineteenth Century Barbados". *Journal of Ecclesiastical History* 30 (1979): 461–74.

Rep

Gimbel, John. *Science, Technology, and Reparations: Exploitation and Plunder in Postwar Germany*. Palo Alto, CA: Stanford University Press, 1990.

Rep

Goldin, Claudia. "The Economics of Emancipation". *Journal of Economic History* 33 (1973): 66–85.

Gomez, Michael. *Exchanging our Country Marks: The Transformation of African Identities in the Colonial and Antebellum South*. Chapel Hill: University of North Carolina Press, 1998.

Bernie Grant Speech [handwritten annotations]

Goveia, Elsa V. *Slave Society in the British Leeward Islands at the End of the Eighteenth Century*. New Haven: Yale University Press, 1965.

———. *The West Indian Slave Laws of the 18th Century*. St Lawrence, Barbados: Caribbean Universities Press, 1970.

Gragg, Larry. "To Procure Negroes: The English Slave Trade to Barbados, 1627–60". *Slavery and Abolition* 16 (1995): 65–84.

Grant, Bernie. "Reparations or Bust". Speech, 12 November 1993, Birmingham Town Hall, Birmingham. See Bernie Grant Archives, Middlesex University, BG/ARM /16/4/4.

Green, William A. *British Slave Emancipation: The Sugar Colonies and the Great Experiment, 1830–1865*. Oxford: Clarendon Press, 1976.

———. "The Planter Class and British West Indian Sugar Production, Before and After Emancipation". *Economic History Review* 26 (1973): 448–63.

———. "Race and Slavery: Considerations of the Williams Thesis". In *British Capitalism and Slavery: The Legacy of Eric Williams*, edited by Barbara L. Solow and Stanley L. Engerman. Cambridge: Cambridge University Press, 2004.

Greene, Jack P. *The Intellectual Construction of America: Exceptionalism and Identity from 1492 to 1800*. Chapel Hill: University of North Carolina Press, 1993.

———. "Society and Economy in the British Caribbean during the Seventeenth and Eighteenth Centuries". *American Historical Review* 79 (1974): 1499–1517.

Gross, Izhak. "The Abolition of Negro Slavery and British Parliamentary Politics, 1832–3". *Historical Journal* 23, no. 1 (1980): 63–85.

Gullick, C. "Black Caribs Origins and Early Society". In *Transactions of the Seventh International Congress on Pre-Columbian Cultures of the Lesser Antilles*, 283–87. Montreal: Centre de Recherches Caraïbes, 1978.

Hall, Catherine. *Civilising Subjects: Metropole and Colony in the English Imagination, 1830–1867*. Cambridge: Polity Press, 2002.

Hall, Catherine, and Sonya Rose, eds. *At Home with the Empire: Metropolitan Culture and the Imperial World*. Cambridge: Cambridge University Press, 2006.

Hall, Douglas. "Absentee Proprietorship in the British West Indies to about 1850". *Jamaican Historical Review* 4 (1964): 15–35.

———. *Five of the Leewards, 1834–1870*. St Lawrence, Barbados: Caribbean Universities Press, 1971.

———. *Free Jamaica, 1838–1865*. New Haven: Yale University Press, 1959.

Hall, Richard. *Acts Passed in the Island of Barbados, 1643–1762*. London, 1764.

Hamilton, Douglas. *Scotland, the Caribbean, and the Atlantic World, 1750–1820*. Manchester: Manchester University Press, 2005.

Handler, Jerome S. "The Amerindian Slave Population of Barbados in the Seventeenth and Early Eighteenth Centuries". *Caribbean Studies* 8 (1969): 38–64.

———. *The Unappropriated People: Freedmen in the Slave Society of Barbados*. Baltimore: Johns Hopkins University Press, 1974.

[handwritten annotations in margins: "Barny", "Barny", "X", "Black Carib", "Read white old woman", "Barny", "Her put", "Little England / Barny"]

Handler, Jerome S., and Frederick W. Lange. *Plantation Slavery in Barbados: An Archaeological and Historical Investigation.* Cambridge, MA: Harvard University Press, 1978.

Harlow, Vincent T. *Christopher Codrington, 1668–1710.* London: Oxford University Press, 1928.

Hart, Richard. *Slaves Who Abolished Slavery.* 2 vols. Kingston: Institute of Social and Economic Research, University of the West Indies, 1980–85.

Heuman, Gad J. *Between Black and White: Race, Politics and the Free Coloreds in Jamaica, 1792–1865.* Westport, CT: Greenwood Press, 1981.

Higman, B.W. "Growth in the Afro-Caribbean Slave Populations". *American Journal of Physical Anthropology* 50 (1979): 373–86.

———. "The Internal Economy of the Jamaican Pens, 1760–1890". *Social and Economic Studies* 38 (1989): 61–86.

———. "The Slave Family and Household in the British West Indies, 1800–1824". *Journal of Interdisciplinary History* 6 (1975): 261–87.

———. *Slave Population and Economy in Jamaica, 1807–1834.* Cambridge: Cambridge University Press, 1976.

———. *Slave Populations of the British Caribbean, 1807–1834.* Baltimore: Johns Hopkins University Press, 1984.

———. "The Sugar Revolution". *Economic History Review* 53 (2000): 213–36.

———. "The West India 'Interest' in Parliament, 1807–1833". *Historical Studies* 13, no. 49 (1967): 1–19.

Hilberg, Raul. *The Destruction of the European Jews.* New York: Holmes and Meiers, 1985.

Holt, Thomas. *The Problem of Freedom: Race, Labor, and Politics in Jamaica and Britain, 1832–1958.* Baltimore: Johns Hopkins University Press, 1992.

Horowitz, David. "Ten Reasons Why Reparations Is a Bad Idea for Blacks – and Racist Too". FrontPageMag.com, 3 January 2001. http://archive.frontpagemag.com/readArticle.aspx?ARTID=24317.

———. *Uncivil Wars: The Controversy over Reparations for Slavery.* San Francisco: Encounter Books, 2002.

Howard-Hassmann, Rhoda E., and Anthony P. Lombardo. "Framing Reparations Claims: Differences between the African and Jewish Social Movements for Reparations". *African Studies Review* 50, no. 1 (April 2007): 27–48.

Huggins, Nathan I. *Black Odyssey: The African-American Ordeal in Slavery.* New York: Vintage Books, 1990.

Inikori, Joseph E. *Africans and the Industrial Revolution in England: A Study in International and Economic Development.* Cambridge, Cambridge University Press, 2002.

———. "Export versus Domestic Demand: The Determinants of Sex Ratios in the Transatlantic Slave Trade". *Research in Economic History* 14 (1992): 117–66.

———. "Measuring the Unmeasured Hazards of the Atlantic Slave Trade: Documents Relating to the British Trade". *Revue Francaise d'Histoire d'Outre* 83 (1996): 53–92.

———. "Slavery and the Development of Industrial Capitalism in England". In *British Capitalism and Caribbean Slavery: The Legacy of Eric Williams*, edited by Barbara L. Solow and Stanley L. Engerman, 79–102. Cambridge: Cambridge University Press, 2004.

Irons, Peter. *Justice at War: The Story of the Japanese Internment Cases*. Oxford: Oxford University Press, 1983.

James, C.L.R. *The Black Jacobins: Toussaint L'Ouverture and the San Domingo Revolution*. New York: Vintage, 1963.

Jamison, Sandra. "A Permanent International Criminal Court: A Proposal That Overcomes Past Objections". *Denver Journal of International Law and Policy* 23 (1995): 419–32.

Jenkinson, Hilary. "The Records of the English African Companies". *Transactions of the Royal Historical Society* 6 (1912): 185–220.

Jennings, Lawrence. "French Perceptions of British Slave Emancipation". *French Colonial Studies* 3 (1979): 72–85.

———. "The French Press and Great Britain's Campaign against the Slave Trade". *Revue Francaise d'Histoire Outre-mer* 67 (1980): 5–24.

Jensen, Richard, and Richard Steckel. "New Evidence on the Causes of Slave and Crew Mortality in the Transatlantic Slave Trade". *Journal of Economic History* 46 (1986): 57–78.

Jeremie, John. *Four Essays on Colonial Slavery*. London: Hatchard and Son, 1831.

Jesse, Rev. C. "Barbadians Buy St Lucia from Caribs". *Journal of the Barbados Museum and Historical Society* 32 (1968): 180–82.

Jordan, Winthrop. "The Influence of the West Indies on the Origins of New England Slavery". *William and Mary Quarterly* 18 (1961): 243–50.

———. *White over Black: American Attitudes toward the Negro, 1550–1812*. Chapel Hill: University of North Carolina Press, 1968.

Karras, Alan L. *Sojourners in the Sun: Scottish Migrants in Jamaica and Chesapeake, 1740–1800*. Ithaca: Cornell University Press, 1992.

Katz, Stephen T. *Post-Holocaust Dialogues: Critical Issues in Modern Jewish Thought*. New York: New York University Press, 1983.

Kea, Ray. "Firearms and Warfare on the Gold and Slave Coasts from the Sixteenth Century to the Nineteenth Century". *Journal of African History* 12 (1971): 185–213.

Kiple, Kenneth. "Deficiency Diseases in the Caribbean". *Journal of Interdisciplinary History* 11 (1980): 197–215.

Klein, Herbert S. *The Middle Passage: Comparative Studies in the Atlantic Slave Trade*. Princeton, NJ: Princeton University Press, 1978.

Klein, Herbert S., and Stanley L. Engerman. "Fertility Differentials between Slaves in the United States and the British West Indies". *William and Mary Quarterly* 35 (1978): 358–73.

Klingberg, Frank J. *The Anti-Slavery Movement in England: A Study in British Humani-tarism.* New Haven: Yale University Press, 1926.

———, ed. *Codrington Chronicle: An Experiment in Anglican Altruism on a Barbados Plan-tation, 1710–1834.* Berkeley: University of California Press, 1949.

Kopytoff, Igor, and Suzanne Miers, eds. *Slavery in Africa: Historical and Anthropological Perspectives.* Madison: University of Wisconsin Press, 1977.

Kovel, Joel. *White Racism: A Psychohistory.* New York: Vintage Books, 1971.

Kupperman, Karen. *Providence Island, 1630–1641: The Other Puritan Colony.* Cambridge: Cambridge University Press, 1993.

Lascelles, Edwin, James Colleton, Edwin Drax, Francis Ford, Reverend John Brathwaite, John Walter, William Holder, James Holder, Phillip Gibbes and John Barney. *The Following Instructions are offered for the consideration of Proprietors and Managers of a Plantation in Barbados and for the Treatment of Negroes* (London, 1786). Reprinted in *Journal of Barbados Museum and Historical Society* 11, no. 1 (1934): 23–31

Law, Robin. "Ethnicity and the Slave Trade: 'Lucumi' and 'Nago' as Ethnyms in West Africa". *History in Africa* 24 (1997): 205–19.

———. " 'Here Is No Resisting the Country': The Realities of Power in Afro-European Relations on the West African 'Slave Coast'". *Itinerario: European Journal of Overseas History* 18 (1994): 50–64.

———. *The Slave Coast of West Africa, 1550–1750.* Oxford: Oxford University Press, 1991.

Lecky, Robert S., and H. Elliott Wright, eds. *The Black Manifesto: Religion, Racism, and Reparations.* New York: Sheed and Ward, 1969.

Levy, Claude. "Barbados: The Last Years of Slavery, 1823–1833". *Journal of Negro History* 44 (1959): 308–45.

———. *Emancipation, Sugar, and Federalism: Barbados and the West Indies, 1833–1876.* Gainesville: University of Florida Press, 1980.

Lewis, G.K. *Main Currents in Caribbean Thought: The Historical Evolution of Caribbean Society in its Ideological Aspects.* London: Heinemann, 1983.

Lipson, E. *The Economic History of England.* London: A. and C. Black, 1943.

Long, Edward. *The History of Jamaica.* 3 vols. London, 1774.

Lovejoy, Paul E. *Transformations in Slavery: A History of Slavery in Africa.* Cambridge: Cambridge University Press, 1983.

———. "The Volume of the Atlantic Slave Trade: A Synthesis". *Journal of African History* 23 (1982): 474–501.

Mandle, Jay R. *The Plantation Economy: Population and Economic Change in Guyana, 1838–1960.* Philadelphia, PA: Temple University Press, 1973.

Manning, Patrick. *Slavery and African Life: Occidental, Oriental, and African Slave Trades.* Cambridge: Cambridge University Press, 1990.

———. "The Slave Trade in the Bight of Benin, 1640–1890". In *The Uncommon Market: Essays in the Economic History of the Transatlantic Slave Trade*, edited by Henry Gemery and Jan Hogendorn, 107–40. New York: Academic Press, 1979.

Marable, Manning. *How Capitalism Underdeveloped Black America*. Washington, DC: Howard University Press, 1981.

———. *Speaking Truth to Power: Essays on Race, Resistance, and Radicalism*. Boulder: Westview Press, 1996.

Marshall, Bernard. *Slavery, Law, and Society in the British Windward Islands, 1763–1823*. Kingston: Arawak, 2007.

Marshall, Peter. *Bristol and the Abolition of Slavery: The Politics of Emancipation*. Bristol: Bristol Historical Association, 1975.

Martin, Michael T., and Marilyn Yaquinto, eds. *Redress for Historical Injustices in the United States: On Reparations for Slavery, Jim Crow, and Their Legacies*. Durham, NC: Duke University Press, 2007.

Martin, Robert. *History of the Colonies of the British Empire*. London: Whittaker, 1843.

———. *Statistics of the Colonies of the British Empire*. London: Allen, 1839.

Mathieson, William. *British Slavery and Its Abolition, 1823–1838*. London: Longman, 1926.

Mathurin-Mair, Lucille. "Women Field Workers in Jamaica during Slavery". Elsa Goveia Lecture, University of the West Indies, Mona, Jamaica, 1986.

Matsuda, Mari J. "Looking to the Bottom: Critical Legal Studies and Reparations". *Harvard Civil Rights–Civil Liberties Law Review* 22, no. 323 (1987): 362–97.

Mazrui, Ali, and Alamin Mazrui. *Black Reparations in the Era of Globalization*. Binghamton, NY: Institute of Global Cultural Studies, 2002.

McCusker, John J., and Russell R. Menard. *The Economy of British America, 1607–1789*. Chapel Hill: University of North Carolina Press, 1985.

McDonald, Roderick A. "Measuring the British Slave Trade to Jamaica, 1789–1808: A Comment". *Economic History Review*, n.s., 33, no. 2 (1980): 253–58.

McGowan, Winston. "African Resistance to the Atlantic Slave Trade in West Africa". *Slavery and Abolition* 11, no. 1 (May 1990): 5–29.

Menezes, Mary Noel. *British Policy towards the Amerindians in British Guiana, 1803–1873*. Oxford: Clarendon Press, 1977.

Michie, R.C., ed. *The Development of London as a Financial Centre*. 4 vols. London: I.B. Tauris, 2005.

Midgley, Clare. "Slave Sugar Boycotts, Female Activism and the Domestic Base of British Anti-Slavery Culture". *Slavery and Abolition* 17, no. 3 (1996): 137–62.

Miller, Joseph C. "Capitalism and Slaving: The Financial and Commercial Organisation of the Angolan Slave Trade". *International Journal of African Historical Studies* 17 (1984): 1–52.

———. "The Significance of Drought, Disease, and Famine in the Agriculturally Marginal Zones of West-Central Africa". *Journal of African History* 23 (1982): 17–61.

———. *Way of Death: Merchant Capitalism and the Angolan Slave Trade, 1730–1830*. Madison: University of Wisconsin Press, 1988.

Mintz, Sidney W. "Slavery and the Rise of Peasantries". *Historical Reflection* 6 (1979): 213–42.

————. "Was the Plantation Slave a Proletariat?" *Fernand Braudel Center Review* 2 (1978): 81–98.

Mintz, Sidney W., and Richard Price. *An Anthropological Approach to the Afro-American Past: A Caribbean Perspective*. Philadelphia, PA: Institute for the Study of Human Issues, 1976.

Moohr, Michael. "The Economic Impact of Slave Emancipation in British Guiana, 1832–1852". *Economic History Review* 25, no. 4 (1972): 588–607.

Moore, Brian L. *Race, Power, and Social Segmentation in Colonial Society; Guyana after Slavery, 1838–1891*. New York: Gordon and Breach, 1987.

Moreton, J.B. *Manners and Customs in the West India Islands*. London: W. Richardson, 1790.

Morgan, Edmund S. "The First American Boom: Virginia, 1618 to 1630". *William and Mary Quarterly* 28 (1971): 178–79.

————. "Slavery and Freedom: The American Paradox". *Journal of American History* 59 (1972): 169–98.

Morgan, Kenneth. *Bristol and the Atlantic Trade in the Eighteenth Century*. Cambridge: Cambridge University Press, 1993.

————. *Slavery, Atlantic Trade and the British Economy, 1660–1800*. Cambridge: Cambridge University Press, 2000.

Morgan, Philip D. "The Cultural Implications of the Atlantic Slave Trade: African Regional Origins, American Destinations, and New World Developments". *Slavery and Abolition* 18 (1997): 122–45.

————. "Work and Culture: The Task System and the World of Low Country Blacks, 1700–1880". *William and Mary Quarterly* 39 (1982): 563–99.

Morgan, Philip D., and David Eltis. "New Perspectives on the Transatlantic Slave Trade". *William and Mary Quarterly* 58 (2001): 551–96.

Morrissey, Marietta. *Slave Women in the New World: Gender Stratification in the Caribbean*. Lawrence, KS: University Press of Kansas, 1989.

Munford, Clarence J. *The Black Ordeal of Slavery and Slave Trading in the French West Indies, 1625–1715*. 3 vols. New York: Edwin Mellen Press, 1991.

————. *Race and Reparations: A Black Perspective for the Twenty-first Century*. Trenton, NJ: Africa World Press, 1996.

Murray, David John. *The West Indies and the Development of Colonial Government, 1801–1834*. Oxford: Clarendon Press, 1965.

Newson, Linda A. *Aboriginal and Spanish Colonial Trinidad: A Study in Culture Contact*. London: Academic Press, 1976.

Newton, Nell. "Compensation, Reparations, and Restitution: Indian Property Claims in the United States". *Georgia Law Review* 28 (1994): 453–60.

Nichols, Charles H. *Many Thousand Gone: The Ex-Slaves' Account of Their Bondage and Freedom*. Leiden: E.J. Brill, 1963.

Northrup, David. *Trade without Rulers: Pre-Colonial Economic Development in South-Eastern Nigeria.* Oxford: Oxford University Press, 1978.

O'Brien, Patrick. "European Economic Development: The Contribution of the Periphery". *Economic History Review* 35 (1982): 1–18.

O'Brien, Patrick Karl, and Louis Prados de la Escosura, "The Costs and Benefits for Europeans from Their Empires Overseas". *Revista de Historia Economica* 16 (1988): 29–89.

Oldmixon, John. *The British Empire in America.* 2 vols. London: Mapp, 1708.

Oliver, Melvin, and Thomas Shapiro. *Black Wealth/White Wealth: A New Perspective on Race Equality.* New York: Routledge, 1995.

Oliver, Vere Langford. *The History of the Island of Antigua.* 3 vols. London: Mitchell and Hughes, 1894–99.

Oostindie, Gert, ed. *Facing Up to the Past: Perspectives on the Commemoration of Slavery from Africa, the Americas, and Europe.* Kingston: Ian Randle, 2001.

O'Shaughnessy, Andrew Jackson. *An Empire Divided: The American Revolution and the British Caribbean.* Philadelphia: University of Pennsylvania Press, 2000.

———. "The Formation of a Commercial Lobby: The West Indies, British Colonial Policy, and the American Revolution". *Historical Journal* 40 (1997): 71–95.

Owen, N. "Conflict and Ethnic Boundaries: A Study of Carib-Black Relations". *Social and Economic Studies* 29 (1990): 264–74.

———. "Land, Politics, and Ethnicity in a Carib Indian Community". *Ethnology* 14, no. 4 (1975): 385–393.

Packwood, Cyril. *Chained on the Rock: Slavery in Bermuda.* New York: Elisco Press, 1975.

Palmer, Colin A. *Human Cargoes: The British Slave Trades to Spanish America, 1700–1739.* Urbana: University of Illinois Press, 1981.

———. "The Slave Trade, African Slavers and the Demography of the Caribbean to 1750". In *General History of the Caribbean.* Vol. 3, *The Slave Societies of the Caribbean,* edited by Franklin W. Knight, 9–44. London: UNESCO, 1997.

Pares, Richard. "The London Sugar Market, 1740–1769". *Economic History Review* 9 (1956): 254–70.

———. "Merchants and Planters". *Economic History Review,* supplement, no. 4 (1960).

———. *A West-India Fortune.* London: Longman, 1950.

Parry, John H. "The English in the New World". In *The Westward Enterprise: English Activities in Ireland, the Atlantic and America, 1480–1650,* edited by K.R. Andrews, N.P. Canny, P.E.H. Hair and D.B. Quinn, 1–3. Liverpool: Liverpool University Press, 1978.

Parry, J.H., and P.A. Sherlock. *A Short History of the West Indies.* 3rd ed. London: Longman, 1971.

Patterson, Orlando. *Freedom: Freedom in the Making of Western Culture.* New York: Basic Books, 1991.

———. "On Slavery and Slave Formations". *New Left Review* 117 (1979): 31–69.

———. *Slavery and Social Death: A Comparative Study.* Cambridge: Cambridge University Press, 1982.

———. *The Sociology of Slavery: An Analysis of the Origins, Development, and Structure of Negro Slave Society in Jamaica*. London: MacGibbon and Kee, 1967.

Peabody, Sue. *"There Are No Slaves in France": The Political Culture of Race and Slavery in the Ancient Regime*. New York: Oxford University Press, 1996.

Pigou, A.C. "Problems of Compensation". *Economic Journal* 35, no. 140 (1925): 568–82.

Pinckard, George. *Notes on the West Indies*. 3 vols. London: Longman, 1806.

Pitman, Frank. "The Treatment of the British West Indian Slaves in Law and Custom". *Journal of Negro History* 11, no. 4 (1926): 610–28.

Pope, D. "The Wealth and Social Aspirations of Liverpool's Slave Merchants of the Second Half of the Eighteenth Century". In *Liverpool and Transatlantic Slavery*, edited by David Richardson, Anthony Tibbles and Suzanne Schwarz, 164–226. Liverpool: Liverpool University Press, 2007.

Price, Richard, ed. *Maroon Societies: Rebel Slave Communities in the Americas*. New York: Anchor Books, 1973.

Puckerin, Gary. *Little England: Plantation Society and Anglo-Barbadian Politics, 1627–1700*. New York: New York University Press, 1984.

Ragatz, Lowell. *The Fall of the Planter Class in the British Caribbean, 1763–1833*. 1928; reprint, New York: Octagon.

Rathbone, Richard. "Some Thoughts on Resistance to Enslavement in West Africa". *Slavery and Abolition* 6 (1986): 5–22.

Rawley, James A. *The Transatlantic Slave Trade: A History*. New York: Norton, 1981.

Rawls, John. *A Theory of Justice*. Cambridge, MA: Harvard University Press, 1971.

Rediker, Marcus. *The Slave Ship: A Human History*. New York: Viking, 2007.

Report of a Committee of the Council of Barbados, Appointed to Inquire into the Actual Conditions of the Slaves of this Island. Bridgetown: W. Walker, 1822.

Richardson, David. "Profits in the Liverpool Slave Trade: The Accounts of William Davenport, 1757–1784". In *Liverpool, the African Slave Trade, and Abolition*, edited by Roger Anstey and P.E.H. Hair, vol. 2, 69–90. Bristol: Historical Society of Lancashire and Cheshire, Occasional Series, 1976.

———. "Slavery and Bristol's 'Golden Age' ". *Slavery and Abolition* 26, no. 1 (2005): 35–54.

———. "The Slave Trade, Sugar, and British Economic Growth, 1748–1776". In *British Capitalism and Caribbean Slavery: The Legacy of Eric Williams*, edited by Barbara L. Solow and Stanley L. Engerman, 103–34. Cambridge: Cambridge University Press, 1987.

Richardson, David, Anthony Tibbles, and Suzanne Schwarz, eds. *Liverpool and Transatlantic Slavery*. Liverpool: Liverpool University Press, 2007.

Roberts, G.W. "A Life Table of a West Indian Slave Population". *Population Studies* 5 (1952): 238–43.

Robertson, Claire, and Martin Klein, eds. *Women and Slavery in Africa*. Madison: University of Wisconsin Press, 1983.

Robinson, Cedric J. "Capitalism, Slavery and Bourgeois Historiography". *History Workshop: A Journal of Socialist and Feminist Historians* 23, no. 1 (1987): 122–140.

Robinson, Randall. *The Debt: What America Owes to Blacks*. New York: Dutton, 2000.

Rodney, Walter. "African Slavery and Other Forms of Social Oppression on the Upper Guinea Coast in the Context of the Atlantic Slave Trade". *Journal of African History* 7 (1966): 131–43.

———. "Gold and Slaves on the Gold Coast". *Transactions of the Historical Society of Ghana* 10 (1969): 13–28.

———. *How Europe Underdeveloped Africa*. London: Bogle L'Ouverture, 1972.

Rubinstein, W.D. "British Millionaires, 1809–1949". *Bulletin of the Institute of Historical Research* 47, no. 116 (1974): 202–23.

———. "The End of 'Old Corruption' in Britain, 1780–1860". *Past and Present* 101 (1983): 55–86.

———. *Men of Property: The Very Wealthy in Britain since the Industrial Revolution*. 2nd ed. London: The Social Affairs Unit, 2006.

Rupprecht, Anita. "Excessive Memories: Slavery, Insurance and Resistance". *History Workshop: A Journal of Socialist and Feminist Historians* 64, no. 1 (2007): 6–28.

Ryden, David. "Does Decline Make Sense? The West Indian Economy and the Abolition of the British Slave Trade". *Journal of Interdisciplinary History* 31 (2001): 347–74.

Sauer, Carl Ortwin. *The Early Spanish Main*. Berkeley: University of California Press, 1966.

———. " 'One of the Fertilist Pleasantest Spotts': An Analysis of the Slave Economy in Jamaica's St. Andrew Parish, 1753". *Slavery and Abolition* 21 (2000): 32–55.

Schama, Simon. *Rough Crossing: Britain, the Slaves, and the American Revolution*. New York: Harper Collins, 2006.

Schomburgk, Robert. *The History of Barbados*. London: Longman, 1848.

Schumpeter, Elizabeth B. *English Overseas Trade Statistics, 1697–1808*. Oxford: Clarendon Press, 1960.

Schwartz, Stuart. *Sugar Plantations in the Formation of Brazilian Society*. Cambridge: Cambridge University Press, 1985.

———. *Tropical Babylons: Sugar and the Making of the Atlantic World, 1450–1680*. Chapel Hill: University of North Carolina Press, 2004.

Scott, Rebecca. "Comparing Emancipations: A Review Essay". *Journal of Social History* 20 (1987): 565–83.

Searing, James F. *West African Slavery and Atlantic Commerce: The Senegal River Valley, 1700–1860*. Cambridge: Cambridge University Press, 1993.

Semmel, Bernard. *The Governor Eyre Controversy*. London: MacGibbon and Kee, 1962.

Shepherd, Verene A., ed. *Engendering Caribbean History: Cross-Cultural Perspectives*. Kingston: Ian Randle, 2011.

———. "Livestock and Sugar: Aspects of Jamaica's Agricultural Development from the

Late Seventeenth to the Early Nineteenth Century". *Historical Journal* 34, no. 3 (1991): 627–43.

———, ed. *Slavery without Sugar: Diversity in Caribbean Economy and Society since the Seventeenth Century.* Gainesville: University of Florida Press, 2002.

Sheridan, Richard B. "The Commercial and Financial Organisation of the British Slave Trade, 1750–1907". *Journal of Economic History* 53, no. 1 (1987): 249–63.

———. "The Plantation Revolution and the Industrial Revolution, 1625–1775". *Caribbean Studies* 9 (1969): 5–25.

———. "The Rise of a Colonial Gentry: A Case Study of Antigua, 1730–1775". *Economic History Review*, n.s., 13, no. 3 (1961): 342–57.

———. "Simon Taylor, Sugar Tycoon in Jamaica, 1740–1813". *Agricultural History* 45 (1971): 285–96.

———. "Sir William Young (1749–1815): Planter and Politician with Special Reference to Slavery in the British West Indies". *Journal of Caribbean History* 33, no. 1–2 (1999): 1–26.

———. *Sugar and Slavery: An Economic History of the British West Indies, 1623–1775.* St Lawrence, Barbados: Caribbean Universities Press, 1974.

———. "The Wealth of Jamaica in the Eighteenth Century". *Economic History Review*, n.s., 18, no. 2 (1965): 292–311.

———. "The Wealth of Jamaica in the Eighteenth Century: A Rejoinder". *Economic History Review*, n.s., 21, no. 1 (1968): 46–61.

———. "The West India Sugar Crisis and British Slave Emancipation, 1830–1833". *Journal of Economic History* 21 (1961): 539–51.

Smith, Abbot Emerson. *Colonists in Bondage: White Servitude and Convict Labor in America, 1607–1776.* Chapel Hill: University of North Carolina Press, 1947.

Smith, Adam. *An Inquiry into the Nature and Causes of the Wealth of Nations*, edited by Edwin Cannan. 2 vols. 1776; repr. New York: Modern Library, 1937.

Smith, James. *Slavery in Bermuda.* New York: Vantage Press, 1976.

Smith, S.D. "Merchants and Planters Revisited". *Economic History Review*, n.s., 55, no. 3 (2002): 434–65.

———. "Gedney Clarke of Salem and Barbados: Transatlantic Super-Merchant". *New England Quarterly* 76 (2003): 499–51.

———. *Slavery, Family, and Gentry Capitalism in the British Atlantic: The World of the Lascelles, 1648–1834.* Cambridge: Cambridge University Press, 2006.

———. "Sugar's Poor Relations: British Coffee Planting in The West Indies, 1720–1833". *Slavery and Abolition* 19 (1998): 68–89.

Solow, Barbara L. "Capitalism and Slavery in the Exceedingly Long Run". In *British Capitalism and Caribbean Slavery: The Legacy of Eric Williams*, edited by Barbara L. Solow and Stanley L. Engerman, 51–77. Cambridge: Cambridge University Press, 1987.

———. "Caribbean Slavery and British Growth: The Eric Williams Hypothesis". *Journal of Developmental Economics* 17 (1985): 99–115.

Solow, Barbara L., and Stanley L. Engerman, eds. *British Capitalism and Caribbean Slavery: The Legacy of Eric Williams*. Cambridge: Cambridge University Press, 1987.

Stein, Robert. "The Revolution of 1789 and the Abolition of Slavery". *Canadian Journal of History* 17 (1982): 447–67.

Stephen, James. *The Slavery of the British West India Colonies Delineated*. 2 vols. London, 1824–30.

Stinchcombe, Arthur L. *Sugar Island Slavery in the Age of Emancipation: The Political Economy of the Caribbean World*. Princeton, NJ: Princeton University Press, 1995.

Stock, Leo, ed. *Proceedings and Debates in the British Parliament Respecting North America*. Vol. 1. Washington, DC: Carnegie Institute, 1924–41.

Sturge, J., and Harvey T. *The West Indies in 1837*. London: Hamilton and Adams, 1837.

Sued-Badillo, Jalil. "Ethnohistorical Research in the Hispanic Caribbean". In *General History of the Caribbean*. Vol. 1, *Autochthonous Societies*, edited by Jalil Sued-Badillo, 8–29. London: UNESCO, 2003.

Tadman, Michael. "The Demographic Cost of Sugar: Debates on Slave Societies and Natural Increases in the Americas". *American Historical Review* 105, no. 1 (2000): 534–75.

Taylor, D. "Our Man in London: John Pollard Mayers, Agent for Barbados and the British Abolition Act 1832–33". *Caribbean Studies* 16 (1977): 60–74.

Taylor, Jared. *Paved with Good Intentions: The Failure of Race Relations in Contemporary America*. New York: Carroll and Graf, 1992.

Temperly, Howard. *British Anti-Slavery, 1830–1870*. Columbia, SC: University of South Carolina Press, 1972.

———. "Capitalism, Slavery, and Ideology". *Past and Present* 75 (1977): 94–118.

Thomas, Sir Dalby. *An Historical Account of the Rise and Growth of the West India Colonies*. London, 1690.

Thomas, Hugh. *The Slave Trade: The History of the Atlantic Slave Trade, 1440–1870*. London: Papermac, 1997.

Thomas, J. Paul. "The Caribs of St Vincent: A Study in Imperial Maladministration, 1763–73". *Journal of Caribbean History* 18, no. 2 (1984): 60–73.

Thomas, Robert Paul. "The Sugar Colonies of the Old Empire: Profit or Loss for Great Britain?" *Economic History Review*, n.s., 21, no. 1 (1968): 30–45.

Thompson, Alvin O. *Confronting Slavery: Breaking through the Corridors of Silence*. Bridgetown: Thompson Business Associates, 2010.

Thornton, A.P. *West India Policy under the Restoration*. Oxford: Clarendon Press, 1956.

Thornton, John. *Africa and Africans in the Making of the Atlantic World, 1400–1800*. Cambridge: Cambridge University Press, 1992.

———. "The Slave Trade in Eighteenth Century Angola: Effects On Demographic Structures". *Canadian Journal of African Studies* 14 (1980): 417–27.

Thornton, Russell. *American Indian Holocaust and Survival: A Population History since 1492*. Norman, OK: University of Oklahoma Press, 1987.

Topley, John. "'Making Whole What Has Been Smashed': Reflections on Reparations". *Journal of Modern History* 73 (2001): 331–61.

Turley, David. *The Culture of English Antislavery, 1780–1860*. London: Routledge, 1991.

Turner, Mary. *Slaves and Missionaries: The Disintegration of Jamaican Slave Society, 1787–1834*. Urbana, IL: University of Illinois Press, 1982.

Tyrrell, Alex. "A House Divided Against Itself: The British Abolitionists Revisited". *Journal of Caribbean History* 22, no. 1–2 (1988): 42–67.

Van den Boogart, Ernst. "The Trade between West Africa and the Atlantic World, 1600–1690". *Journal of African History* 33 (1992): 369–85.

Waller, John Augustine. *A Voyage in the West Indies*. London: Richard Phillips, 1820.

Walvin, James. *Black Ivory: A History of British Slavery*. London: Fontana Press, 1993.

———. "The Colonial Origins of British Wealth: The Harewoods of Yorkshire". *Journal of Caribbean History* 39, no. 1 (2005): 38–53.

Ward, J.R. *British West Indian Slavery: The Process of Amelioration, 1750–1834*. Oxford: Clarendon Press, 1988.

———. "Emancipation and the Planters". *Journal of Caribbean History* 22, no. 1–2 (1988): 116–37.

———. "The Profitability of Sugar Planting in the British West Indies, 1650–1834". *Economic History Review*, n.s., 31, no. 2 (1978): 197–213.

Wastell, R.E.P. "The History of Slave Compensation, 1833 to 1845". MA thesis, London University, 1932.

Wedd, A.F., ed. *The Fate of the Fenwicks: Letters to Mary Hays, 1798–1828*. London: Methuen, 1927.

Welch, Pedro L.V. "The Lascelles and their Contemporaries: Fraud in Little England, 1700–1820". *Journal of the Barbados Museum and Historical Society* 48 (2002): 175–91.

———. *Slave Society in the City: Bridgetown, Barbados, 1680–1834*. Kingston: Ian Randle, 2003.

Weskett, John. *A Complete Digest of the Laws, Theory and Practice of Insurance*. London, 1781.

Williams, Eric. "The British West Indian Slave Trade after Its Abolition in 1807". *Journal of Negro History* 27, no. 2 (1942): 17–91.

———. *Capitalism and Slavery*. Chapel Hill: University of North Carolina Press, 1944.

———. *From Columbus to Castro: The History of the Caribbean, 1492–1969*. London: Andre Deutsch, 1970.

Wilmot, Swithin, ed. *Freedom: Retrospective and Prospective*. Kingston: Ian Randle, 2009.

Wright, James Martin. *History of the Bahamas Islands, with a Special Study of the Abolition of Slavery in the Colony*. Baltimore: Friedenwald, 1905.

Young, Arthur. "An Inquiry into the Situation of the Kingdom on the Conclusion of the Late Treaty". In *Annals of Agriculture and Other Useful Arts*. London, 1784.

Young, William. *An Account of the Black Caribs in the Island of St Vincent's*. 1795; reprint, London: Frank Cass, 1971.

Zehedieh, Nuala. "Making Mercantilism Work: London Merchants and Atlantic Trade in the Seventeenth Century". *Transactions of the Royal Historical Society* 9 (1999): 152–58.

———. "Trade, Plunder, and Economic Development in Early English Jamaica". *Economic History Review* 38 (1986): 205–22.

Ziegler, Jean. *The Swiss, the Gold, and the Dead: How Swiss Bankers Helped Finance the Nazi War Machine*. Translated by John Brownjohn. New York: Harcourt Brace, 1997.

Zook, George Frederick. *The Company of Royal Adventurers Trading into Africa*. Lancaster, PA: New Era, 1919.

The Company of
Royal
Adventures.

Index

slave owners in, 123–24, 130, 139
slave trade inquiry (1790–91), 79, 80
slave traders in, 98–99
House of Lords. *See also* Parliament
bicentenary debate (2007), 207–10,
211
reparations debate (1996), 207–8
Houston, James, 58
Howells, Rosalind, 207–8, 210
Howick, Viscount, 147
Human Rights Watch, 185
Hume, Joseph, 133

imperialism, 91–92. *See also* colonialism
indentured labour, 18, 58–59, 65–67,
86–87
India, 199
Indians. *See* Kalinagos
Industrial Revolution, 100, 101, 102, 108
Industry and Empire (Hobsbawm), 101,
102
Inikori, Joseph, 50
*Instructions for the Management of a Plan-
tation in Barbadoes . . .* (1786), 125–27
insurance sector, 72–73, 98. *See also* Zong
case
Inter-African Union for Human Rights,
180–83
International Court of Justice, 13
International Covenant on Civil and
Political Rights (1966), 15–16
International Criminal Court, 17
International Monetary Fund, 170
Ireland, 199
Irvine, Charles, 115

Jagdeo, Bharrat, 225
Jamaica
bicentenary events (2007), 225
British colonization of, 85, 97
and Haiti, 218, 219
Rastafarians in, 225, 226–27
rebellions in, 147, 196

Reparations Commission, 226, 227–
28, 229
slavery in, 63, 78, 83, 88, 92, 93, 104
sugar plantations in, 87, 104, 140, 141,
205
at WCAR, 191
Jamaica Labour Party, 228, 229
James, C.L.R., 94
James I, 40–41
James II, 44
as Duke of York, 41–42, 92
Jemenema (slave), 79
Jews, 12, 16, 141, 198
Jibril, Abdelbagi G., 181
Jobson, Richard, 40
Jubah (slave), 79
justice (reparations as), 1–2, 13

Kalinagos, 24–36, 85
British campaign against, 28, 31–34
and enslaved, 29–30
in Leeward Islands, 25, 26, 32–34
treaties with British, 31, 34–35
Karifunas, 30, 34–36
Kelsall, James, 73
Kenya, 191
King, Oona, 201
King's College (London University), 136
Klein, Herbert, 50
Klu, Kofi Mawuli, 201
Komenda (Africa), 38
Kufuor, John, 198, 199

Labat, Père Jean-Baptiste, 29–30
Labour Party (UK), 197–98, 200, 203–7
labour systems (colonial), 20–21, 58–60,
86–87
children in, 115
demographic decline and, 113–14
indentured, 18, 58–59, 65–67, 86–87
post-emancipation, 144, 148, 212
racial basis, 65–67
reform attempts, 116–18

Crimes of aggression   Sun 31st
                                          March
                                          2019

aggression   Noun.

1. an attack or harmful action,
esp an unprovoked attack by one
country against another,

2. any offensive activity,
practise, etc. Example: an
aggression against personal
liberty.

3. psychology a hostile or
destructive mental attitude
or behaviour.
[C17: from Latin aggression -
from aggredi to attack]
Managers & Staff British Library + National
  aggressor   noun.   Archives:
Jews, lying —   White Supremacists
     White women, Asians,
Africans + others who consider
              themselves 'better'.

CPSIA information can be obtained
at www.ICGtesting.com
Printed in the USA
LVHW04s1622300918
591853LV00003B/8/P

9 789766 402686

behave like school children & gang-membe